some sins
are not crimes

some sins are not crimes

A PLEA FOR REFORM OF THE CRIMINAL LAW

ALEXANDER B. SMITH & HARRIET POLLACK

New Viewpoints/A Division of Franklin Watts, Inc./New York 1975

Library of Congress Cataloging in Publication Data

Smith, Alexander B   1909–
    Some sins are not crimes.

    Includes bibliographical references.
    1. Criminal justice, Administration of—United
States. 2. Criminal law—United States. I. Pol-
lack, Harriet, 1925–   joint author. II. Title.
KF9223.S56   345'.73   75-5953
ISBN 0-531-05369-5
ISBN 0-531-05576-0 pbk.

To our children
Lynn Smith
Amy Pollack
Deborah and David Bowers

table of contents

foreword

There is no more disheartening vantage point from which to observe the criminal life of a great city than that of a judge in a criminal court. For over twenty-five years I presided over such a court, the Supreme Court of Kings County, perhaps the busiest in the Nation. During that period I presided at 2,000 criminal trials and imposed sentence on 20,000 defendants.

These include many petty offenders but these also include serious offenders—robbers, burglars, forcible rapists, and murderers. With respect to the latter, what quickly becomes apparent to the judge is that he is dealing only with the tip of the iceberg. Only those who are arrested—"cleared by arrest" is the police term—are processed through the criminal justice system. The robber, the burglar, the rapist who is not "caught" and arrested escapes prosecution and punishment at least until the next or the next or the next time. It is generally recognized that the police clear by arrest less than 10 percent of these serious crimes. This is no fault of the police: unless these serious criminals are caught in the act or at the scene or were previously known to the victim, the prospect of arrest is slim indeed. The point of the foregoing is that in dealing with these serious criminals we never really know, for the record cannot accurately inform, whether we are dealing with a first offender or a truly "professional" criminal.

What also becomes apparent to the judge among this conglomerate of petty, serious, and depraved criminals is that criminals display emotions common to all of us—remorse, fear, despair, and occasionally antagonism. The judge, if he looks, will observe that they have families who are often the principal sufferers—anguished, grieved, and frightened of the future. The victims too are there in court—sometimes scarred physically or psychologically by a violent crime: There are others who are fearful and still others who are bored or outraged by the inconvenience of their role in the proceedings.

This endless stream of societal problems is sad indeed to contemplate. It is also depressing to observe, by weight of numbers alone, how inadequately each of these problems must be handled. By the time any of these defendants come before the court for disposition, trial, and punishment, his case has been grinding through the mill for weeks and months and sometimes longer. There has been an arrest and arraignment, a bail hearing, a preliminary examination, a grand jury proceeding, pretrial motions, and several adjournments of the trial. Most of these preliminary proceedings require the presence of the defendant, his attorney, the district attorney, the victim, his witnesses, and the police. Illness of any participant, other engagements of the attorneys, and the sheer length of the calendars result in endless delay.

Finally and only when the preliminary proceedings are completed and all other factors coalesce does the judge obtain his first knowledge, purely surface, of the nature of the offense, the weight of the evidence, and the kind of person who is before him. Most often, indeed in some 90 percent of the cases, a "bargain" is struck after ten minutes of discussion and the defendant will plead guilty. True, at sentence time, some weeks later, the judge will have a sentencing report always enlightening—the defendant's family, his record at school, his employment record, and the "opinion" of family, friends, neighbors, employers, etc. From the viewpoint of the judge the defendant will be adequately punished; from the defendant's overpunished; and from the prosecutor's underpunished. The alternative is a trial in which guilt is determined by the jury, and the judge learns a little more, but not much, about the defendant as a human being.

Every judge is overcome at times with the feeling of futility. Some dangerous criminals—but only a very small percentage (those who had the misfortune to be caught)—will be removed and only temporarily from the community. Society has been served! Perhaps too, but only to the tiniest extent, punishment of this criminal may deter others.

The judge knows from experience that the future is bleak for both society and the defendant. Most criminals, after release, despite supervision, will return to criminality either because this is a way of life or because of economic pressures. And the whole process will be repeated and continued over and over again until the person "burns out"—a prison term describing those who are simply too old, too scared, too bored, or too tired for further criminal adventures.

Of course, the best and brightest hope lies in crime prevention. But those who have studied the "science" of criminology with particular reference to causation cannot pretend that there is anything much which can be done about the many many aspects of that problem. We must confess that recent efforts as well as efforts of all previous generations have left us hopeless and defeated.

The brightest immediate hope—and this is the basic theme of this book by Professors Smith and Pollack—is to remove some of the heaviest traffic from the courts. This theme is set forth practically, lucidly and thoughtfully in *Some Sins Are Not Crimes*.

Keep as many crimes out of the criminal justice system as possible! There are agencies other than the overwhelmed courts better fitted to deal with deviant behavior, drunkenness, and many other less than serious offenses. Only serious crimes, those which are violent or destructive, should remain in the courts as the prime concern of the police, prosecutors, and judges. Only if the vast number of petty offenses are removed from our too congested calendars, will the judge have adequate time to make a thoughtful appraisal of the serious offender as an individual, the degree of his guilt, and an appropriate determination of the punishment to be imposed.

Some sin, suggest Professors Smith and Pollack, may very well be left to good taste and manners, to the churches, and the disapprobation of families and friends. We will have to become more tolerant of conduct which is not socially destructive. And certainly we must weigh logically rather than irrationally the impact of such conduct. We need acceptance and perhaps kindness and compassion for those persons in our midst whose conduct is neither violent, dangerous, nor hostile.

The authors of *Some Sins Are Not Crimes* are certainly competent by long experience and studied research to make these and many more practical suggestions.

Professor Smith, for many years, was a Supervisor of Probation in my court. He was responsible for putting into operation the first self-help clinic for narcotic addicts, a project which received wide community and public support. He also put into practical application many of the precepts here presented. In recent years he has entered academia and his and Professor Pollack's research, writing, and teaching have produced a blend of perspectives that have proved useful and fruitful.

Smith and Pollack are much too practical to suggest a blueprint for utopia. They are however suggesting a modest but important step forward. "It is not incumbent upon us to finish the task; neither may we desist from it altogether."

Nathan R. Sobel
Surrogate of the County of Kings

preface

The theme developed in these pages initially came to mind while working on an earlier book, *Crime and Justice in a Mass Society.* Classroom interaction with police and other practitioner students stimulated us to set down our notions of the important unresolved issues facing the criminal justice system today. Having thus surveyed the problems in *Crime and Justice,* however, it became apparent that the area most in need of reform was the substance of the criminal law itself, an area that has received relatively little attention from those concerned with the shortcomings of our criminal justice system. Most suggestions for change relate to procedural reform, i.e., *how* the system does what it does. Very few people have concerned themselves with substantive reform: *what* the system does, and whether it should be doing it at all.

As always, if we have succeeded at all it is in large part owing to the help we have received from others. We wish particularly to thank Judge Nathan R. Sobel, Surrogate of Kings County, New York, and an outstanding legal scholar; the Honorable Samuel S. Leibowitz, retired Justice of the New York State Supreme Court; the Honorable Joel Tyler and the Honorable William Shea, Judges of the New York City Criminal Court; the Honorable Meyer H. Diskind, Assistant Commissioner of the New York State Drug Abuse Control Commission; the Honorable Charles Fastov, Director, Probation Department, New York City; William Gallagher, Legal Aid Society of New York City; Dr. Charles Winick, Professor of Sociology at the Graduate Center of the City University of New York; Dr. Thomas H. Bewley of Tooting Bec Hospital, London, England; Mr. C. G. Jeffrey, Chief Inspector, Drugs Branch, The Home Office, London, England; and Chief Superintendent Steven O'Brien, New Scotland Yard, London, England. Above all, we wish to thank our students, who provided a receptive and resilient sounding board for our ideas, kept us intellectually honest, and stimulated us at least as much as we stimulated them. In particular we are grateful to Dorothy Schulz, whose research in the field of obscenity was helpful, and to Inspector Ralph Cohen of the New York City Police Department, who gave us valuable insight into the police perspective of the criminal justice field. Sylvia Rothberg and Betty Goldstein, both of John Jay College, provided the best secretarial services two authors could hope for, and have earned our deepest appreciation. Finally, we wish to thank Donald H. Riddle, President of John Jay College, for his encouragement and for providing an atmosphere in which scholarly research and writing can take place.

chapter one

LESS NOT MORE: POLICE, COURTS, PRISONS

Well, I think that the American criminal justice system needs a revolution. I think it's in shambles in the big cities. And as a lawyer, I want it to be revolutionized.

Edward Bennett Williams, as interviewed by Edwin Newman, NBC News, "Speaking Freely," November 20, 1970

Lost is our old simplicity of times. The world abounds with laws, and teems with crimes.

Anonymous

Even when laws have been written down, they ought not always to remain unaltered.

Aristotle, *Politics, Book II*

Political candidates like to argue over whether law and order or justice should be our prime consideration. In the big cities of America we have neither. The criminal justice systems of our metropolitan areas are in such precarious condition that only a degree of nonenforcement by police, nonprosecution by prosecutors, and nondefending by defense counsel saves these systems from a complete breakdown. If every violation witnessed by the police were to result in an arrest, if every accused person were presented to the courts for prosecution, if every defendant were to have a trial, the result, literally, would be anarchy within a few days.

Americans are a law-minded people. If there is something wrong with the world their impulse is to pass a law against it. Our penal codes are, among other things, the heritage of two hundred years of reforming impulses; yet despite all our laws, at night we are afraid to walk the streets of our big cities. Something has gone wrong, and in our anguish our first impulse is to call for *more:* more police, more judges, more courts, more jails, more money to deal with the increasingly insistent problem of crime. But more is not the answer.

What we need is *less:* less crime, fewer criminals, arrests, prosecutions, and prisoners. What we want more of is justice and order, which, paradoxically, we can hope to achieve only through decreasing rather than increasing the scope and sweep of our criminal justice system.

A brief examination of how criminal justice works explains this seeming contradiction. The easiest part of the criminal justice system to expand is the police force, because the policeman is the visible symbol of protection, and when the taxpayer feels insecure, he is quite willing to pay for a larger police force. But more policemen on the street inevitably will fail to provide the sense of security that the public desperately wants, because more police means *more reported crime,* not less. As the number of police officers increases, and as their efficiency and productivity improve, *more* crime will be detected and *more* arrests made, and crime rates, which are simply the ratio of *reported* crime to population, will go up, not down. As crime rates mount, public uneasiness and demands for protection will increase, creating more pressure to hire more police, thus repeating the cycle.

Aside from the admitted artificiality of the crime rate, however, an increased number of police on the streets may not decrease real crime either. There cannot, after all, be a policeman on every block. Purse snatchings, muggings, and assaults inevitably will occur despite stepped-up foot and radio police patrols. Not every section of a city can be simultaneously saturated with police, and experience has shown that rigorous patrolling of one area frequently results merely in displacing crime to another neighborhood. Furthermore, a good deal of crime occurs within the confines of the home, where additional policemen will have no effect. (Most homicides involve perpetrators and victims who are known to each other, and who frequently are related. Similarly, many assaults result from arguments among family members or friends.) The cost of increasing the number of patrolmen on the street at any one time is, moreover, enormous. New York City police administrators estimate that allowing for the necessity of mounting three shifts a day, vacation time, sick time, and the need for administrative and other back-up personnel, six policemen must be hired for every one who eventually ends up walking the beat.

Enlarging the size of the police force will also have a disastrous effect on the rest of the criminal justice system, unless financial provision is made for the simultaneous expansion of courts and prisons. An increased number of arrested persons means more work for the grand jury, more arraignments, more bail hearings, more trials, more appeals, more probation investigations, more prisoners, more parolees, and more probationers to be supervised. The failure in the past to increase the component parts of the criminal justice system other than the police has led to such episodes as the suspension of the civil calendar in the Bronx County Supreme Court in January 1968, so that all judges could work on the backlog of criminal cases, or the 1970 riots in the Tombs precipitated by the tripling up of prisoners in cells designed for one.

Again, the costs of such expansion are very great, and the possibilities of funding are slim. To add a single judge to the bench of the New York State Supreme Court in New York City (the trial court for felony cases) requires an additional outlay of approximately $500,000 a year. In addition to the judge's salary ($43,317 per year in 1974), law clerks, a secretary, the courtroom attendants, a court reporter, etc. must also be paid. A courtroom must be provided, along with facilities for prospective jurors and additional detention space for prisoners.* Since the bulk of the tax money raised in the United States goes to the federal government, there perpetually is a severe shortage of funds at the local level for education, pollution control, mass transit, welfare, and housing. The political reality is that in the scramble for funds the groups that can exert the strongest political pressure get the money. The voters who perceive the need for clean air, better subways, more adequate schools, and new housing are more numerous and influential than the relative few who know of the desperate need for probation officers and prison counseling programs. An Attica or a Tombs riot may make a temporary impression, but what taxpayer is as concerned by the size of the probation officer's case load as by the size of his child's class? The public can and

* The costs cited are for New York City, which means perhaps that they are somewhat higher than they might be elsewhere. The problems of the Criminal Justice system are probably also more acute in New York City than they are elsewhere, especially some of our smaller towns and cities. New York City, however, is a prototype for the large cities of the United States: Whatever happens in New York City does to a considerable extent happen in the other major cities. New York's problems are not different—only larger.

does clamor for more police, but it will not pay for those things which are concomittant to an increase in the police force: more prosecutors, courts, detention facilities, and prisons.

Even if the public were willing to pay for these concommitants, however, we would be accomplishing no more than the perpetuation in our courtrooms of the bureaucratization and mass production of justice that we call plea bargaining. In August 1970, Chief Justice Warren E. Burger stated in a nationally televised speech that 90 percent of all criminal suspects plead guilty and do not stand trial. These suspects elect not to stand trial because they are given an opportunity to plead guilty to an offense less serious than the one with which they were originally charged. Frequently, they also receive informal assurances of relatively light punishment. District attorneys and judges make these offers because a guilty plea can be processed in a fraction of the time required for a formal trial. There is also less likelihood of the defendant's appealing a sentence based on a plea bargain rather than a trial, so that the time of the appellate courts is saved as well. The defense attorney acts as a middle man in this process, negotiating with the district attorney and the judge in the "best interest" of his client. The result is that through plea bargaining, the criminal justice system is able to dispose quickly of a large number of criminal cases, usually by diminishing the punishment of each defendant. Given the fact that severe prison sentences seem to be no more rehabilitative than shorter prison sentences, the acceptance of lesser pleas may not harm society. On the other hand, detention does at least keep the convicted criminal off the streets and away from the rest of the community. To the extent that the plea-bargaining system permits dangerous guilty persons to return to society at large after little or no detention, the criminal justice system has failed to perform even the minimal function of isolation of antisocial persons.

The plea bargaining of the criminal justice system is far from the adversary model of Anglo-American criminal procedure. Criminal defendants are adjudicated, not by a trial involving two evenly matched lawyer-champions, arguing before a neutral judge and jury, but by private negotiations between actors who have at least as much claim on each other as the defendant has on any one of them. The prosecutor, the judge, and even the defense attorney will be around and have to work with each other long after a particular defendant has come and gone. The disposition of a case has to facilitate the working relationship of the judge, prosecutor, and defense attorney, as well as to do justice to the defendant and the community.

The plea-bargaining system is particularly hard on the defendant with a previous criminal record. There are probably few persons in prison who are totally innocent; * there are many more who are innocent of the specific crime for which they were convicted, but who *are or were guilty of something else.* The defense attorney considers (probably correctly) that such a past record impairs his bargaining power *vis à vis* the district attorney, and that the latter will not settle for anything less than a plea of guilty to something. The result is that any defendant with a questionable past record is going to be pleaded by his attorney, even if he is innocent of the specific charge against him.

On the other hand, the plea-bargaining system also results in the kind of revolving door justice of which the police complain so bitterly. Arrested persons plead guilty, are minimally sentenced, and are quickly out on the streets again unsupervised, repeating their crimes partly because of the terrible pressures of crowded calendars and jails. Occasionally, a defense attorney will cooperate with the prosecutor in seeing that a particularly "bad apple" is sent away for a long time. While in one sense this may be reassuring to the public, at the same time, it is a clear indication of how, under the plea-bargaining system, determination of guilt is removed from the hands of the judge and jury to the hands of the defense attorney and prosecutor.

One further drawback of the plea-bargaining system, less apparent than its other faults, is that because negotiations are conducted privately, public surveillance of the criminal justice process is curtailed. The courtroom processes provide an opportunity for the

* Exceptions to this statement occur when political pressure is put on the system. When the Washington, D.C. police, for example, were forced to resort to wholesale, illegal arrests in the spring of 1971, in order to prevent antiwar protestors from disrupting the government, many innocent persons were caught in the dragnet. If a community is upset by a particularly vicious crime or an especially outrageous affront to law and order, great public pressure will be exerted on the police to make an arrest. An innocent person is then more likely to be detained, arrested, convicted, and committed than would normally be the case. Experienced civil rights lawyers also claim that there is a greater possibility of innocent people being detained for misdemeanors than for felonies.

community at large to observe how suspects are handled, how effectively the law is being enforced, and how relevant the law is to the needs of society. When the defendant is handled through private agreements made by prosecutor, defense attorney, and judge, the public has no opportunity to review the police practices that led to the arrest of the defendant, the pretrial interrogation conducted by police and prosecutors, the defendant's opportunity to obtain counsel, the fairness of the trial procedures, etc. Worst of all, perhaps, no participant in the plea-bargaining system is likely to evaluate the law itself for its shortcomings, inadequacies, outmodedness or irrelevance. When a numbers runner, for example, is picked up, the plea-bargaining negotiations focus on what is to be done with the defendant. No one concerned is likely to raise the question of whether the conduct charged to the defendant should in fact be considered criminal.

Another consequence of increased numbers of defendants is the crowding of the jails. Periodic riots, journalistic exposés of rampant homosexuality and corrupt or brutal guards, frequent inmate suicides, all testify to the disastrous conditions of the institutions that hold accused persons prior to trial, or for the serving of short sentences after conviction. Conditions in local jails are so notorious that there is universal agreement on the need for more facilities—but the money is seldom, if ever, forthcoming. The politics of the budgetary process are such that the building of new jails, or even the rehabilitation of old ones, is an almost impossible feat.

Not only are more jails needed, however, but theoretically, at least, there must be more prisons for the detention of those convicted of serious crimes.* In actuality, criminologists and others who work with convicts are not at all sure that a prison sentence accomplishes much beyond keeping the prisoner out of circulation for the length of his sentence. Ultimately, however, almost all prisoners are released, and there is very little evidence that their sentences have been either deterrent or rehabilitative. Such statistics as we have indicate the

---

* Jails are institutions for short-term confinement: either for those awaiting trial, awaiting sentence, or waiting transfer to another institution. They also serve to house those serving sentences of less than one year. Prisons, penitentiaries, and reformatories house only those convicted of crimes serious enough to incur a sentence of more than one year.

contrary: two-thirds of all prison inmates are recidivists, and similarly a large percentage of all crimes committed is committed by those who have already served a prison sentence. Many experts argue that prisons are counter-productive in that they tend further to corrupt young prisoners. Under the circumstances it is questionable to advocate large outlays of public funds for more prisons, unless and until corrections programs can be devised that both deter crime and rehabilitate offenders. One obstacle, to deterrence at least, is that no prison program, no matter how sophisticated and brilliant, can deter potential criminals as long as the chances of arrest are small and the delay between the commission of the crime, the appearance in court, and the ultimate prison sentence is a matter of months or years, rather than days or weeks. Psychologically, it is unsound to expect any punishment to act as a deterrent if it is not both swift and relatively certain, and our prison sentences are neither. Rehabilitative programs on the other hand, have not met with any great degree of success, in part at least, owing to shortages of public funds for creating and implementing such programs. The result is that in recent years there has been a tendency to imprison only those convicted persons so hardened or so vicious that they are a danger to their communities. Thus, while our prisons have not felt the impact of increasing numbers of criminal defendants to the same extent as the police and the courts, our probation and parole systems have become increasingly overburdened. If we further increase the numbers of criminal defendants to be handled by our criminal justice system, the immediate pressure will be for more jails and more probation and parole services; ultimately we also will need more prisons.

From any realistic point of view, to expand the criminal justice system is an exercise in futility. The system cannot handle even the defendants who are currently funneled into it, much less the larger number that would be created by more intensive law enforcement. The amount of expansion that would be needed for the kind of crash program that "law and order" advocates suggest would involve sums of money and an allocation of social resources far beyond the ability of society to pay for it and remain viable. What then do we do?

The answer is obvious: not more—but less: *fewer defendants.* The number of criminal defendants handled by the system can be reduced in two ways: either, through the processes of education and acculturation, people can be convinced to refrain from committing those acts we call crimes; or, the laws themselves can be changed so that fewer acts will be considered crimes. Ideally, the first method, i.e., motivating people to be law abiding, is best. We do not, however, know how to accomplish this goal. We do not really know what makes some people break the law, even though we know that family breakdown, poor school attendance, bad housing, racial discrimination, poverty, and possibly even poor health and poor nutrition are related to the incidence of crime in a particular segment of the population. Preventing crime is, in any case, a very long-range proposition, and the criminal justice system needs help *now*.

The second alternative is far more feasible: to reexamine our penal codes to determine whether all the acts prohibited by them are so antisocial in nature that we must take cognizance of them by handling them as crimes. Some, of course, are. No society can tolerate such acts as murder, rape, arson, and robbery—and survive. The part of the penal code that deals with acts such as these, which are *malum in se* (evil in themselves), needs no revision in terms of defining forbidden conduct. We must and should prohibit violent assaults on both people and property.

A good part of our penal code, however, is concerned with acts of another nature—those that are not universally condemned as evil, but which our society for a variety of reasons has labeled as sufficiently undesirable to warrant punishment by the criminal justice system. While we think gambling, for example, is wrong, many societies do not, and, indeed, *we* do not in all places and circumstances. At the same time that we prohibit off-track betting by private persons, we organize state-run lotteries. New York State has gone so far as to organize state-sponsored book-making establishments. We forbid the use of marihuana and heroin but tolerate the limited use of amphetamines and barbiturates and encourage in our advertising the widespread, indiscriminate sale of pills and potions to pep us up, calm us down, or make us sleep soundly.

Hundreds of sections of our penal codes are concerned with acts that are criminal mainly because we say they are: homosexuality between consenting adults, prostitution, gambling, adultery, marihuana use, possession of obscene and pornographic materials. We also have Sunday closing laws, restrictions on the sale of liquor, and housing, labor, and sanitary code violations that carry criminal penalties. No accurate figures exist on the percentage of the cases in our criminal courts that stem from violations of these sections of the penal code, but anyone familiar with our criminal courts system can attest that only a small fraction of the time of police officers, judges, prosecutors, and corrections officials is spent in handling those offenses that are always criminal, such as rape, murder, arson, and aggravated assault. For every murderer processed through the system there are dozens of gamblers, prostitutes, pushers, and alcoholics. If our criminal justice system is breaking down, it is the processing of the latter type of offender that is causing the breakdown. We have sufficient resources—enough police, courts, etc.—to handle quickly and efficiently every apprehended perpetrator of every serious crime, *if we could remove petty offenders and morals offenders from the system.*

If we stop processing malum prohibitum (*evil because prohibited*) *offenses, the way we process* malum in se (*evil in themselves*) *acts, we can halt the deterioration of our criminal justice; we can thus do more to restore order and safe streets without the sacrifice of civil liberties than by any other single method now available to us.*

Though politically controversial, by far the best method of handling morals offenses is to remove them from the penal code. Admittedly, such a deliberate legislative policy would fly in the face of all American historical experience. As Morris Ernst, the well known lawyer and civil libertarian, once observed, Americans do not repeal morals legislation: they simply allow such laws to fall into desuetude. Sunday blue laws are a classic example of this process. The New York State Sunday closing law currently on the books has in the past been read to forbid movie, stage, and radio performances on Sunday, a view that is now archaic because the courts have stopped interpreting the law in so restrictive a manner and the police, unconcerned with enforcing the law, ignore violations. In 1971, New York City Police Commissioner Murphy, in recognition of the fact that no one cared about Sunday closing laws any longer, announced that his men would not even attempt to enforce them. Such forthrightness on the part of an administrative official is unusual; most laws go unenforced by default rather than by deliberate policy. Despite the commissioner's forthrightness and the inutility of the law, the legislature has not removed it from the books. The reasons are obvious: any such attempt would lead to an outcry by small but militant minority groups who would convert a simple act of legislative housekeeping into a debate over morality. No legislator wants to be cast in the role of the defender of immorality, even an immorality that is widely accepted and practiced by a large part of his constituents. It is much easier, and politically much more sensible simply to sweep the issue under the rug by ignoring it.* Even an honest, forthright, well-intentioned legislator is better advised to approach the repeal of morals legislation with the utmost caution. Many of these issues do, after all, go away if ignored, and the legislator would not have wasted his time, energy, and political capital in fighting a trivial battle. Thus, the historical trend to allow morals legislation simply to fall into disuse through administrative inaction, rather than to recognize its outmodedness, has very good pragmatic reasons behind it. Unfortunately, we no longer can afford the luxury of waiting for administrative policy to catch up with public morality. Possibly because of the great changes in public mores in a relatively short time, we have too many laws (gambling, prostitution, drugs) that the police are attempting to enforce and the courts to handle, which large segments of the public simply will not abide by.

There is something very frightening to most people in advocating the repeal of morals laws. It is as though by advocating repeal, we are endorsing conduct that heretofore has been forbidden. Nothing could be further from the truth. By repealing morals laws we are simply declaring that the criminal sanction will no longer be used to enforce a particular mode of conduct. Most human conduct is, after all, regulated by such nonlegal institutions as the home, the school, the church, the family, and the peer group. Most husbands work hard and support their wives and children because they respond to cultural demands, rather than because they could be put in jail for nonsupport if they fail to do so. The unpalatable truth is that passing a law does not ensure that it will be obeyed, or that it can be enforced. Conversely, to repeal the law does not necessarily mean an increase in undesirable conduct. Prohibition is probably the most clear-cut example of the effect of passing and then repealing a morals law. The

* The above discussion does not mean to imply that individual communities may not have valid reasons to opt for Sunday business closings for *secular* reasons such as diminution of traffic or consideration for the needs of employees. What is irrational and archaic are sweeping statewide *religiously* based statutes.

Eighteenth Amendment had virtually no effect in reducing *per capita* alcohol consumption in this country; and its repeal did not increase either the amount of drinking or the problems of alcoholism. The only effect of the Eighteenth Amendment was to create a thriving illegal bootlegging industry, and it was this spin-off—the rise in serious crime due to an unenforceable law—that constituted one of the principal reasons for repeal.

We are in a similar position today. Our gambling and drug laws, particularly, have created a consumer demand that nourishes an enormous organized crime industry. Worse yet, by making heroin impossible to obtain legally, our drug laws have so inflated the cost of addiction that we have created an army of amateur criminals who prey upon the public.* But perhaps the most terrible consequence of all is that the effort to cope with the crime that directly results from our unenforceable drug and gambling laws is destroying our criminal justice system and rendering it incapable of dealing with criminals who violate laws that might, under better circumstances, be reasonably enforceable.

Of all morals laws, the prohibition on the possession and sale of heroin is the sanction the public is most hesitant to repeal or modify. There is, of course, a risk in repealing the ban on heroin. Many people, including a large number of policemen, believe that lifting the ban would greatly increase experimentation with the drug, especially among youngsters, and would lead to lifelong addiction. Removing heroin from the penal code does not, however, mean permitting its sale in every candy store. As with many other pharmaceuticals, distribution can be regulated by prescription. Medical handling may, in fact, make it harder to obtain heroin for unauthorized use because the present law is totally ineffectual as a deterrent. Despite the law and the entire criminal justice system arrayed in its support, it is easy to get heroin in New York City today. Apparently, those of us who are not using heroin are not addicted because we

* In 1973, interviews with Criminal Court judges and correction officials in New York City indicated that probably two-thirds of the defendants arraigned in Criminal Court were currently heroin users or had a history of recent heroin use; and three-quarters of the adolescent boys (16–21) confined in the Adolescent Remand Shelter in Rikers Island awaiting trial or sentencing were heroin addicts on admission.

don't want to be. If this assumption is true, then the risk we run in repealing the drug laws is minimal, and the benefits we stand to gain are very great.

A common characteristic of violations of morals laws (including drug laws) is that the resulting crimes have no victims. The prostitute's client has not been forcibly seduced; the housewife who makes a twenty-five-cent bet on the numbers has not been robbed; the drug user has directly harmed only himself. There are, in a very real sense, no complaining witnesses who can help the police in establishing the case against the accused offender. Because of the fact that there are no aggrieved victims ready and willing to testify for the state, the burden of producing evidence for the prosecution rests entirely on the police. It is the search for evidence to make morals offense violations stick that produces the greatest number of violations of civil liberties by the police. Prostitutes are frequently the victims of entrapment by plainclothes officers. If her customers will not testify, who besides the plainclothes officer can, and what better way of establishing a case than to offer an obviously willing girl a little "encouragement?" Official police records indicate that an incredible number of gamblers and drug pushers "drop" gambling slips and narcotics at the mere approach of a policeman. This so-called "dropsie" evidence is, in reality, often a euphemism for an illegal search. The police can, and do, search people who appear to be suspicious to them without proper legal cause. Since the United States Supreme Court decision in *Mapp* v. *Ohio*,[1] illegally secured evidence cannot be used to obtain a conviction—hence, the startling increase in "dropsie" evidence in post-Mapp cases. Such violations of civil liberties occur not because the police prefer to act illegally, but because it is difficult, if not impossible, to build a legitimate case where there is no real victim. It is worth noting that at the United States Supreme Court level, most decisions restricting police conduct deal with state and local, rather than federal, enforcement procedures. This is not because FBI agents are inherently more civil libertarian or law abiding than local policemen, but, because they deal with different kinds of crimes. In a kidnapping or bank robbery or counterfeiting case there are real victims, and police agents can build their case in an ethical, professional manner: obtaining statements from the victims, interviewing eyewitnesses, obtaining fingerprints, weapons, contraband, etc.* Local police who have to deal with pimps, prostitutes, and illegal abortionists are not afforded this luxury. They must make a case the best way they can, and frequently this involves illegal snooping, searching, and arrests.

The enforcement of morals laws not only involves the police in violations of civil liberties, but is the source of most of the corruption within the police department. All police departments are plagued with a small number of dishonest members who join forces with the criminals they are supposed to apprehend and who participate in such crimes as burglaries, holdups, and extortions. This kind of corruption is, however, relatively rare and usually not too difficult to handle. Rarely does such corruption extend to the top administrative levels. The most common kind of police corruption is the pay-offs policemen receive (and pass along to their superior officers) from gamblers, pushers, and pimps. This kind of graft is almost impossible to eradicate, partly because the illegal activities involved are so profitable, and the pay-offs so lucrative; and partly because the activities themselves do not seem so immoral to the police, possibly because the crimes have no real victims. Most policemen are willing to accept human fraility, at least insofar as gambling, liquor, and prostitution are concerned. Until recent years police mores allegedly frowned upon taking pay-offs from drug pushers, but with the increase in the use of drugs, this taboo seems to have diminished. This type of police corruption is intractible because as long as a large segment of the population is willing not only to break morals laws, but to pay a great deal of money for illegal services rendered, there will be lawbreakers to provide the service and policemen willing, for a fee, to participate in the trade. Such corruption is intractible because it spreads throughout entire departments, from the patrolman on the beat through top administrators, and sometimes even to the commissioner, the mayor, and elected officials.

Periodic exposés reveal a pattern that has varied little from the one laid bare at the turn of the century by Lincoln Steffens in *The Shame of the Cities;* however, the waves of reform following such exposés lead to little more than temporary remissions. No way has yet

* There have unfortunately been notable exceptions to FBI legality, usually in cases involving national security or defendants who have been considered politically dangerous.

been found to eliminate this kind of corruption as long as the public wants to gamble, take illegal drugs, frequent prostitutes, etc., and as long as immense profits can be earned by criminals meeting these desires. (Eliminating gambling, narcotics, and prostitution laws, would, incidentally, virtually eliminate the bulk of the business on which organized crime thrives.)

The most important benefit, however, that would result from the elimination of morals offenses from the penal code would be the relief of the criminal justice system. No one knows how much of the time of the police, prosecutors, and courts is spent in processing morals defendants, but it has been estimated that as little as 10 percent of the courtroom hours available in our criminal courts are now devoted to the processing of serious crimes. If we were free to devote the remaining 90 percent of our courtroom hours to the handling of dangerous offenders or of serious crimes of property, we would be able to overcome most of the shortcomings of our present criminal justice system. With fewer offenders to concern them, the police could become more thorough and more legitimate. The decongestion of court calendars would reduce the pressure for plea bargaining, as would, incidentally, more carefully prepared cases based on legally gathered evidence. The burden on probation and parole officers would also be lighter, and if the likelihood of arrest were greater as the result of better police work, then corrections programs might be more likely to act as a deterrent. Though the public is fond of criticizing the courts for coddling criminals and supports the imposition of more severe prison sentences on convicted defendants, no sentence can deter if it is unlikely to be imposed at all. As things stand now, the likelihood of even an apprehended law-breaker's being sent to prison is so small that realistically we must assume that fear of imprisonment plays little part in the thinking of a potential criminal. If, however, the full resources of our criminal justice system were devoted to those who commit serious crimes, the likelihood of speedy trials and felony punishments for felony offenses would be greatly increased.

At the moment, proposals to repeal morals legislation are neither popular nor acceptable. Such proposals are attacked from both ends of the morality spectrum. On the one hand, guardians of public order are outraged at the prospect of "legalizing" gambling, drug sales, and sexual soliciting. "How would you feel if it were your sixteen-year-old daughter who became hooked on heroin?" "Terrible. But thousands are hooked now, and if she does become hooked, at least she will not have to steal, prostitute herself, victimize other people, or die of an overdose."

The response in the imaginary colloquy is correct, but probably unconvincing to those who look at the printed word of the law as an amulet to ward off evil. The police, on the whole, do not favor the repeal of morals laws, in part because they see repeal as an admission of their limited role in society, i.e., they can enforce only those laws the general public is willing to obey. Such an admission is not only ego-bruising but a distinct handicap in the annual race for their share of the public budget.

On the other hand, many people make large profits from such activities as dope peddling and gambling and they are not likely to give up their livelihood without a struggle. No one knows the extent of the ties between the underworld and elected and appointed officials but it is certain that organized crime is capable of exerting pressure behind the scenes to discourage the passage of unfavorable legislation.

One can only hope that the uncommitted majority will come to realize the price we pay in corruption, the denial of civil liberties, and the overburdening of our criminal justice system for the luxury of using our penal code to enforce our currently fashionable behavior preferences. We need courage enough to admit that certain kinds of behavior cannot be controlled through the penal sanction and faith enough to believe that cultural pressure (or innate decency) will keep us from mass dissipation and self-destruction. And we need political leaders strong enough to get up and say so.

chapter two

DEVIANCE:
SIN, CRIME,
AND THE LAW

> The subject of this book is knavery, skul-
> duggery, cheating, unfairness, crime, sneaki-
> ness, malingering, cutting corners, immorality,
> dishonesty, betrayal, graft, corruption, wicked-
> ness, and sin—in short, deviance.
>
> Albert K. Cohen, *Deviance and Control.*

> . . . *deviant behavior is behavior that people
> so label.*
>
> Howard S. Becker, *Outsiders.*

> *Obscenity, at bottom, is not a crime. Obscenity
> is sin.*
>
> Louis Henkin, "Morals and the Constitution:
> The Sin of Obscenity." *Columbia Law Review.*

Superficially, it is very easy to define deviance. A deviant person is one who does something we would not do. He is, in the words of Howard Becker, an outsider, one who is outside the consensus of what constitutes proper conduct. The problem is that from someone's point of view we are all outsiders in one respect or another. Discussions of deviance, therefore, really turn on searches for universals, for modes of conduct that all human societies consider unacceptable.

In the classroom, anthropology professors like to upset their students by pointing out that there are no such universally disapproved modes of conduct. Even a killing that we would consider murder is acceptable in some societies: the infanticide practiced by the Spartans and the deliberate starvation of old people by Eskimos. In actuality, however, assaultive acts against the persons or property of others, such as murder, assault, rape, and robbery, are considered taboo in almost all human societies, and people who perform such acts are clearly deviant. These acts, however, constitute only a tiny fraction of all the modes of conduct that our own and other societies have from time to time labeled as wrong.

If today, we were to ask a middle-class, middle-aged, white American what kinds of acts (outside of assaultive crime), he considered deviant, he might respond as follows:

> Being a homosexual; reading dirty books or seeing pornographic movies; going to prostitutes; engaging in sex outside of marriage; having illegitimate children (especially if the children wind up on welfare).

> Using drugs—not prescription drugs or over-the-counter items like Alka Seltzer or Geritol or Vitamin E—but heroin, LSD, and pep pills.

> Drinking too much; eating enough to make you fat; smoking cigarettes (maybe); smoking marihuana (positively).

> Not taking care of your obligations; being lazy or shiftless; losing money at gambling; swearing and using bad language publicly.

If we accept this list as typical, it is as interesting for the conduct it omits as for that which it includes. Many acts that were in the past or are now attacked as highly immoral are not even mentioned: contraception, abortion, sex and race discrimination to mention just a few. Our Everyman also seems unconcerned about profiteering, sharp-dealing, tax evasion, consumer fraud, and other kinds of white-collar crime. To be sure, if questioned specifically about these unmentioned acts, he would disapprove of all of them (except for contraception, possibly), but the term "deviant conduct" would not bring them immediately to mind, as it does for the acts listed.

The reason for our Everyman's selective perception of deviance lies in our description of Everyman: middle-class, middle-aged, and white. From where he stands some acts affect his world adversely, others have little effect, and some are simply irrelevant. He does not especially care about racial or sexual discrimination because he is neither black nor female. He believes in sexual regularity because he is a family man whose world is stabilized by the nuclear families of his friends and neighbors. Furthermore, illegitimacy (as he sees it) is a direct and undeserved burden on taxpayers such as himself because of its effect on welfare rolls. On the other hand, contraception does not seem wrong to him since his middle-class status was probably dependent on his own success in limiting the size of his family. Even abortion has much to be said for it, since anyone can get into trouble, and, anyway, maybe abortion will keep some of those babies off welfare. He does not worry too much about tax evasion because he is not aware of the activities of large-scale tax evaders, such as giant corporations and wealthy individuals whose accountants and tax lawyers have created tax shelters for them; and small-scale tax evasion is probably a fairly common and socially acceptable activity in his milieu. Sharp dealing (such as exploitive landlord-tenant or consumer-purchaser transactions) also provides a living for some middle-class individuals; and in any case, middle-class people are frequently able to cope with dishonest landlords or tradesmen. On the other hand, individuals who take or sell drugs are enormously threatening both because drug use frequently leads to assaultive or dangerous criminal conduct, and because drug addicts, by their aberrant attitudes toward work and other social obligations, threaten the stability of the social system. In fact, if there is one thread which runs through the fabric of our Everyman's scheme of acceptable social conduct, it is the desire to maintain stability, to preserve the status quo. As a middle-class individual, he has made it, and he recognizes that life is as good for him as it is ever likely to be. He does not want to lose what he has. Change is threatening and makes him very uncomfortable.

The laundry list of unacceptable conduct varies with the age and status of the individual compiling it. Inner-city blacks, for example, might list racial discrimination first and not list gambling at all. Smoking marihuana might be quite acceptable to middle-class university students, but tax evasion, sharp dealing, and profiteering would be high on their lists of forbidden conduct. In the Bible Belt of the deep South, blasphemy, secularism, and atheism are still heinous offenses, yet relatively free use of firearms, moonshining, and blatant racial discrimination are regarded with considerable tolerance.

Obviously, deviance is to some extent in the eye of the beholder—but only to some extent. All classes and status groups reject violent assaultive crime.* They differ, however, with respect to other

---

* An exception might be black revolutionaries such as George Jackson, who while imprisoned in San Quentin for armed robbery, wrote extensively on the place of blacks in white society. Jackson felt that because "Amerika" was a "society above society" in which blacks were "captive," they were

types of unacceptable conduct, some of which are illegal in our system, some of which are immoral, and some of which are merely matters of good taste. In considering these widely varying perceptions of what constitutes deviant conduct, the basic question must be not who is right and who is wrong, but what kinds of conduct society can tolerate and still exist as a viable society, and what kinds it cannot accept. Part of the answer, of course, must lie in one's perception of a desirable society. For purposes of this discussion we are assuming an ideal closely akin to the traditional Jeffersonian model: an open society predicated on a belief in equality of opportunity and equality before the law, with a reasonable level of material comfort and economic security for all. In such a society, what kinds of behavior are necessarily beyond the pale?

Deviance: Crime

Clearly, heading the list are murder, rape, arson, assault, robbery, burglary, and larceny, acts that are totally unacceptable, and condoned, if at all, only on an ad hoc basis and under very special circumstances.* We label these acts *crimes*, meaning that they are offenses against the public order sufficiently severe so as to require handling punitively and coercively by the police, courts, and prisons. Even the perpetrators agree that their conduct is wrong. A housebreaker does not want his house to be burglarized, and, except in legends such as Robin Hood, robbers do not argue that what they do is legitimate. This type of conduct is taboo, because a viable society cannot be maintained if such acts are tolerated. Throughout history the control of such conduct is indeed one of the central problems

under no obligation to obey the laws. All crime, therefore, was an act of rebellion. Even Jackson concedes, however, that noneconomic crime, e.g., "the rape of a black woman by a black man," is an expression of racial violence turned inward. It is "autodestructive" and hence presumably wrong, even if understandable. Tad Szulc, "George Jackson Radicalizes the Brothers in Soledad and San Quentin," *New York Times Magazine,* August 1, 1971, p. 10.

* We are referring here, of course, to random acts by individuals or small groups such as gangs and omitting discussion of governmentally organized and sponsored violence such as that practiced under Hitler in Germany, during the Spanish Inquisition, or in any war. Whether this kind of organized violence is ever justifiable depends on one's politics, religion, nationality, and time in history.

faced by philosophers who have attempted to construct model societies. Whatever their point of view and whatever type of Utopia they have created, they all have at least agreed that this type of act must be forbidden. While Hobbes and Locke, for example, were diametrically opposed in their perceptions of the fundamental nature of man and in their prescriptions for social control of human conduct, they agreed that the principal difficulty in human society is the regulation of assaultive, violent acts of one individual upon another.

Assaultive conduct, however, is only one category of crime. So-called "white-collar crime," while nonviolent, is basically an attack on legitimate property arrangements in society. Acts such as tax fraud, stock manipulations, commercial bribery, misrepresentation in advertising and salesmanship, short weighting and misgrading of commodities, and embezzlement are all methods of illegitimately obtaining money or other property. Since the function of an economic system is to prescribe how one may properly obtain property, white-collar criminals are subversive of accepted economic relationships. As such, they, like their more violent criminal counterparts, are a threat to a viable society, and it is reasonable that their acts be included in the penal code.* We do in fact so label them, but, although the prescribed penalties may sometimes be as severe as those for burglary or larceny, these acts do not carry the stigma or the punishment of violent crimes. In 1961, some forty-five executives of electrical equipment manufacturing companies (including General Electric and Westinghouse vice-presidents) were convicted in Federal Court of having fixed prices and rigged bids for government contracts. The dollar value of the funds they thereby illegally misappropriated from the public treasury probably exceeded the amount stolen by a thousand ordinary burglars in their lifetimes. Yet, the heaviest sentence imposed on any individual involved was a thirty-day jail sentence and a fine. The case, moreover, was newsworthy not because of the magnitude of the fraud, but because of the unusual *severity* of the sentences imposed. It is true, of course, that the high socioeconomic

* While many political theorists have attacked the American economic system and consequent property arrangements as illegitimate in terms of natural justice, no one has seriously suggested that the types of fraud usually encompassed by the term "white-collar crime" are justified as an attempt to remedy economic inequity. The embezzlers and stock manipulators have not yet produced their George Jackson.

status of the defendants was, in part, responsible for their lenient treatment; lower-middle-class embezzlers and stock manipulators are treated more harshly. Nevertheless, white-collar criminals are among the elite as criminals go. Their neighbors may be disapproving, but not disgusted. In fact, most of the defendants in the electrical conspiracy case did not even lose their jobs, and those who did had little trouble finding employment elsewhere at the same level.

We also are relatively tolerant of businessmen who stay within the technical limits of the law while they are in fact behaving fraudulently. Merchants who sell poor people shoddy merchandise or arrange for installment sales at usurious rates of interest; landlords who take advantage of housing shortages by remodeling dwellings into single-room occupancy units at unconscionable rents; "charitable" organizations that divert the bulk of the funds they collect toward high salaries and administrative expenses; advertisers who exaggerate the virtues of the product they sell—all these are examples of businessmen who are within the law but who are not honest. There is obviously a certain ambivalence in a society that considers conduct destructive enough to be labeled criminal, and then imposes relatively little social stigma upon those who engage in such conduct. The reasons for this ambivalence are not clear, but they probably stem from conflicting norms within the American system. On the one hand we believe in doing business by the rules and with honesty and reliability. Our whole credit system is a testimonial to the fact that most people are honest. Hertz and Avis are highly profitable businesses that operate by trusting total strangers to take possession of valuable automobiles, drive them thousands of miles away, return them in good condition, and pay for the service. On the other hand, American society also places a high premium on individual success, so high in fact that the illegitimacy of dubious means of achieving wealth is mitigated if the individual succeeds in his quest. The Robber Barons were prime examples of this process, but even less successful white-collar criminals farther down the social scale are treated relatively leniently.

Another variable in the treatment of white-collar criminals is the impact of the crime upon the victim or victims. When the impact is widespread and fairly minimal on any one individual, the impetus for punishment is blunted. This is true also when the impact is not fully perceived by the victim, as, for example, in the manufacture of defective automobiles that cause accidents. The accident victim may not realize that the automobile manufacturer was at fault. On the other hand, the embezzler who steals $1,000 from a small business-man or poor widow will be dealt with quite severely unless he makes restitution.

The basic ambivalence, however, remains. Property crimes are not really heinous if they are not violent or potentially violent. It is interesting to note that in the Soviet Union far less ambivalence is exhibited in regard to so-called "economic crimes." Some such of-fenses, such as currency manipulation, are punishable by death sen-tences, whereas certain kinds of homicide are treated with relative leniency. This difference probably reflects the orientation of the So-viet legal system toward the preservation of its economic and social system, rather than, as in this country, toward the protection of indi-vidual rights. From this point of view, the inconsistency of the Ameri-can system, which punishes personal crimes more severely than property crimes, is understandable. Whatever our ambivalences, however, it is clear that nonviolent crimes of property must be han-dled punitively, at least to the extent necessary to maintain the legiti-macy of both our property arrangements and our system of law. The latent admiration of Americans for Robber Baron types may never disappear, but if business is to be conducted in an orderly way, and if prohibitions on assaultive crimes are to be taken seriously, there must be reasonable enforcement of the law relating to white-collar of-fenses. Moreover, as the public conscience increases in sensitivity the criminal sanction will be extended to dealings that are now con-sidered unsavory but not illegal. The basic notion behind the devel-oping field of poverty law is, in fact, the extension of the criminal or civil law to cover some actions of landlords against tenants and of merchants against customers, neither of which has ever before been considered illegal. Can a landlord, for example, continue to demand rent from his tenants if he has failed to provide the agreed-upon level of services? Can a merchant misrepresent the quality of his merchan-dise and demand continued performance of a time payment contract if the goods in question have already deteriorated? The trend toward making such actions illegal is probably an indication of the feeling that even nonassaultive crimes of property are a threat to the viability of American society.

Our penal law thus contains prohibitions against both assaultive crimes against persons and property and nonassaultive crimes against property. Assaultive crimes offend our notions of natural justice; nonassaultive property crimes undermine the economic arrangements that are basic to the stability of society. The penal code (which is the most emphatic and in many ways the most important method of declaring social policy) logically contains such prohibitions. It also contains, however, strictures against a number of modes of conduct that are included because of a relatively parochial cultural determination that they are immoral: drinking, gambling, homosexuality, doing business on Sunday, prostitution, drug addiction, etc. While the legislators who enacted these prohibitions doubtlessly felt they were preventing subversion of the legitimate social system, there are many societies similar to our own in which such conduct is either tolerated quite well or handled nonpunitively. Many of these regulations are, moreover, both inconsistent and incomplete in their regulatory schemes. Prostitutes are punished, for example, but not their customers; heroin is forbidden, but not amphetamines; football betting, but not horse-race betting, etc.

Deviance: Sin

Many of these modes of conduct were originally thought of as sin, and *religiously* prohibited. Our use of secular law to regulate them is a hangover from the time when the authority of the state was used to enforce the rules of an established church. That era is past, but we can see our cultural heritage most clearly perhaps in the laws we inherited from the Puritan theocracy in New England. We have (or have had in the recent past) laws against blasphemy, obscenity, contraception, Sabbath breaking, extramarital sexual relations, lewdness, homosexuality, gambling, and drunkenness. (We also have inherited a distrust of self-indulgence and hedonism: even a rich man is expected to be constructively, if not gainfully, employed.)

Actually, this heritage is a reflection of a social culture of which religion once was a dominant part. As our culture has changed, as religion has waned in importance, as our economic system has developed, as scientific discoveries have occurred, and as improved communications and the development of the mass media have reduced both social and cultural isolation, our feelings about what constitutes sin have undergone a marked change. Some behavior, such as blasphemy, has become virtually acceptable today; other behavior, such as heroin use, is still taboo. We have highly ambivalent feelings about other forms of conduct, such as gambling, drinking, homosexuality, and abortion. While some of this conduct is still subject to the criminal sanction, some is not. If we remove the religious component, the criterion for whether the conduct in question should be forbidden should rest on whether there is *any demonstrable, objectively measurable social harm resulting from such conduct.* To determine this, each mode of conduct must be separately considered and evaluated. If this were a totally rational world, we would expect there to be a correlation between the prohibition of conduct and its objective harmfulness. Unfortunately, this is not a rational world, and the correlation does not exist.

Of all the modes of conduct in this culturally determined category, drinking is probably the most harmful and also the most widely accepted. Alcohol is involved in, among other things, at least half of all fatal automobile accidents, a majority of private airline crashes, thousands of industrial accidents, and millions of lost man-days annually. There are approximately 9 million alcoholics in the United States who are unable to support their families, do their jobs, or function normally in the community.[1] Alcohol use is involved in 55 percent of the arrests made by American police officers. From a medical point of view, even moderate drinking puts a strain on the liver and complicates many other diseases, such as diabetes and heart disease.

Yet today alcohol consumption is widely accepted in the United States, and absolute nondrinkers constitute only a small minority of the population. Historically, the temperance movement waxed and waned in strength for over a century before it culminated in the "noble experiment" of Prohibition in 1920. Within a few years after the enactment of the Eighteenth Amendment, however, it became apparent that Prohibition was a disaster, and since Repeal in 1933, the temperance movement appears to be all but moribund. Moderate social drinking is fully acceptable behavior except among members of strict religious sects, such as the Mormons. Problem drinkers, moreover, are considered sick rather than evil (or at least so we say, although in practice the handling of some alcoholics, particularly derelicts, is more punitive than therapeutic). Drinking, thus, has been handled both coercively through the criminal sanction (in the past) and noncoercively (at present), and while our current noncoercive approach has fewer adverse side effects in the form of enforcement difficulties and police corruption, alcohol abuse still presents a problem—a problem, however, that is not reflected in public attitudes.

Even more permissive than our attitude toward drinking are our feelings about cigarette smoking and overeating. The medical evidence against smoking and obesity is overwhelming, with both being major public health problems, but to forbid such conduct by law would be ludicrous and horrifying in terms of civil liberties. Even attempts to regulate cigarette advertising have met with great resistance. While there is considerable consensus that people ought not smoke or get fat, many, if not most, people do. The number of Americans who neither smoke nor are overweight is probably a minority, yet, medically and sociologically speaking, both are seriously harmful practices.

In contrast to drinking, smoking, and overeating, there is no medical evidence that moderate marihuana smoking is harmful, nor is there medical evidence of physiological harm due to reasonable heroin consumption. It is undoubtedly true that many heroin or marihuana users exhibit undesirable psychological symptoms, but it is not clear whether these symptoms are a result of drug use, or whether both drug use and behavioral dysfunction result from a prior existing pathological, psychological, or sociological condition. Most of the other adverse sociological effects of drug use, such as crime and prostitution, result from our present coercive handling of the drug problem rather than from drug use per se. In terms of social attitudes, however, there are few modes of conduct that are looked upon with more social disapproval than heroin use, and only recently is a similar attitude toward marihuana softening. Our method of handling drug use has, moreover, in certain respects been precisely opposite our handling of alcohol: alcohol, which formerly was handled punitively, is now handled nonpunitively; opiates and marihuana, which were formerly handled nonpunitively, are now handled punitively. (Until the passage of the Harrison Act in 1914, the sale and consumption of opium derivatives were unregulated in the United States. Administrative and judicial interpretations of the Harrison Act since 1914 have led to a total prohibition on the sale and distribution of heroin, and, since 1937, of marihuana as well.)

Neither punitive handling, moreover, nor extreme social disapproval has resulted in a decline (or even a stabilization) of the number of marihuana and heroin users in the United States. Marihuana use, which during the thirties was a relatively isolated phenomenon confined to some Spanish-speaking and black groups, spread during the 1960s to the extent that today a majority of college students is thought to use marihuana at least occasionally, and a large proportion of middle-class individuals between the ages of fifteen and thirty-five are considered to be regular users. Heroin use, similarly, has increased sharply. Where, in 1967, it was estimated that there were 100,000 addicts in the United States, of whom 50,000 were in New York City, five years later the estimates had precisely tripled: 300,000 in the United States and 150,000 in New York City. Not only has punitive handling failed to reduce the incidence of marihuana and heroin use, but it has also produced a number of very undesirable side-effects. The effect of punitive handling on the incidence of crime has already been mentioned, as well as its connection with the growth of organized crime and its impact on the criminal justice system. What we are less aware of, perhaps, is that we have simultaneously produced a public health problem and virtually eliminated opportunities for research into its alleviation. Heroin addicts are today a focal point in the spread of hepatitis. They frequently become victims of the disease because of the unsanitary conditions under which they inject the drug and, once having become infected, they spread the infection either through direct contact with other people or through subsequent sale of their blood to blood banks. The infections, malnutrition, and other pathological conditions associated with the life of the drug addict, moreover, have made drug addiction the leading cause of death among young adults. One of these pathological factors is the difficulty of obtaining unadulterated drug supplies that are uniform in quality. The drugs purchased by the addict may at any time be either stronger or weaker than the dosage to which his body has become accustomed. If the overdose is too great he will die. Drug supplies are, moreover, diluted with many different types of adulterants, ranging from milk sugar and quinine to rat poison. Presumably, the more lethal adulterants are not used frequently since the addict population has not declined. In the criminal subculture, however, of which drug use is a part, the use of poisons as adulterants is a convenient way of disposing of those individuals who are suspected of being potentially dangerous to suppliers.

Despite the epidemic proportions of drug use, however, we

know very little, medically speaking, about either the physiological or psychological mechanisms relating to drug use. We have only a hazy idea of why people become addicted. We don't really know what the nature of addiction is: whether there is a chemical imbalance of the make-up of some individuals which makes them prone to drug addiction; whether addiction has unknown physiological and chemical effects; what the distinction between physiological and psychological dependence is. We don't know the chemistry of addiction: how the drug produces the effect that it does on the body. We don't know why some users become addicted and some do not. We know virtually nothing about curing addicts once they have a firm commitment to the drug. We don't know why addiction seems to be concentrated among young adults, and why older people seldom appear in the ranks of addicts. An important reason why we know so little is because the total ban on heroin has had a chilling effect on medical research. It is difficult if not impossible for doctors to obtain supplies of heroin for research purposes, and even when and if such supplies can be obtained, they must of necessity be hedged about with so many restrictions and precautions against improper use that research is inhibited. Physicians and other research workers, if they are to work with addicts, must by definition work with members of a criminal subculture who are unpleasant, undependable, and frequently dangerous. It is understandable that medical schools are reluctant to undertake such research, and government and foundation money is scarce. In short, no matter what position one takes in regard to either the morality or legality of drug use, it is extremely difficult to find a single positive result of our present method of handling the problem. Like Prohibition, our present drug policy can only be described as a disaster.

In contrast to our attitude towards alcohol and drug use, which have fluctuated between acceptance and rejection, our attitudes toward deviant sexual conduct have grown rather consistently more permissive. During the eighteenth and nineteenth centuries in this country, the etiquette of behavior between men and women reflected a society that placed high value on premarital chastity and monogamy. Divorce was frowned upon, and premarital dalliance (except possibly for young men who were sowing their "wild oats") was strictly taboo. Prostitution, at least from the middle-class point of view, was considered degrading and abhorrent, and the fallen woman became a stock figure in literature. In the same period, homosexuality seems to have been considered so dreadful that there appears to have been neither public discussion of the subject nor literary reference to the problem, except for some very guarded indirect references. Today we are permissive in regard to premarital sex; we sanction divorce; we have ambivalent attitudes toward prostitution; and we are slowly coming to a grudging acceptance of homosexual conduct. Some of these attitudinal changes have been reflected in changes in either the criminal law or its application; others have not. Nevertheless, few people would dispute the proposition that our attitudes toward sexual conduct have changed substantially even if the conduct in question has not.

To understand this phenomenon one must appreciate that the older rules for sexual conduct were drawn up in a society that had vastly different needs: until the twentieth century the need was for more population rather than less; venereal disease was an uncontrollable plague; and production of goods and services was directly dependent on the family in a way that no longer exists. Before twentieth-century advances in public health and medical knowledge, infant mortality rates were high, large numbers of women died in childbirth, and young adults in their prime were struck down by contagious disease. Demographically, this meant that a high birth rate was necessary to balance a high death rate. Sociologically, in an agricultural society with a relatively weak decentralized governmental structure, monogamous marriages were the most feasible way of caring for the large numbers of children that needed to be born. Any sexual conduct that tended to undermine monogamous marriages, such as homosexuality, prostitution, or premarital sex, was subversive in a sense, of society itself. Even contraception and abortion were dangerous in an age that needed people.

Promiscuous sexuality, moreover, posed a threat of uncontrollable epidemics of venereal disease. Until the advent of modern drugs and pharmaceuticals, the most practicable way of containing the damage done by venereal disease was to limit the sexual contacts of each individual. While it was true that in any case syphilis was passed on congenitally to newborn infants, the spread would have been worse if the syphilitic parent had had contact with a variety of sexual partners.

The economy was tied, moreover, to the family unit in a way that is hard for us to appreciate today. The United States was predominantly agricultural until the Civil War, and even after the Civil War, well into the twentieth century, a majority of Americans lived on the land. While American farming since colonial times tended to be of a commercial rather than a subsistence type, until quite recently, farming was a family enterprise rather than the agribusiness type of establishment found today in the vast wheat and cattle ranches of the West, and the huge fruit and vegetable farms of California. A family farm requires a family to run it: mother, father, and above all, children who become economic assets by the time they are seven or eight years old. Even in industrial areas, moreover, the family operated as a unit. In coal mining areas, youngsters went down into the mines to do work within their physical capacity, and contributed their pittance wages to the household so that the family might survive. Children worked in the factories in much the same way. It is estimated that in the early part of the twentieth century, as much as one-tenth of American industrial production was produced by children under the age of fourteen. In some of the large cities where immigrant populations were concentrated, women and children worked in their homes, producing caps, waists, artificial flowers, and a variety of other items in order to supplement the salary of the principal wage earner. In an era of low wage rates, it was the earnings of wife and children that spelled the difference between survival and disaster, and in a very real sense the entire American economy was based on the assumption that the family as a unit could produce.

Medical knowledge and technology have turned the older rationale for monogamous units upside-down. Whereas one hundred years ago, a couple might have to produce ten or a dozen children in order to produce four or six live adults, today the parents of two can reasonably expect to raise both to adulthood. Whereas previously men buried two or three wives who died in childbirth, and women survived two or three husbands who were killed by typhoid, yellow fever, or industrial accidents, the thrice married individual today is more likely to be a divorced rather than a widowed person. Where sexual promiscuity used to result in either an unwanted pregnancy or even more unwanted venereal disease, with minimal care today's gay blades need suffer neither; and if he or she is careless, the consequences may still be avoided through abortion and medical care. Perhaps most significant of all is that where formerly children represented a source of income and social security for one's old age, children today are economic liabilities at least until they reach adulthood, and sometimes thereafter. Unionization and the changing pattern of industrialization have, moreover, raised wage levels to a point where the earnings of children are no longer essential, and the increased emphasis on social security and medicare have removed primary responsibility for the care of older people from the family unit to impersonal governmental units.

In the face of these substantial scientific and technological changes, it is understandable that many of the older rules of sexual conduct are anachronistic. This is not to say that our commitment to monogamous unions, as the basis of our family structure, has weakened. Nor does it mean that actual sexual practices (as opposed to the accepted social standards for what those practices should be) have changed very much. What it means is that deviation from these sexual norms is accepted more readily and less fearfully than was previously the case. We are not so hysterically defensive about our rules of sexual conduct because we no longer see deviations from those rules as subversive of the entire social order. We no longer need a strict sexual code to provide for population maintenance or growth, industrial or agricultural production, or as a prophylactic against rampant venereal disease. Our family structure, and thus our sexual code, is adhered to more for the fulfillment of individual, rather than for societal needs, i.e., the achievement of personal happiness and an optimal setting in which to raise children. Under those circumstances the desire of some individuals to find personal happiness through premarital sex, homosexuality, prostitution, etc., becomes less terrifying and, if not acceptable, is at least understandable.

On the whole, our penal codes have lagged behind public attitudes and behavior in the field of sexual practices. Relatively little change has occurred in the statutory prohibitions in this area. Contraception has to all intents and purposes been legalized throughout the United States, and abortion in the first six months of pregnancy has been declared permissible by the United States Supreme Court. The statute books, however, still hold both homosexual acts between consenting adults and prostitution to be a crime. This, however, presents a deceptive picture of actual practice. Police, prosecutors, and courts rarely concern themselves with sexual conduct that is kept private enough to avoid offending the sensibilities of those not party to it. The laws on the books, moreover, even if they were enforced, are illogical and ineffective. As indicated previously, it is unfair and counterproductive to prosecute only prostitutes and not their customers. Surely, if we wanted to rid ourselves of prostitution, it would be eminently sensible, as well as just, to apply the law to both parties to the transaction. Secondly, if we are concerned, as we still must be to some extent, with the spread of venereal disease, it would be more practical to license prostitutes and require regular medical examinations than to try to eliminate a practice that is probably as old as recorded history.

Actually, proposals to license prostitutes have very few supporters. There are also very few groups, including the police, that are anxious to eliminate prostitution. What most people seem to want is that prostitutes be kept out of sight. It is the appearance of the street walker, rather than what she does, that is offensive. If all prostitutes were high-priced call girls operating discreetly, their conduct would cause hardly a ripple of public disapproval. The same is true of homosexuality and other unorthodox sexual behavior. We are willing to accept it if we don't see it. These public attitudes are illustrated by the current results of the struggle over obscene and pornographic literature. For years the courts, including the United States Supreme Court, wrestled with the problem of defining obscenity and pornography, finally by their failure conceding that there is no clear standard for such determination. While the range or scope of what can be published in the way of erotic materials has been broadened, however, the way in which such materials can be marketed has been limited. Ralph Ginzburg's offense for which he was committed for three years to federal prison was not that he published obscene materials, but that he "pandered," i.e., he merchandised those materials in an offensive way. Police today are far less concerned with the sale of pornographic materials or the showing of pornographic movies than they are with sidewalk or window displays advertising such wares. As long as such shops and movie houses present a discreet face to the general public, they are unlikely to be prosecuted. This is a tacit recognition of the fact that we consider deviant sexual behavior for the most part to be tasteless, unpleasant, and perhaps unwise, but not dangerous.*

Our attitudes toward deviant sexual practices thus have become more permissive but have stopped short of achieving full acceptance. Gambling, however, is a mode of conduct that probably has come closest of all to shedding the stigma of immorality inherited from the past. American attitudes toward gambling have always been ambivalent. Even in Puritan times we find mention of gaming and lotteries at the same time the churches were exhorting against such worldly pleasures. The 1821 case of *Cohens* v. *Virginia*,[2] concerning the degree of sovereignty reserved to the states under the federal Constitution, arose because of a conflict between the laws of Virginia, which forbade the selling of lottery tickets, and the laws of the District of Columbia, which permitted such sales. By the end of the nineteenth century most Protestant denominations opposed gambling, partly because of its self-indulgent character, and partly because of the fear that the poor would gamble their way into destitution. (In an era of private religiously centered charity rather than public assistance for the needy, this was doubtless a practical consideration.) Gradually, however, during the twentieth century the Catholic church, which had never quite shared the enthusiasm of the Protestants for condemning earthly pleasures, became more openly accepting of gambling (particularly when Bingo and other games of chance proved a lucrative source of church income). Protestants until recently still lined up fairly rigidly against state sponsored or state permitted gambling in any form.† Slowly, however, the Protestant at-

---

* In 1973, the United States Supreme Court decided a group of obscenity cases, *Miller* v. *California,* 413 U.S. 15 (1973), et al., in which the Court upheld the rights of local communities to set their own standards for obscenity. This may lead to a reversion to earlier police practices, where the emphasis was more on the substance of the materials in question, rather than on the way they were marketed. The *Miller* decision presents a number of problems however (cf. Ch. V) and it is too soon to predict what the impact on the police and prosecutors will be, or whether the decision itself is likely to be modified.

† The Northeastern states (New York, Massachusetts, and Connecticut), where Catholic influence was strongest in the two decades after World War II, in many respects demonstrated conflicting religious patterns of morality: the Catholics lining up *for* released time for religious instruction in the public

titudes have softened, probably because of the general relaxation of the personal standards of behavior, and perhaps because of the possibilities of relief for the hard-pressed taxpayer through state sponsored lotteries. In any case, at the present time, not only does Nevada have legalized gambling, and New York OTB (a public corporation to conduct off-track betting), but increasingly the criminal justice system is refusing to use its resources to enforce antigambling laws. The police protest openly at the futility of picking up small-time gamblers who are doing no more than the employees of the state-owned Off-Track Betting Corporation, and the courts handle such gamblers as are prosecuted in a perfunctory and minimally punitive manner. The change in public opinion, the negative attitudes of police and prosecutors toward gambling law enforcement, combined with public awareness of the fact that illegal gambling is a major source of income for organized criminal syndicates, appears to be hastening the day when many if not all gambling statutes will actually be repealed. There is virtually no effective interest group in the United States today that has espoused the cause of retaining gambling laws on the books. Public apathy and the fear of criticism by zealots are apparently the major factors retarding legislative repeal today.

Deviance: Poor Taste

In contrast to acts that are crimes and/or sins, there are some aspects of human behavior that are considered matters of taste, and which even when disapproved of, are rarely regulated by law. Manners and style fall within this category. Women in pants were once objects of scandal, and girls' bobbed hair during the 1920s was viewed as dubiously as boys' long hair in the 1960s. In Puritan New England it was a misdemeanor for a man and woman to kiss in public even if they were married; we think nothing of more overt expressions of affection, although we become increasingly offended as the conduct becomes more explicitly sexual. Adults smile benignly at little Boy Scouts and Girl Scouts in their uniforms, but glare at black-jacketed Hell's Angels and similarly dressed members of youth

schools, and legalization of Bingo, and *against* relaxation of laws against birth control, abortion, and divorce; the Protestants taking precisely the opposite positions *for* birth control, divorce, and abortion and *against* Bingo and religious released time for public schools.

gangs. Frenchmen may kiss each other heartily; American men may not. It is all right to wear a cross or a mezuzah, but a swastika armband, a hooded sheet, a clenched fist salute are perceived with considerable hostility and, under certain circumstances are forbidden by the authorities.

To the visitor from Mars all of this can be very confusing. Why, for example, is it all right for adults to wear skimpy bathing suits in public but never their underwear? To us, however, it is not confusing at all, although few people when pressed could rationalize all the idiosyncracies of manners and style that comprise taste. It is clear that to a great extent these modes of conduct are cultural accidents. Pants are no more ordained by nature for men than skirts are for women, and in some tribal societies men do wear skirts and women pants. There is nothing in the shape of a cross that inherently suggests Christianity, nor in the shape of the swastika that inherently equals fascism. Handshaking is neither more nor less rational as a method of greeting than a kiss on the cheek, or a deep curtsy.

While such conduct itself may be irrational, the inferences drawn from it may be highly rational. The wearing of the swastika by American fascists is a reliable indicator of a belief in racial inequality, a totalitarian system of government, etc. A man who appears in public in a woman's dress probably is sexually deviant. What we object to in these modes of conduct, therefore, is that they suggest or anticipate other actions to which we take exception. They are in a sense *symbolic* conduct, symbolic of some type of overt action to which there is or may be a rational objection. Thus, the objection to the swastika is an objection to fascism, and the more closely the swastika is related in reality to fascism, and the more we object to fascism as a mode of conduct, the more we will object to the swastika. Many modes of dress are objectionable because they appear to anticipate undesirable sexual conduct: slacks and bikinis on women, long hair and feminine looking clothing on men. Interpersonal conduct—modes of greeting and communicating with other people—are evaluated by our interpretation of the hidden messages those modes send out. When attempts are made to change matters of manner and style, objection is frequently vigorous simply because such changes are viewed as a precedent to change in more serious forms of nonsymbolic conduct. It is at the point where the symbolic conduct is recognized as having lost its symbolism that opposition fades away.

In Victorian times a woman who showed her ankles freely was considered a fast woman, aggressively inviting promiscuous conduct. When enough women started to wear short skirts without the anticipated undesirable sexual conduct resulting, short skirts became acceptable. The first men to wear their hair in the current style were considered to be homosexually inclined. When the majority of adolescent youths and young men adopted the fashion, long hair as a symbol of homosexuality faded.

Thus the problem in regard to matters of taste is to recognize, first of all, that they are cultural accidents and may be intrinsically quite irrational. We must also recognize, however, that such conduct is symbolic conduct and may be the surface manifestation of far more meaningful attitudes and actions. In regulating such matters of taste then, the problem is to know when the surface conduct is truly symbolic and when it has lost its symbolism. If the symbolism is extant, and if the conduct to which it refers is truly harmful, then it is possible that even symbolic action may need to be regulated socially. One of the most difficult problems in law enforcement, for example, is when and how to control inflammatory street demonstrations that frequently rely on dress, political insignia, and stylized methods of speaking to incite a group to potentially antisocial action. Consider the problems of policing the massive peace demonstrations in Washington, D.C. during the Nixon administration, where as many as a quarter of a million people participated, a large proportion of whom wore long hair, hippie headbands, black armbands, and who carried posters with abusive and insulting language, candles in memory of the dead, and caskets; or consider the 1966 situation where a couple of dozen white robed and hooded Klansmen held a rally in the center of a Southern town with a large Negro population, during which they broadcast by loud speaker racial epithets and violent and provocative anti-Negro sentiments. What modes of conduct or dress, if any, should the police have controlled? Was it worse to wear a white sheet and hood than hippie beads and a black armband? Was it worse to yell fascist or nigger? Was it worse to gather in a group of 250,000 calling for peace than in a group of 25 calling for riot?

The seemingly unimportant problem of regulating matters of taste is actually quite complex because it is in these matters of taste that social change frequently has its first impact. The degree of resistance to change in these matters is a reflection of the rigidity of society itself. To remain viable, a society that encourages a high degree of technical innovation must display as the price of such innovation a reasonable amount of flexibility in accepting change in these symbolic modes of conduct.

The range of deviant conduct is extensive: from personal violence and dishonesty to the latest fad in hairdos or adolescent dress. The very term deviant suggests that there is a norm to which society thinks its members ought to return. To effectuate that return social policies, of which the penal code is but one expression, exert pressures on nonconforming individuals. The current popular clamor against "permissiveness" implies that not enough social pressure is being exerted against deviants. An analysis of types of deviant conduct however, suggests that heavy social pressure may be desirable in only a small number of the kinds of behavior we label deviant; in other cases such behavior may be counterproductive and represent a form of overkill. Why this is so becomes more readily apparent if we examine some of the ways we currently handle the most important kinds of deviance.

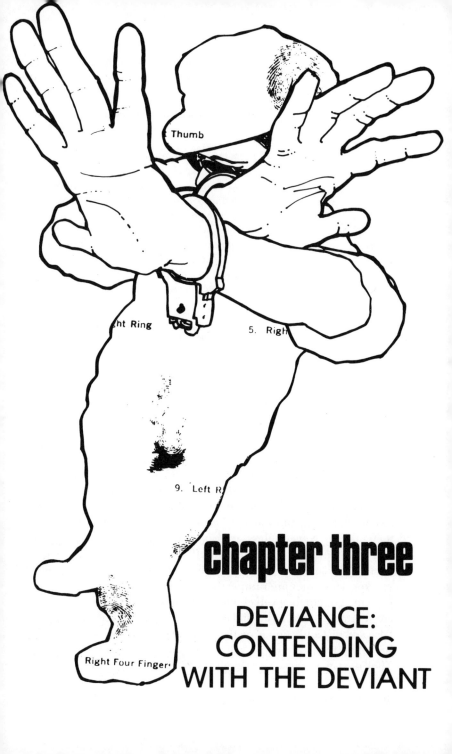

chapter three

DEVIANCE: CONTENDING WITH THE DEVIANT

Deviance is, to use Albert K. Cohen's definition, "behavior which violates institutionalized expectations . . . expectations which are
shared and recognized as legitimate within a social system." [1] This is
an admirable definition, but its difficulties lie in determining precisely what the institutionalized expectations are and how legitimate
they may be. Nevertheless, in many situations there is widespread
agreement, even by the actor himself, that a particular mode of conduct is deviant. Burglars know they are doing wrong, cigarette
smokers know they are ruining their health, alcoholics know they are
bringing grief to themselves and their families, fat people know they
are shortening their lives, and drug users know that their euphoria is
false and that addiction is really an unsatisfactory way of coping with
life. Why then do people rob, drink, smoke, overeat, take drugs?
They deviate because society places great stresses on every individ-

ual, and when those stresses become too great, individuals make adjustments in their conduct which may, from a medical, psychological, or sociological standpoint be highly unsatisfactory, but which may nevertheless be the optimum that they are able to achieve at that particular point. *Deviance is, in short, an attempt to cope. From this point of view, almost everyone is deviant in some respect.* Almost everyone smokes, overeats, drives too fast, drinks too much, or does something else that is personally or socially destructive.

Deviant conduct, moreover, is not necessarily related to personality abnormality. To put it another way, if everyone who is deviant were considered abnormal, the definition of abnormality would be so broad as to be virtually meaningless. Without becoming involved in the ongoing controversy over what constitutes personality abnormality, for the purposes of this discussion, let us define as psychotic an individual who is out of touch with reality with respect to time, place, or circumstance. All other individuals, i.e., all those who are in touch with reality are nonpsychotic. Within this nonpsychotic group are many neurotic individuals, i.e., individuals who can cope with reality but at some psychic cost. Some neurotics develop facial tics; some develop stomach ulcers; others indulge in various forms of deviant behavior. It is difficult to determine in any group who is neurotic and who is not, partly because the criteria for neurotic behavior are ill defined, and partly because neurotic and normal behavior are not clearly separated from each other, but in fact form a continuum. The kinds of deviant behavior we have been discussing here can be found widely dispersed among all groups: psychotic, neurotic, and normal, and the degree of social destructiveness exhibited by various kinds of deviant behavior is not necessarily related to the degree of personality disorganization of those performing such behavior. The Puerto Rican boy in *el barrio* who conforms to the drug-taking habits of his peers may be far less "neurotic" than the successful businessman who is thirty pounds overweight and smokes three packs of cigarettes a day.

The well-springs of deviant behavior, thus, lie not so much in personality as in society. It is the stresses that society creates interacting with the personality of a given individual that is the determinant of behavior, whether deviant or otherwise. This is not to say, however, that deviance is mechanically foreordained by the individual's place in society. While there is probably a causal relationship between poverty and crime, for example, not every poor person becomes a criminal, and middle-class children with every advantage sometimes go wrong. No individual, no matter how pressing the claims that society makes upon him, ever entirely escapes some degree of personal responsibility for his behavior. It may be very difficult for a person to avoid socially disapproved or socially destructive conduct, but the fact that individuals under the most adverse circumstances have survived crushing pressures indicates that behavior is more than mechanically determined. The assumption that there is some area in which free will operates is, moreover, an assumption that is absolutely basic to any type of free society. To deny this assumption is to accept the legitimacy of infinite bureaucratic manipulation of individuals "for their own good." If man is a robot, then Big Brother must be the robot-master. It is the continuing belief that individuals count, and can to some degree affect their personal destinies, which makes possible the democratic faith.

If deviant behavior, thus, is an attempt to cope, the form that deviance takes depends on the total circumstances of the individual plus the opportunities that his culture offers him. Ninety-eight pound weaklings do not become second story men because it takes physical strength, coordination, and stamina to be a competent burglar. Adolescents with problems in isolated rural communities may burn down barns but do not become drug addicts because drugs are not available in such communities and barns are. Jews seldom become alcoholics but have a strong tendency to overeat. Food rather than drink will normally be chosen as the vehicle for deviance simply because it is a form of deviance more acceptable to Jewish culture. Deviants, on the other hand, who wish to shock by their behavior will choose a mode of conduct that is as abrasive or unacceptable as possible. Thus, rebellious adolescents in our culture will smoke hashish; in a Moslem society they will drink whiskey. Before the discovery of tobacco there were no smokers; before the development of the distillation of spirits only wine and beer were consumed. In the nineteenth century Jesse James held up trains and stagecoaches. Today we have airplane hijackers. Our social culture provides the means for deviance as well as the pressures that lead to it. The individual's personality, physical makeup, and environment determine the form deviant conduct will assume, or whether indeed he will become deviant at all. Aggressive tendencies, for example, may, in the ghetto, be translated into rape or assault; in a middle-class community they may be transmuted into the ambition that leads to professional accomplishment and advancement; in a war-time army, such aggression may produce a Congressional Medal winner.

While insight into the nature of deviant conduct and its causes is interesting intellectually, in practical terms such insight is useful primarily in answering the most important question of all: What do we do about deviant behavior in society? This question is essentially similar to the new mother's inquiry about what to do with her crying baby. What one does about a crying baby depends upon why the baby is crying; what society does about deviant conduct depends on what kind of adaptation the deviant is attempting to make by his deviance.

Deviance: A Conceptual Framework

Robert K. Merton, in one of the most seminal of twentieth-century sociological writings, has categorized the ways in which individuals adapt to society.[2] His hypothesis, stated in simplified terms, is that society imposes certain goals on its members and indicates legitimate means by which these goals may be achieved. Individuals who accept both the goals and the means specified are conformists who, for purposes of this discussion, pose no problems. Other individuals, who may accept the goals of society, reject the indicated legitimate means either because they cannot, or will not, use these means; and still other individuals may use legitimate means to achieve goals that are not socially approved. Both of these latter categories engage in deviant conduct, though the type of conduct and its significance varies between the two groups. Those who accept society's goals but reject the legitimate means for attaining them may, for example, become burglars or swindlers. They accept the goal of acquiring material goods but they reject the prescribed means of hard work and individual effort. For them crime is a short cut to the attainment of a socially acceptable goal which they see (realistically or unrealistically) as otherwise unattainable for them.

The conduct of those who accept legitimate means but reject the approved goals of society is not so obviously deviant as is the conduct of the first group. Into this group of means acceptors-goals rejectors fall such individuals as the stereotype of the bureaucrat: the clerk who exists for the purpose of perpetuating his job rather than serving the overall function of his agency or the organization of which it is a part. These individuals invent nitpicking regulations, find reasons to refuse service on picayune grounds, fight to the death any attempt at administrative innovation or reform, and generally constitute a burden on a mass society that must deliver services on a large scale if it is to survive. In the sense that they act as a brake on progress and needed change their conduct is not only counterproductive but is deviant in the sense that "it violates institutionalized expectations" by preventing the agency from performing as well as society has a right to expect. An extreme example of this type of bureaucratic means acceptor-goals rejector is Adolph Eichmann. From the point of view of the Israeli prosecutors, at least, Eichmann's crime lay precisely in the fact that he followed Hitler's orders to the letter, without perceiving that these orders were completely beyond the pale of legitimate goals for legislation. To put it another way, Eichmann saw the whole of his duty as following legitimate bureaucratic means. The unsympathetic Israelis, on the other hand, saw his supreme efficiency in killing masses of Jews as deviant conduct.*

A fourth group that Merton discusses is composed of those who reject both the goals and the means imposed by society. In this group are people who "cop out": psychotics, outcasts, vagrants, tramps, chronic drunkards, and drug addicts.†

Deviant conduct, thus, must be analyzed in terms of what the deviant is trying to tell us by his conduct, and what we do about him depends on why he is doing whatever it is that we feel is wrong. Con-

---

* For a discussion of deviant conduct more typical of bureaucrats see Arthur H. Levin, *The Satisficers* (New York: McCall Publishers, 1970). Levin's book is a scathing indictment of officials of the U.S. Department of Health, Education and Welfare for their tendency to "satisfice," i.e., to do a job that is good enough to get by, but which does not truly meet the needs of the public they are supposed to be serving.

† Merton's paradigm includes a fifth category of individuals who reject society's goals and means but who wish to substitute other, more legitimate goals and means to which they would then conform. In this group are rebels, revolutionaries, and the more militant of social reformers. We have not discussed this category since it is not germane to the central purposes of this chapter.

sider, for example, the following case histories.* They are in no way remarkable. Indeed, their value lies in that they are typical of the ways in which the common forms of deviance—crime, alcoholism, drug abuse, sexual misconduct, smoking, gambling, and overeating— manifest themselves, and the ways in which our society handles such deviance.

Case Histories in Deviance:

	Name	*Type of Conduct*
Case 1	Bernard Lewis	Homicide
Case 2	John Mahon	Robbery
	Malcolm Lane	
	Henry Galt	
Case 3	Dirk Van Rijn	Robbery and Drug Abuse
Case 4	Marvin Rothblatt	Embezzlement and Drug Abuse
Case 5	Lars Larsen	Assault and Alcoholism
Case 6	Lucy Comerford	Alcoholism
Case 7	Lincoln Breed	Alcoholism
Case 8	Carlo Traventi	Homosexuality and Making Obscene Telephone Calls
Case 9	Peter Arroyo	Homosexuality
Case 10	Roy Williams	Voyeurism and Homosexuality
Case 11	Olive	Prostitution
Case 12	Jerry Geller	Gambling and Fraud
Case 13	William Tallman	Smoking
Case 14	Lorraine Bendix	Overeating

Case 1: Homicide

Bernard Lewis, a thirty-six-year-old maintenance man, while preparing dinner became involved in an argument with his drunken wife. In a fit of rage Lewis, using the kitchen knife with which he had

---

* Some of the names in these cases are fictitious, although the cases themselves are not. The fictitious names suggest the ethnic background of the real subjects. The cases themselves were drawn from various sources: the records of the New York State Supreme Court (Kings County) Probation Department; Brooklyn Association for the Rehabilitation of Offenders (BARO); scholarly writings in the field; and current periodicals.

been preparing the meal, stabbed and killed his wife. He immediately called for assistance, and readily confessed when the first patrolman appeared on the scene with the ambulance attendant. He pleaded guilty to manslaughter. The probation department's presentence investigation indicated that Lewis was a rigid individual who never drank, worked regularly, and had no previous criminal record. His thirty-year-old deceased wife, and mother of three children, was a "fine girl" when sober but was frequently drunk and on a number of occasions when intoxicated had left their small children unattended. After due consideration of the background of the offense and especially of the plight of the three motherless youngsters, the judge placed Lewis on probation so that he could work, support, and take care of the children. On probation Lewis adjusted well, worked regularly, appeared to be devoted to the children, and a few years later was discharged as "improved" from probation.

Case 2: Robbery

Shortly after World War II, three young men from Boston held up a liquor store in downtown Brooklyn and stole over $300. The robbery was actually committed by John Mahon and Malcolm Lane while Henry Galt waited outside in a getaway car. After the hold up the trio drove away carefully, but nevertheless excited the suspicion of two plainclothes patrolmen in an unmarked car who halted the thieves' automobile. As the police questioned the three young men, a strange license plate inside the car led them to search the vehicle and the loot and the weapons used in the holdup were discovered. The policemen brought the trio into the precinct just as the victim was arriving to make his report. Identification was made and the three young men confessed. They ultimately pleaded guilty to reduced felony charges.

The presentence probation report indicated that Mahon was the illegitimate offspring of parents who never married because of religious differences. He grew up in a boarding school where, as a fine athlete, he was looked up to by other boys, especially Galt, who was at the same school. A marine during World War II, Mahon participated in four landings in a unit that later received a Presidential Citation with a star. After his discharge, at loose ends, he was attracted by acting, and at the time of the liquor store robbery was enrolled under the G.I. Bill in a drama school near Boston.

Lane and Galt were relatively quiet withdrawn young men who were attracted to Mahon and content to follow his lead. Lane grew up in an underprivileged family, and after indifferent success in school had gone to work as a window dresser, a job to which he returned after the war. He was Jewish but had been attracted to a group of Irish Americans and prior to the robbery had been taking instructions preparatory to converting to Catholicism.

Galt was a friendless boy who was placed in a boarding school as a child because of a broken home. He worshipped Mahon, who looked after and protected him in boarding school. After being discharged from the army, Galt obtained a regular, though routine job.

Mahon was the leader of the group. It was he who shook the other two out of their uneventful lives and prevailed upon them to go to New York. While the trio admitted to other holdups they insisted that all the crimes were conceived impetuously when they needed money. (At arrest the three men had little more than the loot from the last holdup.) The trio had been thinking of a large haul that would make them financially independent so that they could live more glamorously than they had in Boston.

The three defendants were committed to the state reformatory for sentences with five year maxima.

Case 3: Robbery and Drug Abuse

Dirk Van Rijn, a nineteen-year-old black youth whose father was a native of Dutch Guiana, together with four other young men, was arrested for a series of liquor store holdups in Brooklyn and Queens. All five pleaded guilty to Robbery I. Probation reports indicated that three of the defendants had minimal criminal records, and appeared likely to stay out of trouble. They were placed on probation. Van Rijn and the leader of the group, however, confessed to about twenty robberies and were committed to the reformatory. Van Rijn was of average intelligence and came from an intact family where both parents worked. He had a previous juvenile court record and (unlike his other four codefendants) was a confirmed user of heroin. He was not employed and met his need for large amounts of money for heroin through increasingly serious and assaultive crime.

Case 4: Embezzlement and Drug Abuse

Marvin Rothblatt, twenty-seven, was charged in Kings County Court with embezzlement, to which charge he pleaded guilty. The presentence investigation disclosed that Rothblatt had grown up in a middle-class Jewish neighborhood, graduated from high school with a mediocre record, and had gone to work as a salesman. At age eighteen he began to associate with a group of boys who were heroin addicts and he became a confirmed user. Shortly thereafter he lost his job and was arrested with others while burglarizing a store. As a first offender, he was permitted to plead guilty to a lesser charge, was placed on probation, and was discharged within a short period of time when it appeared that he was no longer using drugs. Some years later while working as a salesman he was severely injured in an automobile accident and while in the hospital was given narcotic drugs to ease his pain. This rehabituated him and when discharged from the hospital he reverted to the habitual use of drugs. He returned to work as a salesman but very quickly found that he had to defraud his employer to support his drug habit. When the thefts were discovered, he was unable to make restitution and he was taken to court. He pleaded guilty to a felony and was committed to state prison.

Case 5: Assault and Alcoholism

Lars Larsen was born in Brooklyn, but had lived with his grandmother in Sweden from age five to age twenty when he returned to his family in the United States. He was of average intelligence, but had a poor relationship with his father. He had attended school in Sweden for eight years and took further technical courses in the United States for about two years on his return. He had worked as a laborer in Sweden and later was employed as a seaman in the United States. He served with the marines for two years on active duty in Korea where he attained the rank of sergeant. After his return from Korea, and his discharge from the service, at age twenty-seven he beat up a uniformed New York City patrolman who was attempting to break up a barroom brawl between Larsen and another man. Larsen inflicted a fractured right hand and bruises about the body on the patrolman who was confined to his home on sick leave for about two months. Larsen was intoxicated at the time and claimed amnesia for the entire period of this episode. For this assault,

Larsen was arrested and charged with a felony. He pleaded guilty to a lesser charge, was placed on probation on the condition that he undergo group therapy at the BARO (Brooklyn Association for the Rehabilitation of Offenders) Clinic.

At the clinic, he was assigned to a group consisting of ten men convicted of a variety of crimes. The therapeutic approach selected for the group was a technique developed by Carl Rogers, a noted psychologist by which the burden of maintaining verbal interaction is placed on the patients, the therapist remaining relatively inactive. The theory behind this type of group therapy is that interaction within a group of peers permits the participants to ventilate their feelings more easily and accept solutions for problems more readily from their fellow members than they would from a therapist who might be of a different socioeconomic class, and who, in any case, would have a somewhat authoritarian relationship to the participants. In this type of client-centered approach, the subjects for discussion are decided upon by the group members, who almost always choose topics that relate to their jobs, family relationships, and other personal concerns. (Other therapeutic approaches are more directive and under the direct control of the group therapist.)

Larsen participated enthusiastically and was highly regarded by the group. He responded well and was able to stop drinking. After fifteen weeks of therapy, he returned to the individual handling of his probation officer, and at the end of his three-year period of probation was discharged. He was then working regularly and not drinking.

Case 6: Alcoholism

Lucy Comerford was a middle-aged, distinguished looking grandmother who had been active for some years in Alcoholics Anonymous (AA). She related well to the members of her organization and was on a panel of speakers who regularly went out in teams of two or three to address community groups, starting with the statement:

"I am an alcoholic. I will be an alcoholic until the day I die."

In her talk Mrs. Comerford told how as the wife of a successful business executive she had raised four children in a comfortable middle-class home. When her children grew up and left, she became vaguely dissatisfied and uncomfortable, and to overcome these unpleasant feelings, she started to drink more and more. Finally, she found that she could no longer control her craving for alcohol. Her conduct became increasingly unacceptable as she became more desperate in her efforts to obtain liquor. Neither her nor her family's efforts succeeded in controlling her drinking. Ultimately she left home and found herself one of the few women derelicts on the Bowery. After two years of indignities and distress, she accidentally attended an AA meeting. The AA message reached her and gradually she acquired the strength to overcome her need to drink. She attended meetings regularly, and in time felt strong enough to return home. Sometimes when the urge to drink seemed overwhelming she phoned a group member for help in resisting it; at other times she responded to calls from other disturbed AA members. She continued to attend AA meetings and became a speaker and representative of AA. She appeared to have achieved a sort of tranquility through group interaction that she probably had formerly attempted to get through drinking.

Case 7: Alcoholism

During the late thirties, Lincoln Breed, an editor of the prestigious, now defunct, *Morning World*, became an alcoholic, left his family, and finally was reduced to living on public assistance in New York City. For years he lived in a small shabby apartment spending the major part of his welfare food and clothing allowance to buy cheap whiskey. As his case workers changed, each one in turn was impressed by his previous status and obvious intellectual capacity and attainments, and each unsuccessfully attempted to discuss his problem in a meaningful constructive way so that he would stop drinking and become self-supporting. After twenty years of these earnest efforts Breed saw one of his most recent welfare workers in the street, ran after him, and caught up with him. Breed was obviously distraught, and when asked what was wrong, the alcoholic ex-newspaper editor emotionally exclaimed

> *Please get Mr. X (the latest of Mr. Breed's welfare workers) off my back. Please get him to understand that I can't control my drinking. Doesn't he know that I understand better than he that it would be to my best interests to stop drinking? Make him understand that I cannot control this urge.*

Case 8: Homosexuality and Making Obscene Telephone Calls

Carlo Traventi was a short, slight, dark nineteen-year-old youth with regular features and a somewhat effeminate appearance. Born out of wedlock in upstate New York, he was adopted by a hard-working, childless couple who, even after having lived in New York City for many years, spoke English with difficulty and a heavy accent. A high school drop-out, Carlo went from job to job and was the despair of his hard-working, rigid parents. He stayed out late and associated with a gang of toughs. After appearing in juvenile court on a number of occasions Carlo and a companion were arrested for a store burglary and were committed to a New York State reformatory. At the institution he adjusted poorly and at nineteen was paroled to live with his adoptive parents. He could not hold on to a job, and when he swaggered in to report to his parole officer, he bragged about his having contracted a "dose" of gonorrhea, implying that a man of his virility had to expect some such trifling misadventure. His case record on the other hand disclosed that he had engaged in homosexual behavior in the reformatory. Though given the opportunity, he refused to discuss his sexual problems with his parole officer. He was finally arrested after he had made a series of obscene phone calls to women whose numbers he had selected at random from the telephone book. One of his proposals was that if the woman would expose her breasts, Carlo would masturbate in front of the phone at the other end. Later, he arranged to meet a woman he had called in front of a movie theater, and when he appeared and identified himself, detectives arrested him. He was convicted of a minor charge and was returned to the reformatory for parole violation.

Traventi impressed those who worked with him as a youth with severe psychosexual problems involving his masculinity, which he would have liked to work out in a socially acceptable way. His strong homosexual impulses were manifested and nurtured while Carlo was in the reformatory, and when he was on parole he went out of his way to brag to his parole officer about his gonorrhea infection knowing that this incident was a technical violation of parole. Nevertheless, although encouraged to do so, Carlo did not discuss any of his problems of sexual adjustment with his parole officer.

Case 9: Homosexuality

Peter Arroyo, was twenty-two, the only child born of an Oriental father and an Irish-American mother. When he was ten his parents were divorced and he remained with his father who did not remarry. His mother moved out of the city where she married again and had a number of children. Peter was a devout Catholic who graduated from a parochial elementary and secondary school. At seventeen he came to the attention of the Youth Counsel Bureau (a semipublic agency designed to handle arrested youths unofficially so as to avoid, if possible, a criminal record for the youngster) because of the theft of an automobile, but at that time was not referred for treatment. Five years later he voluntarily came into the Youth Counsel Bureau, asked for psychiatric help, and was referred to the BARO Clinic. He was unhappy in his job, was living with a homosexual with whom he had been engaging in sex relations, and complained of his inability to control his excessive masturbation. He was guilt-ridden about his feelings about sex. The closest he ever came to having heterosexual relations was when he was sixteen. At that time he slept at a relative's house and an older girl cousin came into bed with him. He started to have intercourse but was unable to continue. Afterward he was attracted into having homosexual relations.

At the clinic it was felt that his basic difficulty was psychosexual in that his guilt over his homosexual practices caused severe anxiety and other neurotic symptoms. He was assigned for therapy to a group consisting of homosexuals. In the therapy group Peter participated enthusiastically and intelligently, exhibiting a great deal of insight into his problems and the problems of other group members. During the course of the meetings he was able to work out his conflicts regarding his religion and his feelings of guilt relating to his homosexuality. After a time, he ceased his homosexual activity and started to have heterosexual relations, which further eased his religious problems. He also matriculated in the evening session of a college and changed to a job where he was much happier. He continued in the homosexual therapy group for about two years and withdrew when he felt that he had benefited sufficiently to function on his own. The projective drawing tests given to him at the start of therapy, during the course of treatment, and at the conclusion of treatment, showed a marked diminution of anxiety and a greater acceptance of a masculine role. The BARO staff felt he had made marked progress.

Case 10: Voyeurism and Homosexuality

Roy Williams was an unmarried black man in his early thirties born and bred on Staten Island. He was one of five children in a family that was marginally supported by his father, a regularly employed unskilled laborer. Williams dropped out of high school and held a series of poorly paid unskilled jobs. He also became a voyeur. All of his crimes followed the same pattern. At night he crept into homes and watched women undress. At no time did he attack or molest the women, and at no time was any loot found on or near his person at the times of arrest. Each time he was charged with burglary. After his first arrest he pleaded guilty to a misdemeanor and was placed on probation. After his second arrest he was committed to a New York State reformatory. He was paroled, worked regularly, but was soon rearrested for breaking into a home where he watched a woman undress. This time he was sent to state prison where he adjusted fairly well and was paroled at the first meeting of the Parole Board. After his release he was referred to the BARO Clinic, where he became part of a special caseload of sex offenders who were assigned to group therapy. During the sessions he verbalized his problem with some degree of insight and participated constructively in the group sessions. He was under treatment at BARO for two years, worked regularly and was not rearrested. His crimes had apparently been caused by his sex drives, which he had not been able to satisfy in a socially acceptable way.

Case 11: Prostitution

Olive was a call girl treated and studied by Harold Greenwald, a psychoanalyst who discussed her case in *The Elegant Prostitute,* a book dealing with the psychological problems of prostitutes.[3] She was an out of wedlock child born in Pittsburgh, whose mother never acknowledged her. Olive was raised by her grandmother and aunt who lived in different cities. Because of her frequent moving around she never developed a circle of friends. Olive told Dr. Greenwald that when she was six years old a fifteen-year-old male cousin got into bed with her and began caressing her. She found this pleasurable and exciting, and in addition her cousin gave her candy and toys. She loved candy, rarely getting any from her aunt.

Greenwald theorizes that Olive reacted strongly to being rejected by her mother, grandmother, and aunt. The only signs of affection in her life were from her cousin who through his gifts of toys and candy taught her early in life that sex was a commodity that she could barter for some form of emotional contact. This led her to acquire skill in acting seductively and ultimately was influential in her turning to being a call girl as a way of life. This was not socially acceptable but it gave her money, gifts, and some form of emotional acceptance; and it fitted the only successful pattern of interaction she knew.

Case 12: Gambling and Fraud

Jerry Geller grew up in Brooklyn where he became president of his class in high school, graduated from Harvard with honors, married, went to work as a salesman, and became quite successful. In college however, he had started to gamble and continued to do so after graduation. He lost a considerable amount of money and issued checks that initially his father covered. However, when the amounts became too large for his father to handle, Geller's creditors went to the district attorneys of Brooklyn and Manhattan, both of whom indicted Geller. For the bad checks issued in Manhattan, Geller was taken before the Court of General Sessions where he pleaded guilty to a felony. The judge ordered restitution and placed Geller on probation. While on probation, Geller again issued a bad check. The judge then committed him to Sing Sing. In prison, at the school where he had been assigned as a teacher, Geller heard from others about Alcoholics Anonymous. He was so impressed with the approach, that upon his release, he organized Gambler's Anonymous, an organization structured along similar lines. He remained active in GA, was able to stop gambling, and subsequently became quite successful as a businessman.

Case 13: Smoking

Television star William Tallman, in the last days of his life, made a devastating television short urging his audience to stop smoking. Emaciated, ill, a ghost of the robust figure of Hamilton Burger in the Perry Mason series that he was best known for portraying, he told his viewers that his heavy smoking had almost certainly caused the lung cancer which was killing him. Shortly after the film appeared, he died.

The medical evidence against smoking is overwhelming. There is no reputable research group that does not implicate cigarette smoking in the increase in lung cancer during the twentieth century and there is much evidence linking smoking to heart disease, strokes, and other forms of cancer.

By law, a statement that smoking is dangerous to one's health must appear on every package of cigarettes sold in the United States. Yet, the annual consumption of cigarettes continues to rise in America. Although smokers intellectually understand and accept that smoking is not only dangerous to their health and acts to shorten their life spans, they continue to smoke. Many attempt to stop smoking but relatively few succeed. When asked why they continue to smoke in spite of the danger to their health, most smokers say that smoking relaxes them and is difficult to stop. Smoking apparently fills an ill-defined compelling psychological need great enough so that there is a strong compulsion to smoke in spite of the dangers involved.

Case 14: Overeating

Lorraine Bendix is the daughter of the late William Bendix, the well known movie star. Although she grew up in a small family without seeming difficulty, as a teen-ager, she developed a voracious appetite and at age twenty weighed 300 pounds. She consulted numerous physicians and was exposed to a wide variety of treatments, all of which were ineffective. Finally, in desperation, she agreed to a surgical procedure, a jejuno-ileal bypass, an operation that connects the front part of the small intestine to the end part. The small intestine is, in effect, decreased in length from 23 feet to 4½ feet, and the smaller surface for absorption, as well as the shorter time span for digestion, permits food to pass through the body without being absorbed. The theory behind the procedure is that if the patient cannot control her food intake, then altering the digestive process will control the number of calories available to the body. In Miss Bendix's case the procedure was successful in that her weight dropped to 118 pounds.

Such operations are a last resort for the person whose obesity is life-threatening, since they are major surgical procedures that are dangerous in themselves, and which frequently have serious and even fatal side effects. Fortunately, there are not too many 300 pound women among us, but a large proportion of the American public is more than 10 percent above their optimum weight. Insurance statistics clearly reflect the dangers of being even moderately obese, yet many, if not most, Americans continue to overeat, shortening their life-spans and subjecting themselves to a host of dangerous and unpleasant illnesses. Some people are treated by physicians with drugs, and for a short time succeed in reducing their weight, but a large proportion of these patients regain their lost weight relatively quickly after treatment stops. Some people derive help from weight reducing groups, some go on self-imposed diets, but whatever the technique, most fail. Most overweight people continue to remain overweight because they continue to overeat. Evidence suggests that overeating meets some kind of psychological need, even when the subject is aware that overeating is medically dangerous, and the resulting obesity socially unacceptable.

These case histories are a sad catalogue in miniature of society's losers. For different reasons, these are people who have been unable to adapt or conform well enough to function acceptably. Analytically, many of these examples of deviant conduct can be fitted into the framework of Merton's paradigm. Several of the case histories involving crimes, for example, involve individuals who were willing to accept the goals of society but who rejected the accepted institutionalized means for achieving those goals. In Case 2, Mahon, Lane, and Galt wanted to lead comfortable, glamorous lives but attempted to finance themselves through a series of holdups rather than by legitimate work. Not quite so obvious but basically in the same category was Mr. Lewis in Case 1, who killed his wife because she was making his life unbearable. Mr. Lewis was not wrong in wanting to get rid of his wife, or at least of the problems she was creating. Under similar circumstances a middle-class couple might have turned to marriage counseling, but Lewis was unaware of the existence of such services, would have been uncomfortable utilizing them, and, in any case probably would not have had such services available to him at his income and education levels. As a result, tension built up between him and his wife until the explosion that led to the homicide.

Crimes are also sometimes committed not so much for the immediate end achieved by the crime itself, as for the psychological gratification of the criminal. Roy Williams (Case 10), the voyeur who watched women undress, and Carlo Traventi (Case 8), the homosexual who made obscene phone calls, both relieved their feelings of sexual inadequacy through criminal activity. Both cases portray individuals who were trying to achieve the kind of personal fulfillment that conforming persons achieve through legitimate relationships, productive work, creativity in the arts, etc. Again, the goal of personal fulfillment was acceptable but the means were illegitimate.

Some of these case studies, on the other hand, involve persons who, by withdrawing as much as possible from the human scene, rejected not only the means prescribed by society, but the goals themselves as well. Mrs. Comerford, the genteel grandmother (Case 6), and Mr. Breed, the talented editor (Case 7), who as alcoholics renounced completely their customary mode of middle-class existence are examples of this process. Not all withdrawal, of course, is criminal in nature, as for example, the cases of individuals who become recluses. On the other hand, alcoholics and drug addicts frequently get into trouble with the law: alcoholics because of assaultive or unrestrained conduct resulting from the lessening of inhibitions during intoxication; and drug addicts because possession of drugs is a crime per se, and the high price of drugs forces addicts to steal (see Case 4, Marvin Rothblatt or Case 3, Dirk Van Rijn). Psychotics who commit crimes also fall into this category because due to their loss of contact with reality they have no true awareness of either socially accepted goals or means.

Not all addicts and alcoholics, however, have reconciled themselves to total withdrawal from society and abandonment of approved social goals: witness Mrs. Comerford who made a comeback through AA. The alcoholic who repeatedly attempts to control his drinking, and the drug addict too who tries to "kick the habit" have not yet completely given up the struggle for acceptance in our social system. When the pain and discomfort of attempting to make it becomes too great they are forced back into the relief offered by alcohol or drugs as was Mr. Breed, who begged the social worker to get off his back and Mr. Rosenblatt, who permitted himself to become readdicted after his automobile accident. The pain of changing conduct that brings relief from stress also accounts for the case histories of Lorraine Bendix (Case 14), who submitted to a dangerous operation to reduce her weight, and William Tallman (Case 13), who literally smoked himself to death. Most overeaters do not undergo dangerous operations and cigarette smokers do not die so quickly or dramatically, but they harm themselves, admit the harm, deplore the harm, and continue their self-destructive behavior. Despite much private and social effort to control overeating and cigarette smoking, most smokers do not succeed in breaking the habit, and most overeaters continue to remain obese, just as most criminals fail to respond positively to counseling efforts of probation and parole officers.

Handling Deviants

Assuming that Merton's paradigm is useful for the analysis of deviant conduct, what does it tell us in regard to alleviating the problems created by such conduct? What, for example, should we do about crime?

Currently, in our society, criminals are handled punitively, i.e., if and when we catch them they are either imprisoned or required to submit to supervision by probation or parole authorities. The chief purposes, at least in practical terms, of putting a man in prison are physical restraint, i.e., removing him physically from the community at large, and deterrence, or dampening his impulse (and the impulse of others similarly situated) to commit future crimes. The goals of probation and parole are protection of the community through supervision of the criminal, and deterring future crime through rehabilitation of the subject. How effective are prison, probation, and parole as methods of handling criminals?

Without question the goal best achieved in the criminal justice system is that of physical restraint. Our prisons do an admirable job of keeping criminals away from the public for the duration of their sentences. The problem that arises, however, is that at some point almost all criminals must be released and returned to society, and it is at that point that the other goals of the system, deterrence and rehabilitation become important. These goals are achieved by our criminal justice agencies with very limited success.

In prison, and in the course of probation and parole counseling, an attempt is made to convince the prisoner, again using the terms of Merton's paradigm, that he cannot achieve his goals however legitimate and justifiable by illegitimate means. Consider in this light the cases 1, 2, 3, and 4. It would be relatively easy for a probation officer to convince Mr. Lewis that he should never kill again. Lewis was essentially a conforming individual who functioned relatively well in his setting. He simply had been temporarily overwhelmed by a situation he couldn't handle. He was fully aware of the enormity of what he had done and it was highly unlikely that he would ever find himself in such a situation again.

The prognosis in Case 2, involving the three young Bostonians who held up the liquor store, was not nearly so good. In the first place all three men were sentenced to the reformatory, and unfortunately, despite the rehabilitative goals of such institutions the effects of imprisonment are frequently counterproductive in that the prisoner, especially the novice prisoner, becomes both embittered by the conditions under which he is forced to live and more knowledgeable about crime, having absorbed the wisdom of his colleagues in the institutions. Suppose, however, the defendants had been placed on probation. Would the prognosis have been any different? Quite possibly Lane and Galt, the "followers" of Mahon, the leader, would have successfully completed their periods of probation. Both Lane and Galt were attracted to Mahon because they were looking for a warm, protective, dynamic friend who could give purpose and direction to their lives. It is quite conceivable that with a probation officer to whom they related well, and with intelligent and appropriate counseling, Lane and Galt would have adjusted well, since the need that they had for a strong supportive figure could be met quite legitimately.

Mahon's needs, on the other hand, represented a more difficult problem. He apparently had a strong desire to achieve a high status position in life, and a glamorous and exciting career. If Mahon had been the son of the president of General Motors, or even of a well known movie star, he might very reasonably have expected to achieve his ambition. Since he wasn't, he had problems. To the extent that a probation officer might be able to convince him either to scale down his ambitions or to work very hard through legitimate channels accepting the rather dubious chances of success in his endeavors, Mahon might be expected to adjust. If, however, he was unable to accept a humbler status, or unable to put in years of drudgery, or unable to face the probability of failure, then he might be expected to revert to criminal or, at least, antisocial behavior.*

Cases 3 and 4 concern drug addicts who committed crimes to get money with which to purchase drugs; Case 3 involved Dirk Van Rijn, a nineteen-year-old black youth from the ghetto, and Case 4 Marvin Rothblatt, a middle-class young Jew. Both of these defendants were sentenced to prison, and as in Case 2 the prognosis for rehabilitation following a prison sentence is somewhat dubious. Again, however, suppose they had been placed on probation. What then? As drug addicts there is almost no chance that they could have avoided reverting to criminal behavior since the money for drugs could be obtained in no other way, at least by persons of ordinary means. Could they have been withdrawn from drugs? Would they then have "gone straight?" The experience of those who deal with confirmed addicts indicates that very few addicts can be counselled, persuaded, exhorted, or in any noncoercive way influenced to give up drugs. Some addicts do when they enter a therapeutic community, experience a highly emotional religious conversion, or undergo some profound personality change. The vast majority of addicts revert to their addiction.

Suppose, however, Van Rijn and Rothblatt had been placed in some type of drug maintenance program—either an American methadone program, or the British type of heroin maintenance arrangement.† Would they then have been able to lead conforming, produc-

---

* This case was drawn from the files of the New York State Supreme Court (Kings County) Probation Department. At the time of the presentence investigation, the probation officer involved was faced with a dilemma. On the one hand he felt that probation would have been a more appropriate sentence than imprisonment for Lane and Galt; on the other hand to sentence one participant in a holdup to prison while permitting his equally guilty partners to remain free on probation would have created a sentence disparity hard to justify in terms of other goals of the criminal justice system. Unfortunately for Lane and Galt, perhaps, the latter consideration prevailed. This dilemma is of the same type that every judge and probation officer faces in sentencing offenders to prison. The results are so frequently counterproductive in terms of the defendant's rehabilitation that it seems wrong to do so, yet society must be protected from the violent, antisocial criminal. We don't know yet how to do away with prisons.

† See Chapter IV.

tive lives? The answer lies partly in why they turned to drugs in the first place and partly in the supportive help they could expect from friends, family, and the milieu in which they live. Rothblatt was apparently a rebellious adolescent who was attracted into the drug culture as a way of defying authority and resisting parental pressure for academic success, which he felt unable to achieve. Van Rijn also became addicted as an act of protest and rebellion, but against conditions far more difficult to remedy than Rothblatt's. Overbearing parents learn to settle for half a loaf, and academic success doesn't matter after one has passed school age, but Van Rijn's black face meant that he would always be faced with housing problems, job discrimination, social prejudice, and the other attributes of second-class citizenship, along with whatever personal and family problems he may have encountered as an adolescent. Where Rothblatt's community would very likely offer opportunities for rehabilitation and legitimate employment, Van Rijn's community offered very little support, and in any case was without political or economic strength. The chances of Rothblatt's rehabilitation are thus greater than of Van Rijn's; but in both cases, the subjects would be far more likely to give up criminal behavior if placed in a drug maintenance program than if simply sentenced to prison.

Much deviant behavior is of course noncriminal, and the handling of such behavior legally must be noncoercive (except where the subject is thought to have diminished capacity as in the case of children or the mentally ill, who may be handled coercively, theoretically at least, for their own protection). How effective are our noncoercive methods of handling noncriminal deviants? Consider for example, Cases 5, 6, and 7 involving alcoholics.

Lars Larsen was essentially a hardworking, competent young man whose alcoholism led him to lose his job and released such hostility in him that he feloniously assaulted another person.* Lucy Comerford was an upper-middle-class woman, a respected wife and mother who cheated, lied, stole from her family, and eventually wound up on the Bowery. Lincoln Breed was an intellectual member of a high status family who gave up his job, ruined his health, and eked out a miserable existence on public welfare. Ultimately, Larsen

* Larsen's conduct was of course criminal, but his crime was merely an incident in the much broader problem of his alcoholism.

and Mrs. Commerford were rehabilitated: Larsen through group therapy organized by a rehabilitative clinic to which he was referred by the court, and Mrs. Commerford through Alcoholics Anonymous. Mr. Breed was never rehabilitated despite strenuous efforts on the part of his welfare social worker. Why were Larsen and Commerford successful and Breed not? The answer probably lies somewhere in the complex recesses of each subject's personality. Commerford and Larsen, whatever their self-destructive impulses, and whatever the social or personal reasons for their alcoholism, apparently had self-preservative instincts strong enough to respond to the appropriate therapy when it was offered.

Not every kind of therapy will work for every individual. It was fortunate that the interplay with his peers in a group therapy session met Larsen's needs, and that Mrs. Commerford was the type of individual who could respond to the almost religious fervor of an organization such as Alcoholics Anonymous. Some individuals are not fortunate enough to be offered the kind of therapy to which they can respond. Some individuals simply do not have sufficient inner resources to respond to any therapy. Mr. Breed, who was tormented by his social worker, was a person who could not or would not accept salvation.

Smoking and overeating are other forms of noncriminal self-destructive behavior. The alarming precipitous increase in lung cancer in recent years led the American Cancer Society to undertake a series of large-scale studies which led unmistakably to the conclusion that cigarette smoking is by far the most important cause of lung cancer and is also a major factor in deaths from coronary heart disease, chronic bronchitis, emphysema, and other diseases.[4] The evidence was so damning that despite the opposition of tobacco growers and manufacturers, as well as advertisers and others with an economic stake in the future in the tobacco industry, Congress passed several laws which, among other things, provided that a statement warning that cigarettes were dangerous to health be placed on every package of cigarettes manufactured; and which forbade cigarette advertising on radio and television. The evidence against cigarette smoking was so strong, in fact, that a physician as experienced and knowledgeable as Dr. Vincent P. Dole of the Rockefeller University (who along with his wife, Dr. Marie Nyswander, conducted the original methadone pilot program for heroin addicts) said without qualification that "cigarette smoking is unquestionably more damaging to the human body than heroin."[5]

Not only were the medical and legislative communities convinced by the scientific evidence, but cigarette smokers were. A survey conducted by the United States Public Health Service in 1966 among a cross-section of male cigarette smokers disclosed that more than 70 percent agreed that smoking was harmful to their health; and close to 60 percent felt that cigarette smoking was a cause of lung cancer and hoped that their children would never smoke.[6] Nevertheless, despite all the fanfare, hoopla, legislative changes, and widespread acceptance of the harmful effects of cigarette smoking, *the vast majority of cigarette smokers continue to smoke cigarettes,* and from 250,000 to 300,000 smokers a year go right on dying as a result of their smoking.[7] Why?

Brecher and his associates feel that part of the answer may be that nicotine is an addictive substance similar in its ability to create a physical dependency to heroin. Even if true, the problem is more complex. Cigarette smokers start to smoke frequently for a variety of social reasons: their friends are doing it; it seems sophisticated; it is a sign of maturity. They continue to *maintain* an expensive, and, many agree, an inconvenient and even dirty habit, however, for psychological reasons: it makes them feel better. Most cigarette smokers agree that cigarettes relieve tension and help them to relax. Their discomfort, when they stop smoking, may in part be physiological due to the addictive properties of nicotine, but it is even more markedly psychological because they can no longer use the cigarette as a tension relieving agent.

This phenomenon—psychological rather than purely physiological addiction—is best illustrated, perhaps, in the case of food. There is widespread agreement that a large percentage of Americans are obese, i.e., over their maximum healthful weight. There is also widespread agreement that obesity is a strongly contributing factor in heart disease, high blood pressure, diabetes, and a host of other very serious and frequently fatal physical ailments. Overweight people are sicker and die younger than those of normal weight. People become overweight in the vast majority of cases because they eat too much. Once again, despite medical evidence, publicity, and widespread acceptance of the evidence people go right on eating too much and dying too soon. Again, why? For much the same reasons that they continue to smoke cigarettes. It makes them feel better. Most experts in the field will agree that food serves a social and psychological function in our culture as well as a purely physiological one, and that for a majority of obese individuals food serves as an effective tension reliever. It is for this reason that so many people find it hard to diet and once having dieted find it equally difficult to keep from regaining the lost weight. The syndrome is remarkably similar to that seen among cigarette smokers except here there is no physically addictive agent involved.

Cigarette smoking and overeating are illustrations of the kinds of deviant conduct that results from efforts to cope with the pressures that society creates and imposes on every individual. Smokers and eaters, like some heroin addicts, are primarily goal accepters-means rejectors, i.e., they have internalized and accepted as valid the goals that society has created for them, but they find the prescribed means inadequate for the accomplishment of those goals without a psychic cost that is too much for them to bear unaided. At this point the "crutches"—heroin, cigarettes, food—come into use. Can those crutches successfully be removed?

The case of heroin addiction is particularly complex because of the illegality of the behavior involved and because the addiction is physical as well as psychological. The problem will be discussed more fully in the next chapter. In the case of cigarettes and food, however, several kinds of approaches are utilized to help people overcome their dependency. Most obvious is the general cultural pressure to be slim, look attractive, wear stylish clothes, be healthy, have fresh smelling breath, unstained teeth, etc. These pressures are, perhaps, more effective with regard to obesity than with regard to cigarette smokers. Undoubtedly the guilt and shame engendered by not being able to get clothes that fit, or worse yet, having to shop in stout departments are a strong deterrent to overeating. For those for whom these general cultural pressures do not suffice, however, some more organized programs have been developed. These programs are generally of two types: those involving individual therapy and those involving group interaction. The individual therapeutic approaches include psychotherapy and counseling by psychiatrists, psychologists, and social workers and medically prescribed diets with or without supplementary medication handled by physicians who usually dispense supportive therapy as well. Group approaches include smokers' clinics (frequently hospital based and sponsored) weight reduction clubs (such as Weight Watchers), which are most often commercial enterprises; and, psychotherapy groups run by psychiatrists, psychologists, or social workers. The aim in all these approaches is the same: to enable the smoker or overeater to cope with his daily life without the aid of cigarettes or excessive food. In general the success rates are modest. The majority of clients either do not reform or revert to their bad habits once therapy has stopped, indicating needs which are very complex and deeply ingrained in the total makeup of the person. It should be noted moreover, that occasionally individuals under pressure to give up a form of deviant conduct will succeed only at the cost of adopting another, possibly even less desirable, form of deviance. Thus, many overeaters stay slim by smoking, and there is some evidence that heroin addicts frequently turn to alcohol when the difficulties of remaining an addict become too great.

Cases 8, 9, and 10 involve sexually deviant conduct, technically criminal, but which now is almost always handled noncoercively unless as in these cases an unwilling second person is involved. Carlo Traventi made obscene phone calls to women, Roy Williams was a peeping Tom, and Peter Arroyo stole a car because it was a masculine thing to do. The common denominator underlying all three actions was that each of these men was a homosexual and was driven by pressures engendered by his homosexuality into criminal activity. Not all homosexuals, of course, become criminals.* Relatively speaking very few are, yet all homosexuals are considered to be deviants. Their deviance, however, unlike that of the alcoholic, smoker, or overeater, has no objective, measurable harmful results.† Nor is it like the deviance of the criminal who assaults or kills another person. It is, in fact, conduct that is deviant purely because we say it is so. It is not appropriate in this discussion to enter into the controversy over whether homosexuality is or is not "wrong." The taboo against it has very deep religious and cultural roots. Whether these roots lie in anything more than prejudice against a person who is dif-

---

* Except for breaking laws forbidding homosexual behavior.

† Unless one subscribes to the theory that homosexuality is a sickness that is *contagious*, and even then, one would have to prove the harmfulness of the disease itself.

ferent is hard to say. We don't know if there is anything biologically wrong with the homosexual. We don't know if it is "sick" to be a homosexual. We don't know if the tendency is inborn or culturally determined. We don't know whether being "different" in this way is of inconsequential significance, as lefthandedness is, for example, or whether it is an outward manifestation of a deep derangement of the personality.

We do know that homosexuals have great legal and social pressures put upon them. They must keep their sexual activities private in order to avoid arrest, and perhaps even more important, social pressure and disgrace. Most difficult of all they must accept themselves as homosexuals in the face of the disgust and revulsion evidenced by most heterosexuals. The case histories cited are examples of individuals whose personalities were unequal to the double strain of accepting themselves and leading secret lives, and whose deviance took on related but more harmful forms. Traventi, the obscene telephone caller, was drawn into a situation with which he could not contend. He was labeled a criminal, confined in a reformatory, and the combination of his homosexuality, criminal labeling, the subculture of the reformatory, virtually insured that his conduct would become increasingly unacceptable. Williams and Arroyo were fortunate to have had the opportunity to receive therapy that they were able to accept before their personal situations overwhelmed them.

Therapy for homosexuals rarely takes the form of psychiatric handling because most psychiatrists consider homosexuals untreatable. There are occasional rehabilitative clinics where group therapy is offered, and more recently, homosexuals themselves have organized various kinds of clubs and associations to help alleviate their common problems, whether political, social, economic, or psychological. The main thrust of most of these programs is to make homosexuals more comfortable with themselves, enable them to withstand the "slings and arrows of outrageous fortune," and in the nonhomosexual sponsored groups to offer those who wish to reorient their sexual preferences an opportunity to do so.

Prostitution, like homosexuality, is conduct that is deviant almost entirely because we say it is. Like homosexuality it produces no objective measurable physical harm to any of the parties involved. Culturally, however, we think prostitution a degrading activity. Anthropologically, although different cultures accept sexual arrangements other than monogamy, i.e., harem societies in the Moslem world, or polyandrous unions in Tibet, for reasons which are not entirely clear, prostitution where the act is not institutionally sponsored as in the case of certain religious rites, is almost universally disapproved. Even in our own culture, moreover, there is a wide range of roles encompassed in the term prostitute. At one end of the spectrum is the street walker who "turns a trick" with a "John" who is previously unknown to her and whom she solicits literally on the streets. At the other end of the scale is the call girl who is frequently fastidious, quietly and elegantly dressed, and very selective in regard to her male patrons. Call girls, moreover, shade into the category of mistresses who, while they occupy marginal social position, are in fact frequently very highly regarded not only by their lovers, but by those in his social, business, or political circle. (Historically, the mistresses of many royal personages have been far more influential, interesting, and altogether more noteworthy than their legitimate consorts.)

To speak of prostitution as deviant conduct, thus, one must first define precisely what kind of prostitution one is discussing, and in what context it occurs. In the context of the large, urban criminal justice system, we are concerned almost entirely with the lower end of the prostitution scale, the street walker. Street walkers in recent times fall into two groups: those who are drug addicts and those who are not. Most female addicts become prostitutes since this is the easiest way for them to acquire money with which to purchase heroin, and a large proportion of those arrested for prostitution in the large cities are, in fact, addicts. For these women the problem of prostitution is secondary; their addiction must be handled first. As long as we have no viable method of curing their addiction, or enabling them to maintain their habit without expending large sums of money, there is no point in discussing their sexual deviance.

Not all prostitutes, however, are addicts. Some, like Olive in Case 11, have become prostitutes because of psychological and situational circumstances. It is known, for example, that more women become prostitutes during periods of economic depression, or severe economic hardship, as for example, many respectable middle-class women turned to prostitution to keep from starving during the uncontrolled inflation in Germany following World War I. Conversely, during periods when jobs open up for relatively unskilled women, as during World War II in the United States, fewer women tend to become prostitutes. For some women, of course, the motivation is not economic, but psychological, as in the case of Olive. For such women, should they seek help, counseling, group therapy, or psychotherapy is sometimes helpful. For the remainder, those who cannot be helped or persuaded to renounce their calling, the criminal justice system is surely inappropriate. Punitive handling has never been successful historically, and in fact, the fines levied on prostitutes are little more than a license fee to do business, and the earnings of the prostitute herself become a source of income for the pimp and the corrupt policeman.

Case 12, Jerry Geller, the Harvard graduate who issued bad checks to cover his gambling losses, is another illustration of one form of deviance leading to another even less desirable kind of conduct. Geller's problem was his need to gamble, but it was not because he broke laws relating to gambling that he got into trouble. He got into trouble because he couldn't support his habit. It is the fear that everyone who gambles is potentially a Geller, however, that is the justification for laws against gambling. Their purpose is to save us from ourselves.

Geller had problems that he was unable to handle which in turn led to an uncontrollable desire to gamble. When originally placed on probation he recidivated, and only when he found a kind of therapy he could accept in the group interaction of Gamblers Anonymous was he able to give up the habit that was destroying his life. Punishment in a case like this has very little therapeutic effect and the effectiveness of the criminal justice system is limited solely to effectuating restitution if that is possible, and to protecting potential victims of fraud by keeping the gambler out of circulation for a while. If a prison sentence is to be inflicted, it must be with an awareness of what can realistically be expected of such handling, and not with pious hopes of effecting a "cure" or reformation of a deviant person.

Most gamblers, of course, are not like Mr. Geller, any more than social drinkers are like Lucy Commerford or Lincoln Breed. For most people who bet on the numbers, or on the outcome of a football game, the criminal justice system is even less relevant than it is for compulsive gamblers. Some individuals, no doubt, gamble away money that would, from an outsider's point of view, be better spent on food and shoes for the children. Gambling is, however, a form of recreation and serves the purposes that recreation usually serves: relieving tension, blocking out one's immediate problems, and making life more pleasant. To use the criminal justice system to direct people's choice of recreation is, on a pragmatic level, ineffective and self-defeating, and on a philosophical level, a vestige of the more unattractive aspects of our Puritan heritage.

Conclusion

By and large, efforts to control deviant conduct by exhortation or punishment fail. They fail because the roots of deviance lie in the individual's effort to cope with social and psychological pressures that he cannot handle in any other way. If these pressures cannot be relieved deviant conduct will not cease because of sermons or pep talks by well meaning therapists and social workers; nor will such conduct cease when the criminal is released from prison. To recognize the limited value of exhortation, however, does not mean that we can or should cease our attempts to structure rational policy for the handling of deviance. If the foregoing analysis is correct, certain conclusions seem implicit.

1. The most serious form of deviant conduct is crime. In the handling of criminals we must recognize that physical punishment, such as imprisonment, serves almost one function exclusively: restraint. Putting a person in prison effectively takes him off the streets, and keeps him away from the rest of the community. This is a policy that is entirely appropriate for all offenders whose conduct is violent or potentially violent. No viable community can exist if this type of offender is permitted to remain at large. We must recognize, however, that imprisonment is simply a holding action and does little or nothing toward reforming the criminal himself. This is borne out by the statistics relating to the careers of those who have been released from our penitentiaries, as well as the testimony of thousands of convicts and ex-convicts. Imprisonment on the whole tends to embitter the prisoner and teach him new and better ways of committing crime. Again, this does not mean that we should tear down our prisons or abandon incarceration as punishment for crime. It simply means that we must understand the limitations of this form of punishment.

It follows then that imprisonment, except for the purpose of protecting the community from the offender, is utterly pointless. To put gamblers, pornography peddlers, nonviolent drug users, alcoholics, and homosexuals in prison is farcical at best and sadistic at worst.

2. To reform the deviant as opposed to simply restraining him, some sort of nonphysically coercive pressure must be applied. This pressure may take many forms: for some offenders, probation or parole counselling, educational or vocational rehabilitation, or psychiatric therapy; for alcoholics, Alcoholics Anonymous, individual or group counselling or chemotherapy; for drug addicts, drug-free communities such as Synanon, heroin or methadone maintenance programs, psychotherapy, etc. The degree of success that these programs are likely to have depends, at least in part, on how successful the therapist is in teaching the offender to cope with his problems in ways other than through the conduct that we find objectionable. Unfortunately, the reality of the deviant's situation may frequently be the strongest impediment to reform of his conduct. Probation and parole workers, for example, are frequently unable to convince the incompetent burglar that he would be better off as an honest man, because the truth of the matter is that (especially if he is semiliterate, poor, and black) he may *not* be better off if he were an honest man. It is hard to convince such an individual that he shouldn't desire material affluence when the entire society around him is structured in praise of material affluence. Under those circumstances, we must recognize that unless we give up our materially oriented society (which is highly unlikely), or we reduce the disparity of status and opportunity between the bulk of our population and the poor (which at this moment seems only a little less unlikely) we are not going to have too much success with probation and parole.

The same principles apply in the handling of drug addicts and alcoholics. If we cannot relieve sociological and psychological pressures that force such people to take refuge in the surcease provided by such consciousness altering chemicals, alcoholics and heroin users will continue to remain addicted. Again, the roots of such conduct frequently lie in the well-known evils of poverty, racism, broken homes, etc. Again, long-range social efforts to control such conditions are necessary if we expect to correct this type of conduct.

3. The amount of pressure, coercive or noncoercive, that society should apply to a deviant depends on how harmful his conduct is in fact to the entire community. This harm must be real and demon-

strably measurable rather than a behavior preference that exists in the minds of some or many individuals. Violent criminals, as indicated above, must be restrained. In regard to others, the extent of the pressure should vary from intensive efforts in behalf of alcoholics and drug addicts whose conduct brings intense pain and suffering to their families as well as to themselves, to relatively mild pressures on overeaters or smokers. While it is true, for example, that overeating and smoking are physically harmful, it is also true that in the absence of a Utopian society the pressures heaped upon every individual must have some outlet, and to choke off an outlet like smoking or overeating may simply force the individual into some other tension releasing syndrome which may be even more harmful or deviant. A certain amount of tolerance for mildly deviant conduct is probably essential in a society as complex and imperfect as our own.

4. In the light of the above, it is apparent that we should resort to the criminal process sparingly and as a last resort in the handling of deviant conduct. Punishment, after all, is only a stop-gap measure. We keep the offender off the streets to give the community a rest, or in the hope that he will grow physically or emotionally tired as he matures and will lack the energy to continue his antisocial conduct. All deviants cannot be handled that way. To do so would be not only an enormous waste of social resources and the human talents possessed by these deviants, but would be destructive of the basic ideal of an open, free, pluralistic society. If we are not going to imprison, there is far less impetus for the use of the criminal process. Drug addicts and alcoholics, for example, can be handled at least as effectively medically. Gamblers and homosexuals probably should not be handled at all, except insofar as they seek help, since their conduct is very minimally harmful to the community at large.

To sum up, deviant conduct is ubiquitous in a society such as ours. While to some extent, deviance lies in the eye of the beholder, certain forms of conduct which are objectively and measurably harmful to the community, or which violate rational institutionalized expectations are always deviant. The roots of deviance lie in sociological and psychological pressures generated within the individual by social forces frequently beyond his control. Since, however, the very notion of a free society is based on the responsibility of each individual for his own conduct, the responsibility for the control of deviant conduct lies with both the individual and the community at large.

Deviance is an attempt on the part of the individual to cope with the pressures that beset him and he can neither be punished nor persuaded out of or away from his unacceptable conduct unless alternative methods of coping are available and feasible for him. Physically coercive punishment must be used only as a last resort and for the protection of the community, for it has almost no rehabilitative effect, and serves in fact only to keep the offender away from the community. For this reason the criminal process should be reserved almost exclusively for those individuals who either must be restrained at all costs, or whose conduct is so seriously disruptive of the peace and good order of the community (such as swindlers and embezzlers who commit nonviolent property crimes) that rehabilitative counseling should be carried on in a semicoercive setting such as probation. For all others, we should either attempt education and persuasion by appropriate therapists; or for those whose conduct harms really no one but themselves, *we ought to leave them alone*, recognizing that to some extent we are all deviants.

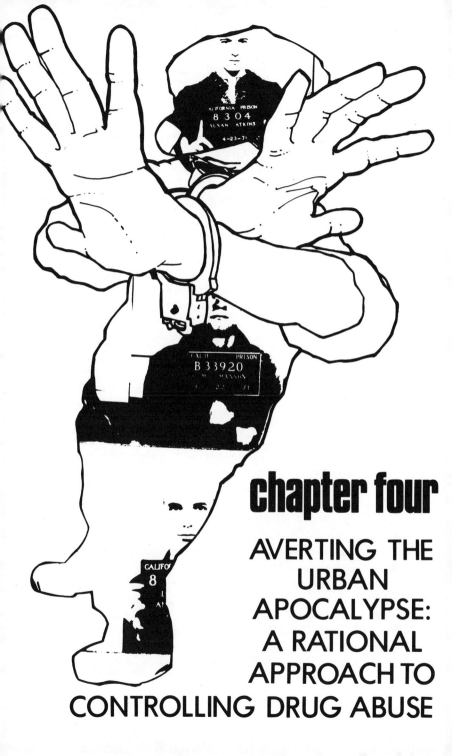

chapter four

AVERTING THE URBAN APOCALYPSE: A RATIONAL APPROACH TO CONTROLLING DRUG ABUSE

*He who tries to determine everything by law
will foment crime rather than lessen it.*

Baruch Spinoza

*We all recognize the gap between the moral law
and the law of the land. . . . The distinction is
well put in the judgment of African elders in a
family dispute: "We have power to make you
divide the crops, for this is our law, and we will
see this is done. But we have not power to make
you behave like an upright man."*

Patrick Devlin, *The Enforcement of Morals*, pp.
19–20.

*. . . The amount of noise made by proponents of
different types of treatment is inversely propor-
tional to the amount of scientific evaluation that
has been made of their effectiveness.*

Thomas H. Bewley, *An Introduction to Drug
Dependence.*

While not every problem besetting our big cities is related to drug
abuse, drug abuse and more specifically heroin addiction is the single factor most responsible for the decline in the quality of life in
urban America. The basic problems of our cities are, as they always
have been, poverty, poor housing, social disorganization, alcoholism,
unemployment, crime, water and air pollution, inadequate transportation, and overcrowding. It is probably fair to say that these problems have been endemic in urban society since the onset of the Industrial Revolution. Certainly they have been with us with only
relatively minor variations as to quantity and quality during the twentieth century. Yet there are few people today who would dispute the
widely held view that the quality of life in New York, Chicago, De-
troit, and Washington, D.C. (to mention just a few cities) has deteriorated substantially from what it was during even such difficult times

as the Great Depression.* The basic problems have not changed much. They are not responsible for the decline. The decline is due to what used to be a minor aspect of urban life: fear. People are afraid today. They are almost hysterical with fear. Some of the fear is unreasonable and self-induced. Some of it stems from the inadequacy and misinterpretation of crime statistics. But much of it is real. People are terribly afraid: of leaving their homes at night, of going to the theater, of opening their doors to strangers, of riding the subways, of taking an evening stroll on a summer's night, of using the public parks, of riding in a taxicab, of sleeping in their homes, of leaving their homes unattended when going on a trip. In short they are afraid to live. They are afraid because they anticipate being robbed, burgled, raped, assaulted, or killed.

It is impossible to say how rational this anticipation is, because no one can say with precision how much crime we have today or how much we had at any other time in the past. Crime statistics are based on reported crime, that is, crime of which the police are aware. Recent studies, however, have shown that the police may be aware of only a fraction of the crimes that actually do occur in a big city. Crime statistics have many other deficiencies: neither arrests nor convictions are accurate barometers of frequency of crime or of the effectiveness of law enforcement; and the wide amount of discretion exercised by police and prosecuters in making arrests or prosecuting defendants also affects the accuracy of the statistical picture. Nevertheless, despite the difficulty of arriving at a true estimate of how much crime we have, and by how much the crime rate has increased, there is an

* Consider for example fireman Dennis Smith's wistful justification for his move to the suburbs:

> Like most firemen who have moved from the city, my children are my first consideration. I want them to be able to go to school without being held up by a fifth-grader for their lunch money. They can ride their bicycles through the neighborhood with a feeling of freedom. They can park their bikes and go rambling through the woods, knowing that the bikes will be there on their return. They can learn to defend themselves, and to stick up for what they think is right by arguing with the kids next door. They won't have to fight their way through a band of marauding youths. There aren't any. They have a good chance of reaching adolescence unscarred. Dennis Smith, Report from Engine Co. 82 (New York: Saturday Review Press, 1972), p. 53.

unshakeable conviction in the public mind (which is in all probability true) that crime has increased appreciably in recent years, especially in relation to muggings, burglaries, and assaults. When we examine the histories, moreover, of those arrested for these crimes, we find that in a very large proportion of the cases, drug abuse plays a part in the crime. Half, and possibly as much as three-quarters of the cases handled in the criminal courts of New York City involve offenses directly relating to heroin use (such as possession or sale of heroin) or indirectly related to such use (such as robbery, burglary, or assault for the purpose of obtaining funds with which to purchase drugs).*

Some observers, such as James M. Markham, a reporter for the *New York Times,* dispute the hypothesis that drug addiction is responsible for the increase in urban crime, especially violent crime.[1] Markham cites studies which show that drug addicts typically were criminals *before* they became addicts, and that addicts in any case tend to commit property crimes rather than crimes of violence. It is probably true that frequently lower-class addicts display criminal tendencies before they become addicts. Drug addiction, after all, is simply another kind of deviant conduct designed to cope with problems that beset a troubled individual. It is also true that addicts tend to commit property crimes more frequently than personal crimes.

Drug addiction, however, greatly increases both the incidence of criminal behavior and the potential for crimes of violence. Crime statistics indicate that property crimes are committed far more frequently than personal offenses. Addiction, however, increases the proportion of violent crimes in both categories. The term property offense, moreover, encompasses many actions that can result in personal violence such as burglary, where the intruder may be surprised by the householder. Addiction, therefore, despite Markham's evidence, is very much involved in the upsurge of urban crime and the fear resulting therefrom. His data, moreover, indicate that with the exception of prostitution every method used by addicts to raise

* This proportion may have dropped since 1972 when large-scale methadone programs became available. See, e.g., "City's Jail Population Fell 20 Percent in Last Year," *New York Times,* January 30, 1974, p. 1, which suggests that the declining rate of addiction and subsequent declining rate of robberies and burglaries may have been partially responsible for the declining jail population.

the funds needed to support their habits either penalizes a victim directly (as in a robbery), or constitutes a drain on the economy (as in stealing from trucks), ultimately borne by consumers in the form of higher prices.

Not only is drug-related crime quantitatively great, it is qualitatively more destructive of society than other types of crime because it is irrational, and its irrationality prevents potential victims from protecting themselves. A nonaddict criminal normally commits crimes in order either to obtain money or to harm a particular victim. An addict must steal so much and so often that he cannot select opportunities that will yield the greatest amounts of money with the least violence and risk to himself. A nonaddict robber, for example, might plan a robbery where he knows there is loot to be had, the prospect of violence is minimal, and the chances that he will get away are great. An addict, on the other hand, will commit this kind of robbery if he can, but such good opportunities may be scarce and if he can't wait he may try an assault on the streets in broad daylight where he may obtain only a trifling sum of money. The Columbia University Law School professor who was murdered in the middle of the afternoon on a busy street adjoining the university, for less than five dollars, was a victim of this type of crime.

The irrational crimes committed by addicts are more frightening than the rational crimes of nonaddicts because they are so unpredictable, and because victims cannot realistically protect themselves from them. Diamond merchants and businessmen who carry large sums of cash know that they are marked as potential targets of robberies, and they can take suitable precautions. People who walk along the streets going about their daily business cannot take any sort of precautions because there is no reason why they should be assaulted. For much the same reasons the police are helpless. A determined addict will not be deterred by even a generous allocation of police to foot and radio patrol, and crimes that take place in hallways, elevators, and the like are completely uncontrollable by law enforcement personnel. It is this sensed inability to carry on one's normal daily activities without fear of personal violence that has eroded the quality of life in our large cities.

The impact of the large numbers of offenders on the criminal justice system has already been discussed. The courts are forced into a demeaning series of plea-bargaining negotiations, and ultimately a tiny fraction of the offenders are sent to prison. Even this tiny fraction, moreover, will be deterred only during the period of incarceration. Offenders emerge from prison no better, and frequently worse, than when they entered. There are other social effects of the increase in drug related crime that are equally significant but perhaps not so obvious. While it is true, for example, that drug addiction makes for an increased amount of crime, the dynamics of this increase, are complex. In an urban society, most crime is committed by boys between the ages of eighteen and twenty-four, and a sizeable proportion of all boys acquire some kind of police record before their twenty-first birthday. A study of 10,000 boys born in Philadelphia in 1945, by Marvin Wolfgang, director of Studies in Criminology and Criminal Law at the University of Pennsylvania, and his associates, showed that before age nineteen one out of every three white boys and one out of every two black boys had become involved with the police at least once to the extent that an official recording of the act resulted. Of this group of 10,000, only about 600, or approximately 6 percent, accounted for more than half of the entire number of crimes committed by the entire group.[2]

Since the incidence of criminality in the adult population, i.e., those over age twenty-four, is not nearly so high, it follows that young people, especially the large group who were only minimally involved with the police, tend to mature out of the tendency to commit crimes. If, however, these eighteen- to twenty-four-year-olds become addicted to heroin and are forced to commit crimes in order to support their habits, will they then be able to mature out of their criminal behavior? As yet we have not amassed the empirical evidence to answer this question, but the prospect is a frightening one. As the proportion of young people in our population grows (as it has in the years since World War II) the amount of crime we suffer will naturally increase because of the relationship between youth and crime. If, however, the upper age limits for criminal behavior become extended because of the need addicts have to commit crime, then the incidence of crime will be even further increased.

The quantitative increase in crime is, moreover, only part of the problem. There are qualitative differences as well. Addiction related crime is different from ordinary adolescent crime in that it tends to be far more irrational and violent. Where the theft of a car for joy-riding is a typical offense of the nonaddict youth, daytime house burglary, shoplifting, or mugging are characteristic of the addict looking for money for a fix.

Not only does addiction have a distorting effect on the incidence of crime, it also distorts the patterns of handling offenders by creating a situation where a far larger proportion of blacks and Puerto Ricans are incarcerated in jails and prisons while white suspects and criminals are released or placed on probation. This is because of the effect of addiction on bail procedures in the first instance, and on sentencing procedures ultimately. When a defendant is brought before a judge for arraignment, the judge must make the decision as to whether or not to set bail. If he sets bail he must decide the amount. In making these decisions he must consider a number of factors: the seriousness of the offense; the defendant's past criminal record; and the defendant's status, including his age, where he lives and for how long he has lived there, his employment record, whether he is married, his ties to the community, whether he is an alcoholic, and whether he is an addict. From all of this information the judge attempts to determine, first of all whether the defendant can be relied upon to return to court for his trial, and secondly, whether his release will be a danger to the community or to himself.

In respect to both of these considerations, addiction weighs heavily against release. If he is an addict he is much less likely to return for trial and his addiction makes it almost certain that he will continue to commit crimes to support his habit as long as he is free. In these cases judges, therefore, tend to set high bail, or to deny bail where possible. Since most heroin addicts are black or Puerto Rican, this means that a disproportionate number of those incarcerated before trial will be black or Puerto Rican, producing jail populations that are largely nonwhite.

Similarly, the sentence that the judge imposes depends on the nature of the offense, the defendant's past record, his social history, and the prognosis for his future conduct. Again, on all scores the drug addict is likely to fare worse than the defendant who is not an addict. He is more likely to have committed a crime of violence, he is more likely to have a previous criminal record of serious offenses, his social history is unattractive, and the likelihood of his rehabilitation is slim. He is therefore far more likely to be sentenced to prison rather than to be placed on probation. Again, since most addicts are black or Puerto Rican, this results in seeming sentence disparities where nonwhites are sent to prison more frequently than whites for similar offenses. Such prison populations, particularly where the institution is located in a rural middle-class white area, present serious administrative problems: the resentment of inmates who feel that they have been unfairly punished because of their color; the hostility between the guards who are drawn largely from the local white population, and the black inmates; and the difficulty of dealing with prisoners who, in addition to all the problems that led to their criminal conduct in the first place, and the usual problems of adjustment to the prison regime, have the added discomfort of an unsatisfied physical hunger for the drug they are not able to obtain.

Perhaps the least appreciated adverse effect of addiction (at least by our predominantly white population) is the effect of heroin addiction on the black community. The black community is doubly victimized by the plague of heroin addiction: they are the first and most frequent victims of the crimes committed by addicts; and it is their own children who are the addicts, who are the criminals, and who are destroying themselves, the community of which they are a part, the group with whom they must primarily identify for the rest of their lives. Surely, there can be no greater anguish for parents than to be the victims of crimes committed by their own children.

The addiction problem is also tearing the black community apart in terms of seeking a solution. On the one hand, blacks desperately need and want police protection and vigorous enforcement of the law.[3] Yet, because the offenders arrested will be their own children, and because the police are suspect due to their past history of brutality in dealing with blacks, the black community is ambivalent in its support of police law enforcement efforts, and the police in turn respond with less than wholehearted efforts to handle the situation. The situation is further complicated by the fact that police corruption is inevitable where there is so much money to be made from the sale of illegal drugs. This further increases the hostility of the black community toward the police. The ultimate result of the inability of the criminal justice system to handle the drug addiction problem and drug related crime has been to convert many black communities into jungles where survival is joyless and precarious.

The hostility and distrust that the black community feels for the white community is also reflected in the ambivalent reaction blacks have toward proposals for handling the drug addiction problem. On the one hand, some blacks, particularly middle-aged, middle-class blacks, in desperation are willing to support even the most Draconian measures against drug pushers such as former Governor Rockefeller of New York's 1973 proposal for mandatory life sentences for all drug dealers, including addict pushers dealing in very small quantities. The effect of such a measure, if carried out, would be devastating to the black community since it would mean life imprisonment without a chance for parole for a substantial proportion of their young men between the ages of fifteen and thirty-five.

Some black leaders, on the other hand, have been extremely hostile to suggestions for drug maintenance programs, either heroin or methadone. They claim that such programs are "genocide," an attempt by the white community to keep the black community in colonial subjugation by keeping its finest young men "on the nod" in a drug induced stupor. Such critics seem to prefer either the drug free ethos of communities such as Synanon, or Daytop Village, or what they call "total law enforcement." They are correct in thinking that it would be preferable for addicts to be treated so as to free them from their addiction, and that the criminal justice system should be made effective enough to prevent dealing in drugs. The problem is that the likelihood of success in both these approaches is very small. Probably fewer than ten percent of those firmly addicted to heroin can be induced to give up the drug by any method short of physical restraint; and the effect of the drug problem on the criminal justice system is such that it is more likely that the drug problem will destroy the criminal justice system than that the system will be able to overcome the problem. Black leaders who express hostility toward maintenance programs frequently are seeking elective office, and it may be that such appeals are structured mainly to overcome traditionally apathetic black voting patterns and are not meant to be taken literally. On the other hand, it is understandable that the black community is even more confused than the white community over the proper approach to the handling of the drug addiction problem and their stake in such handling is even greater.

Another serious adverse effect of the drug problem on the black community is that drug addiction, or, more accurately, the crime associated with drug addiction, has been the single most important factor in preventing housing integration of lower-class blacks with white lower-middle-class neighborhoods. Blacks see the opposition of whites to black housing in their neighborhoods as being entirely based on racial bigotry. Doubtless there is a heavy admixture of racism in the complex of reasons for white hostility to such housing integration, but racism is not the only, or even the most important reason for the furious and implacable opposition of white neighborhoods to racial mixing. At the very same time that middle-class residents of Forest Hills, New York, through street demonstrations and intense political pressure, forced New York City's former Mayor Lindsay substantially to curtail plans for a lower-class predominantly black housing project in their area, considerable housing integration was occurring in New York City in upper-middle-class apartment houses in Manhattan, and even in privately owned middle-class unsubsidized apartment housing in Forest Hills itself. Middle-class *black* residents in Queens, moreover, also objected strongly to city plans to put lower-class housing in their neighborhoods. The single most dominant theme sounded by those who objected to lower-class blacks moving into their neighborhoods was the fear of increased crime. Critics cited the fate of middle- and lower-class housing developments that were destroyed as viable communities when crimes committed by lower-class blacks made life unbearable for tenants. In most of these cases, it was class rather than color that created the problem. Sociologists know that poor people commit more crimes and more serious crimes than middle-class people, and since poor people are disproportionately black, blacks commit more crimes. Attempts to integrate lower-class and middle-class housing are always difficult, but it is crime by addicts (who are overwhelmingly poor and black or Puerto Rican) that has exercerbated the problem beyond all handling.

Whatever the justification of whites for their opposition to integrated housing, the result is that our black communities are being trapped in an unbearable situation. The avenues of escape from the ghetto, as few as they were in the past, are being eliminated, and life in the ghetto itself is even more unbearable than it was in the past. Twenty-five years ago blacks in the United States needed, more than anything else, legal recognition of their claims to first-class citizenship and public acknowledgment of the facts of racial discrimination. The black community today, at least in our large cities, more than anything else, needs relief from the problem of drug addiction.

Heroin Addiction: The Addict's Perception

*To be a confirmed drug addict is to be one of the walking dead.
. . . The teeth have rotted out, the appetite is lost, and the
stomach and intestines don't function properly. The gall blad-
der becomes inflamed; eyes and skin turn a bilious yellow; in
some cases membranes of the nose turn a flaming red; the par-
tition separating the nostrils is eaten away—breathing is difficult. Oxygen in the blood decreases; bronchitis and tuberculosis develop. Good traits of character disappear and bad ones
emerge. Sex organs become affected. Veins collapse and livid
purplish scars remain. Boils and abscesses plague the skin;
gnawing pain racks the body. Nerves snap; vicious twitching
develops. Imaginary and fantastic fears blight the mind and
sometimes complete insanity results. Often times, too, death
comes—much too early in life. . . . Such is the torment of
being a drug addict; such is the plague of being a drug addict;
such is the plague of being one of the walking dead.**

The above description of a drug addict was written by Justice
Potter Stewart of the United States Supreme Court. *It is all wrong
scientifically* but it reflects the popular conception of what being a
drug addict is like. The description of the horrors of addiction is inac-
curate; but the reality is bad enough.

Strangely enough, the physical effects of heroin use on the
body are relatively minor. Brecher and his associates report several
well authenticated studies of morphine and heroin addicts which indicate that contrary to the popular stereotype drug addicts who lead
otherwise healthy lives, and who receive unadulterated supplies of
drugs are not emaciated, do not suffer kidney or liver damage, are not
disproportionately psychotic, do not display reductions in intelligence, and, in general, do not exhibit any indication of physical or
psychological deterioriation. There is some evidence that addiction
does cause a reduction in sexual potency and desire that results in
lessened sexual activity. Some women addicts, although not all, re-

---

* *Robinson* v. *California*, 370 U.S. 660 (1962), cited in Edward M. Brecher et al., *Licit and Illicit Drugs* (Boston: Little, Brown, 1972), p. 21. The authors wish to acknowledge indebtedness for the following discussion of
heroin addiction to the excellent treatment of the subject by Brecher and his
associates.

port irregular menstruation, or a total failure to menstruate, and the likelihood of pregnancy among women addicts appears to be reduced. Some research suggests that pregnant female addicts display a high incidence of maternal complications such as premature delivery, underweight babies, and post partum hemhorrage, but it is difficult to assess the validity of such evidence since many female addicts are also prostitutes, lead unhealthy lives, and are heavy cigarette smokers, all three of which conditions bear on the outcome of pregnancy. There is also conflicting evidence on whether babies born to addictive mothers are themselves addicted and suffer withdrawal symptoms immediately after birth. Some babies born to addictive mothers are in good condition; others are not. Again, how much of this is traceable to conditions in the mother's life other than her addiction is uncertain. Authorities seem to agree that opiates are constipating, and that they do cause variations in mood as the supply of the drug in the body is consumed or replenished.

The fact that the consumption of heroin or morphine per se causes only minor and reversable physical disability should not be taken to mean that addicts do not suffer greatly both physically and psychologically because of their addiction. Most addicts, particularly those from the inner-city ghettos, are very sick individuals. Hepatitis, skin ulcers, infections of all kinds, venereal disease, allergic reactions to adulterants, malnutrition, cirrhosis of the liver, are all conditions endemic among addicts. These ailments relate, however, to the subculture of addiction rather than to the use of drugs per se. The addict buys his drug supplies illegally. He has no way of knowing the potency or purity of the dose he injects.* He uses dirty needles and may inject himself clumsily or too frequently. He has irregular habits: he doesn't eat on time, he doesn't eat the right foods, he may have no regular home. He may be engaging in physically dangerous criminal activities, and in his life on the street he may get into fights or other situations where he suffers physical injury. He may mix his drugs with disastrous physical consequences. Brecher presents a

* Many experienced police officers believe that the quality of drugs sold on the street is so poor that addicts consume far less heroin than they think they are consuming. Indeed, some officers go so far as to speculate that some addicts are not physiologically addicted to the drug at all, but instead are psychologically addicted to the ritual associated with the injection process.

very persuasive argument suggesting that deaths among addicts which are commonly ascribed to heroin overdose are, in fact, due to the consumption of a central nervous system depressant, such as alcohol or barbiturates, along with heroin. While the consumption of heroin itself may not be physically harmful, indiscriminate mixing of drugs can be deadly.

Venereal disease is widely prevalent among addicts. Female addicts are very frequently prostitutes, and presumably at least some male addicts are willing to prostitute themselves to raise the cash needed to support their habits. Addicts' sexual activities, moreover, are no more regular than other aspects of their lives, and promiscuity and personal neglect further contribute to the spread of venereal disease.

Addicts also frequently exhibit personality disturbances. Some are too aggressive, some are too passive, some lie, cheat, steal, deceive themselves and others, have problems of identity, relating to others, and are immature and lack a sense of responsibility. Again, such personality disturbances as were not pre-existing stem more from the addict subculture than from the use of the drug itself. The addict has to be a hustler; he must be a criminal unless he has an independent source of income, and the circumstances of his life would produce much the same type of personality disturbance in nonaddicts leading the same kind of life. The addict, moreover, may very well have had psychological problems to begin with which were at least partly responsible for his becoming addicted in the first place, and the symptoms after his addiction may be no more than a continuation, or exaggeration of personality difficulties predating his addiction.

The studies cited by Brecher indicating that use of opiates per se does not cause physical or mental deterioration were conducted mainly among institutionalized addicts whose nutrition and personal hygiene could be controlled. These studies, however, are not the only evidence we have that the physical and psychological effects commonly associated with drug addiction may not relate to addiction at all. It is an accepted fact that among middle-class addicts the largest single occupational group consists of physicians and nurses, many of whom continue to lead outwardly normal, middle-class lives and who continue to practice their chosen professions successfully. Furthermore, while the sociological pattern of addiction today indicates that the preponderance of heroin addicts are young, male blacks from the inner-city ghettos, during the nineteenth century the distribution of addicts in the general population was entirely different. Morphine addiction* was most prevalent among middle-aged white females and, indeed, was probably most common among menopausal women. It was far more prevalent among the upper and middle classes than among the lower classes, and while women were over-represented, many men, principally physicians and businessmen, were also addicted. Most addicts were in the middle years of life, between forty and sixty, and their addiction seems to have had very little effect on their customary functioning. Housewives continued to run their households, physicians their practices, and businessmen their businesses. This astonishing state of affairs becomes understandable when we realize that these middle-class, middle-aged addicts obtained their supplies of morphine openly, legally, and frequently on the prescription of a physician. Morphine addiction initially started with the use of morphine in the military hospitals during the Civil War, and later spread to the population at large. Although the addictive properties of morphine became known, despite this drawback, the drug became widely used and prescribed because of its usefulness in alleviating various forms of discomfort due to chronic disease or the processes of aging. It was particularly useful in treating the myriad of "female complaints" connected with the processes of childbirth, menstruation, and menopause, thus accounting for its popularity among women. In an age when medical science had very little more than alleviation of pain to offer to its patients, the use of opiates was probably quite rational and enabled many individuals to function perfectly well, possibly better than they would have without such medication, and certainly better than they would after consuming alcohol, the other universal analgesic drug.

Not only were sociological patterns of addiction different dur-

* Heroin is a form of morphine—diacetylmorphine. It is produced by heating morphine in the presence of acetic acid and when introduced into the body is immediately converted back into morphine. The effects of morphine and heroin are virtually identical. Heroin, however, is frequently the drug of choice among addicts because it acts more quickly and more powerfully. The effects of addiction due to morphine are pharmacologically and physiologically very similar to the effects of heroin.

ing the nineteenth century, but social attitudes were also very different. Morphine addiction was disapproved of in somewhat the same way that we disapprove of cigarette smoking. Nonprescription use of morphine was considered somewhat self-indulgent, and rather unwise due to the addictive properties of the drug, yet addicts were, at worst, considered unfortunate. They were not viewed with the horror that today's addicts evoke.* Although statistics in this area are admittedly imprecise, there is considerable evidence that the rate of opiate addiction was much greater in the nineteenth century and the early part of the twentieth century than it is now. Brecher cites the statement of a committee appointed by the United States Secretary of Treasury which estimated that 1 million people were addicted to opium in 1918.[4] While this figure is considered to be an overestimate, it may have been approximately correct in 1900 when the population of the United States was 76 million. In 1972, a reasonably conservative estimate of the number of heroin addicts in the United States was 300,000 out of a population of 210 million. The probabilities are thus that the nineteenth-century rate of addiction was several times that of today. Most significant of all is the almost total lack of social and personal disorganization associated with nineteenth-century opiate use, again indicating that it is not the use of opiates per se that is physically and psychologically destructive to the addict, as much as the subculture resulting from our methods of handling heroin addiction today.

In the nineteenth century, the usual impetus for drug addiction was some type of physical discomfort. Today, however, addiction is far more likely to result from psychological stress within the individual, frequently combined with poverty. About half of the addicts in America are thought to live in New York City.† While there is

* Typical of nineteenth-century attitudes is Dr. Watson's reaction to his friend Sherlock Holmes's use of cocaine and morphine. In the *Sign of the Four*, Watson chides Holmes for his use of the "filthy stuff" and Holmes responds that he needs it to relieve the boredom of life. Holmes is, of course, an entirely respectable, if somewhat eccentric character.

† The Ford Foundation study of drug abuse estimates that 85 percent of our heroin addicts are male, and 60 to 70 percent are black, Puerto Rican, or Mexican-American. Patricia M. Wald and Peter Barton Hutt, et al., *Dealing with Drug Abuse: A Report to the Ford Foundation* (New York: Praeger, 1972), p. 4.

some addiction among white middle-class young people, heroin never really took hold on the campuses even during the most rebellious days of the late 1960s, and heroin addiction among middle-class people simply does not present the same criminal justice problems that it does among lower-class individuals.

Most heroin addicts are introduced to the drug by friends and peer group members. Adolescents are frequently intrigued by the glamour and maturity of using an illegal and "dangerous" substance. Some boys are afraid to refuse lest they be called chicken. Many are curious about the sensation produced by this mysterious substance. Above all, many first-time users are looking for something that will make them "feel better"—that will relieve the problems, anxieties, tensions, insecurities and just plain fear associated with being young, black, and poor. Initially, from what addicts tell us, the drug lives up to most of their expectations. It is a pleasant social activity carried on in a group setting which relieves loneliness and makes the user feel like an "in-person." The sensation produced by the drug itself is euphoric—it is relaxing, warms up cold feet, and chases the butterflies out of the stomach.

Unfortunately, however, the experience is short lived. In a few hours the effect of the drug wears off, and the user is back to facing gray reality. As the user attempts to repeat his experience, however, more problems arise. The drug is expensive and sometimes hard to get. While those familiar with the drug scene agree that despite its illegality heroin can be purchased readily in all our big cities, the purchase is still not quite the same as buying soap in the A & P. The supplier may not be where he says he will be, the quality and the quantity of the drug are uncertain, and the price may vary. Normally, to supply a habit of even moderate size, male addicts are forced into crime and female addicts into crime and prostitution. This change in their life-style is accompanied in many cases by thefts from their immediate relatives and neighbors, leading to disruption of family and neighborhood ties. Increasingly the effort to supply himself with drugs leads the addict into a way of life in which he is isolated from everyone but his fellow addicts and their suppliers, and where activity unrelated to drug use or sale becomes less and less frequent and meaningful.

Why then do heroin addicts continue to use heroin even while recognizing the degradation the drug is imposing upon them? Although it may have been a desire for pleasure and surcease from life's problems that induced the addict to try the drug initially, it is not the euphoric qualities of the drug that make him continue to be a user. The testimony of addicts tells us that once using the drug has become a regular habit, the euphoric sensation becomes less pronounced and even disappears. At that point the addict takes his heroin for a far more pressing reason—to avoid the agonies of withdrawal. Heroin is a physically addictive drug, that is, the body builds up a tolerance for it and larger and larger doses must be used to achieve the same effect. Cessation of use, furthermore, produces very severe physical discomfort:

> *The character and severity of the withdrawal symptoms . . . depend upon many factors, including the particular drug, the total daily dose used, the interval between doses, the duration of use, and the health and personality of the addict. . . . In the case of morphine or heroin lacrimination, running nose, yawning and perspiration appear . . . dilated pupils, loss of appetite, gooseflesh, breathlessness, irritability, and tremor . . . weakness and depression . . . nausea and vomiting . . . intestinal spasm and diarrhea. . . . Marked chilliness, alternating with flushing and excessive sweating . . . abdominal cramps and pains in the bones and muscles of the back . . . occasionally there is cardiovascular collapse.* [5]

The heroin addict who is "hooked" must continue to take the drug if he is to avoid withdrawal symptoms. Worse yet, addicts who are physically withdrawn from heroin, as for example in a hospital or prison, report that months and years after their last shot of heroin they still experience heroin hunger, a longing for the relief of tension that only heroin seems to be able to provide. The strength of this yearning must be very great because it explains why addicts are willing to put up with a life of almost unbelievable degradation and physical danger; why the most intensive rehabilitative efforts in drug-free therapeutic communities are failures for almost all addicts; and why addicts who have served five and even ten years in prison will go back on the drug almost immediately, fully aware that such use virtually assures their prompt return to prison.

Despite the testimony of thousands of addicts as to the compelling nature of heroin addiction, and despite its physically addictive properties, it is not true that taking heroin always and inevitably leads to a lifetime of addiction, nor is it true that it is impossible successfully to kick the heroin habit. There is evidence that there are a considerable number of heroin users who are able to take heroin intermittently without becoming physically addicted. Such individuals, for example, may use heroin on weekends or holidays. There is also some evidence that American soldiers in Vietnam who used heroin there, were able to stop using heroin on their return to the United States.[6] The evaluation of this evidence is complicated by the fact that not only is it difficult to ascertain how many people are occasional heroin users, but we don't know how they use the drug, or at what strength. In Vietnam, for example, reports indicated that while the heroin used was relatively unadulterated by inner-city street standards, many of the GIs were not "mainlining" (injecting the drug into the veins). Many were smoking, some were "snorting" (sniffing into the nostrils), and some were "skin popping" (injecting subcutaneously). In the cities, on the other hand, most addicts appear to be mainliners, but the quality, and the strength of the heroin they use is not accurately known. It is certainly far weaker than that used in Vietnam, and it is possible that for some individuals who use heroin only occasionally, the actual amount used is insufficient to cause physical addiction.

In addition to the evidence that occasional use is possible, an even less understood phenomenon has been observed by those working in the field. *There are relatively few heroin addicts over the age of thirty-five.* All the statistics we have as to the incidence of heroin use (which are gathered mainly from hospitals and prisons) indicate a sharp decline in the number of users starting approximately at age thirty-five. Theoretically, if heroin is a physically addictive drug, the desire for which never leaves the addict, the addict should remain addicted until his death, and there should be no drop off with increasing age, except as addicts die. Yet, the data both statistical and impressionistic, indicate that this is not so. Addicts for the most part are young men. And although we do not know why there are so few older addicts we do know that early death does not account for the skewed statistics. Some addicts do die young; some become alcoholics and derelicts; but some users are, as far as we know, alive and not addicted. The significant point here is that apparently drug addiction may, to some extent, be a self-limiting process. Its onset has been very well documented, but relatively little has been written about its cessation. The best work in this area has been done by Charles Winick, professor of Sociology at the City University of New York, and formerly director of the Narcotic Addiction Program of the American Social Health Association. Winick hypothesizes that drug addiction occurs in the adolescent as an attempt to cope with the strains of growing up, and is relinquished as the strains that caused the addiction are alleviated simply by the passage of time and the processes of maturation.

> *One possible explanation of the cessation of opiate addiction among addicts in their thirties is that they began taking heroin in their late teens or early twenties as their method of coping with the challenges and problems of early adulthood. They may have been faced with compelling personality and social needs to find some expression for impulses involving sex and aggressiveness. They may have confronted vocational decisions and social pressures to help support their parents or families or establish a new family of their own. The use of narcotics may make it possible for the user to evade, mask, or postpone the expression of these needs and these decisions. The narcotics user prefers his drug to sex, and the drug drains off and absorbs his impulse of aggression and hostility. He is so busy getting drugs that he cannot take a regular job or learn a vocational skill. He cannot support his parents or start a family because he needs money for narcotics. He often becomes dependent on his family for money to buy narcotics. On a less conscious level, he may be anticipating becoming dependent on jails and other community resources. By beginning heroin use, he may become a member of a social "hip" or "cool" sub-cultural group which sees its non-involvement in the ordinary concerns of ordinary people as an advantage and as a sign of its elite status. Becoming a narcotics addict in early adulthood thus enables the addict to avoid many decisions, although it implicitly is a major decision. Taking narcotics is not a major decision, it is* the *decision for the young addict.*

> *Maturing out of addiction is the name we can give to the process by which the addict stops taking drugs, as the problems*

for which he began taking drugs become less salient and less urgent, if our hypothesis is correct. It is as if, metaphorically speaking, the addicts' inner fires have become banked by their thirties. They may feel that less is expected of them in the way of sex, aggressiveness, a vocation, helping their parents, or starting a family. As a result of some process of emotional homeostasis, the stresses and strains of life are becoming sufficiently stabilized for the typical addict in his thirties so that he can face them without the support provided by narcotics. This cycle may be analogous to that of the typical delinquent whose delinquency increases during his teens and remains constant till he reaches his late twenties, when it declines. His delinquencies may be his way of meeting the same needs which the addict meets by taking drugs. Since so many addicts are members of a delinquent sub-culture, the approximate consonance in age between addicts and delinquents may well be more than fortuitous. [7]

The Winick hypothesis is unproven, and has been criticized by many sociologists, psychologists, and physicians who feel either that it is too simplistic or that it flies in the face of what is hypothesized about the nature of physical addiction. Yet even the critics are forced to agree that the incidence of drug addiction declines markedly with age and no other explanation for this phenomenon is apparent.

In any case, it is obvious that the impact of heroin addiction on an individual is both complex and quite different from the stereotype commonly held by laymen. While the use of heroin per se, according to the best scientific knowledge available, is only mildly and temporarily psychologically or physiologically harmful, the life of the addict, or at least of the lower-class addict is, nevertheless, a life of intense suffering, physical degradation and danger, and social ostracism, largely attributable to the pattern of life imposed on him by the necessity of obtaining an illegal expensive commodity. A regular user moreover, cannot readily cease his use without experiencing severe physical reactions; yet, there is some evidence that addiction may be a self-limiting process that declines as the addict himself matures. While there is much we do not know about the phenomenon of addiction, it is on the basis of what we *do* know, that various approaches to handling it should be evaluated.

Heroin Addiction: British and American Experiences

Addiction to morphine started in the United States, probably as a result of treatment given to wounded men in military hospitals during the Civil War. Despite their increasing numbers, however, opiate addicts appear not to have been considered a serious problem. They were regarded as individuals with a personality defect or weakness, in much the same way we regard alcoholics today. No particular connection was made between opiate addiction and crime. Opiates were dispensed over the counter by pharmacists by prescriptions from physicians, and as an ingredient in many patent medicines.

In 1914 the Harrison Act was passed, which required all persons and firms handling narcotics to register and pay a nominal excise fee of one cent per ounce on sales. There is no mention of addicts or addiction in the act, the ostensible purpose of which was to make drug distribution a matter of record. Medical practice was exempted:

> *Nothing contained in this section . . . shall . . . apply . . . (t)o the dispensing or distribution of any drugs mentioned . . . to a patient by a physician, dentist, or veterinary surgeon registered under section 4722 in the course of his professional practice only.*

The question of why the Harrison Act was passed at the time that it was and in the form that it assumed is one that cannot be answered conclusively. It seems fairly clear, however, that, whatever the reasons, public clamor for legislation to handle a serious social problem was not one of them. Indeed, the *New York Times Index* for 1914 lists only two brief articles on the passage of the federal legislation. As one student of the Federal Bureau of Narcotics put it:

> *The public's attitude toward drug use had not changed much with the passage of the Act—there was some opposition to drug use, some support of it, and a great many who did not care one way or the other.*[8]

The passage of the Act seems to have been inspired initially by the obligations of the United States as a signatory of the Hague Convention of 1912. Another consideration may have been a desire to protect consumers, a desire which had already resulted in the passage of the Pure Food and Drug Act in 1906. A third consideration may have been the moral crusading of groups such as the WCTU and the antivice societies. In any case, at the time of its passage, the Harrison Act was an uncontroversial, unpublicized law that set up a Narcotics Division in the Internal Revenue Bureau to register and record narcotics transactions in the United States.

Shortly after passage of the act, however, apparently at the instigation of the newly created Narcotics Division, a good deal of publicity regarding the evils of narcotics use was generated, along with a series of test cases regarding the limits of the division's powers. As a result of newly awakened public concern and favorable verdicts from the United States Supreme Court the Narcotics Division was able to expand its function from mere record keeping to policing the entire country in relation to drug use. This meant in practical terms that the medical exception provision of the Harrison Act was effectively eliminated because within a few years it became impossible for physicians to prescribe an opiate for even legitimate purposes.

The Narcotics Division was active in the prosecution of three cases that reached the United States Supreme Court. Two of these cases produced decisions that enabled the division to prohibit totally the use of narcotics. In *Webb* v. *United States*,[9] the physician in question had issued thousands of prescriptions which he sold to addicts for fifty cents a piece. In a second case, *United States* v. *Behrman*,[10] the physician had issued a prescription for a large quantity of narcotics to be used at the addict's discretion. Both of these cases obviously involved improper and unethical medical practices. They nevertheless formed the basis for a general prohibition by the court of medical dispensation of opiates without regard for a specific medical problem. A few years later, a reputable physician named Lindner was convicted under the Harrison Act for prescribing four tablets of a narcotic drug to ease the alleged withdrawal symptoms of a Narcotics Bureau agent posing as an addict. After extensive, and expensive litigation, Dr. Lindner achieved Supreme Court review of his case. The court unanimously reversed the doctor's conviction on the ground that addicts were diseased persons, and proper subjects for bona fide medical treatment. On the surface the *Lindner* decision appeared to reinstate the medical exception of the Harrison Act, and opened the way for medical dispensation of narcotic drugs in appropriate cases. The Narcotics Bureau, however, refused to change its regulations to conform to *Lindner.* As a result physicians, unsure of vindication, were afraid to run the risk of arrest and conviction inherent in prescribing opiates, and preferred to withdraw and leave the field entirely to the Narcotics Bureau.

In retrospect, not only did the Federal Bureau of Narcotics ride roughshod over the medical profession ignoring the rights of doctors and patients, but their enforcement efforts were directed to a large extent against foreign and poor minority groups. David F. Musto, a physician who was consultant to the National Commission on Marihauna and Drug Abuse, shows that efforts at enforcement of the drug laws were made in the context of campaigns against the activities of political radicals, Negroes, Chinese, and Mexicans.

> *The closing of the opiate maintenance clinics in the early 1920's, for example, . . . rode a wave of national hysteria. Addicts were lumped together with Bolsheviks, Wobblies and rebellious youth, fear of crime and addiction closely paralleled our current mood, and even the chiefs of New York City's progressive health department, frustrated by their inability to cure addicts, agreed to abandon maintenance for quarantine . . .*
>
> *At the peak of the lynchings in the South at the turn of the century—while white women were getting through their low moments on opium-laden nostrums like "Mrs. Winslow's Soothing Syrup" and addicting their babies with "Hooper's Anodyne, the Infant's Friend"—wild fears of cocaine-using blacks were rampant. "It has been authoritatively stated," a 1910 Federal survey asserted, "that cocaine is often the direct incentive to the crime of rape by the Negroes of the South and other sections of the country." . . .*
>
> *Prohibitionists . . . conducted a "symbolic crusade" against newly arrived European immigrants who had the habit of lounging around saloons. So, too, the forces that favored a ban on smoking opium had no great empathy for its principal users, Chinese immigrants and coolies. "If the Chinaman cannot get along without 'dope,'" pronounced the American Pharmaceutical Association in 1903, "we can get along without him."* [11]

The net result of federal attempts to regulate drug usage over the past sixty years is that the Federal Bureau of Narcotics has succeeded in imposing on a regulatory tax law the most restrictive inflexible interpretation possible, and it has legitimatized its efforts through an excellent public relations campaign which has created in the public mind the stereotype of a drug user as a dangerous, violent person who, in addition to being a criminal, is sexually dangerous and a member of an unpopular minority group as well.

The impact of the Harrison Act on drug addiction was not quite what was intended by those who passed it, however, because instead of eliminating addiction it simply created a new class of addicts as well as a whole host of problems incident to the enforcement of the act itself rather than to addiction per se. The largely middle-class whites who were addicted at the time of the passage of the Harrison Act probably, for the most part, switched to other drugs, especially the barbiturates which were discovered early in the twentieth century. Some no doubt continued to use drugs illegally, and in some areas of the country opiates were quietly dispensed through physicians and pharmacists until recent times.[12] Addicts who were not so fortunate as to have these quasi-respectable sources of supply, became the vanguard of a new criminal class of addicts who received their supplies through the underworld. Some addicts also shifted to alcohol. Between 1914 and the end of World War II, the number of heroin addicts thus declined (although not the number of those addicted to alcohol or other drugs). After World War II, the underworld (which no longer had bootlegging as a primary source of income), became increasingly interested in the profits to be made from the sale of heroin. Since 1945 the number of heroin addicts in this country has increased sharply, especially in the late 1960s when the rise was meteoric. The reasons for this increase are not altogether clear, but it is reasonable to assume that the interests of organized crime, and the pre-existing nucleus of criminal addicts created by the enforcement of the Harrison Act, combined with the simultaneous sizeable immigration of poor blacks and Puerto Ricans from the farms of the South and Puerto Rico to the slums of our big cities, were probably among the most important factors. Certainly, the existence of the Harrison Act, and the efforts of the Federal Bureau of Narcotics, by themselves do not account for the size of our addict population, since during the period of their administrative suzerainty, the number of addicts both fell and rose, with the rise much the sharper of the two.[13]

The British experience contrasts sharply with our own. Like the United States, the United Kingdom was bound by the Hague Convention for the international control of narcotics, and accordingly, in 1920 Parliament passed the Dangerous Drugs Act, which was designed to regulate the sale and distribution of opiates. The British, however, did not forbid physicians to prescribe opiates for addicted patients. The decision to leave channels of legitimate access to drugs open to addicts was made deliberately after British observation of the effect of the Harrison Act.

> It appears that not only has the Harrison Law failed to diminish the number of drug takers—some contend, indeed, that it has increased their numbers—but, far from bettering the lot of the opium addict, it has actually worsened it; for without curtailing the supply of the drug it has sent the price up tenfold and this had the effect of impoverishing the poorer class of addicts and reducing them to a condition of such abject misery as to render them incapable of gaining an honest livelihood.[14]

The report of the Rolleston Committee, established by the British government to consider drug policy, recommended that addiction to opiates be regarded as a manifestation of a morbid state, or in other words, an illness that could be treated legitimately by physicians caring for such patients through the prescription of the addicting drug. As a result of these recommendations, the Home Office was able to obtain information from physicians and pharmacists on the number of opiate addicts in Great Britain. The number of such addicts declined slowly from 1926 until approximately 1950, at which time there were thought to be between 400 and 600 addicts in Great Britain. These addicts tended to be middle-aged and drawn largely from the medical and paramedical professions. Most cases were therapeutic in origin in that the drug (usually morphine) had originally been prescribed for the relief of pain connected with an illness.[15]

After 1950 a change in the pattern of addiction in Great Britain occurred. The number of addicts increased, the addicts tended to be young males, and the origin of their addiction was nontherapeutic, that is, was not a result of medical treatment. The reasons for these changes are not clear. There is some suggestion that suppression of the use of marihuana immediately following the end of World War II led some marihuana users into opiate addiction. In addition, immigrant Canadian and American youths seemed to have come to Great Britain with the heroin habit firmly entrenched. Several large robberies of hospitals and wholesale pharmaceutical suppliers seemed to have supplied a black market somewhat similar to the American type. An Interdepartmental Committee on Drug Addiction chaired by Sir Russell Brain, nevertheless reaffirmed the policies that had evolved from the original Rolleston Committee report. In the early 1960s, however, the number of addicts in Great Britain increased sharply, more than doubling between 1961 and 1965. The Brain Committee was reconvened, and in its report recommended the first significant modification of the system of drug distribution since 1926.

The increase in the number of addicts was thought to be the result of unethical and ill-advised overprescription by a handful of physicians in London. The chief recommendation of the committee, therefore, was to limit the power of dispensing opiates to clinics, which were to be set up for that purpose, and to make it a statutory offense for other physicians to prescribe heroin and cocaine. The committee also recommended tightening up recording procedures so that the Home Office would have a more accurate count of the number of addicts involved. Following the implementation of the Brain Committee report, the number of addicts at first sharply increased. In 1966 the Home Office was aware of 1,349 drug addicts; in 1967, 1,729, and in 1968, 2,782. This increase, however, is thought to be in large part the result of tightened up reporting procedures. Physicians bent over backward to include all patients for whom they had prescribed opiates, however briefly, during the year. Also, many addicts were apparently reported twice. To eliminate these statistical inaccuracies, the Home Office began to report the number of addicts on record as of a particular day: on December 31, 1968, 1,746; December 31, 1969, 1,466; December 31, 1970, 1,430; December 31, 1971, 1,555; December 31, 1972, 1,619. The most recent statistics available indicate virtual stabilization in the number of persons addicted to opiates. This is in sharp contrast to the American experience, which shows a fivefold increase during roughly the same period of time.

In Great Britain today, if a person is addicted to an opiate such as heroin or methadone, he can go to one of the centers established for the treatment of addiction. These centers are mostly in the London area and are frequently part of a general hospital. A case history is taken for new patients who are then examined to determine whether they are using drugs and are physically addicted. The patient is interviewed to determine whether he wishes to come off drugs completely. If he does not, a prescription will be issued for him. The amount prescribed for him is determined by a conference of the physicians working in the clinic. These prescriptions are sent to the patient's local drug store, made out in such a way that the patient can get one day's supply at a time on Mondays through Fridays and two day's supply on Saturday. The patient returns to the clinic weekly for a new prescription; at that time his urine is checked to determine how much, and what kind of drugs he is taking. He also will be offered whatever therapy or rehabilitative treatment the clinic staff may feel is appropriate.

The clinic reports the numbers of such patients and the amount and type of drug supplied to the Home Office, as do the pharmacists filling the prescriptions. Statistics are believed to be quite accurate although the Home Office maintains a continuing check to determine whether there is a group of addicts unknown to the authorities who are being supplied by illegally obtained drugs. Arrested persons, patients admitted to hospitals, and all autopsied bodies are routinely checked for drug addiction. As a result of this continuing check, it is believed that not more than 3 or 4 percent of the addicts in Great Britain are unknown to the authorities. In any event, if there is a large subterranean group of addicts who have escaped detection, they do not present a social problem since they neither get arrested, nor become seriously ill, nor die.

American handling of drug addicts is, of course, very different from the British approach. Generally, four different types of programs have evolved in the years since the enactment of the Harrison Act. The most common method of handling addiction is the straight punitive approach. The addict who has committed a crime (whether of the laws relating to drugs or to other laws) is arrested, placed in a jail or hospital until he is physically withdrawn from the drug to which he is addicted, tried, and if convicted, handled as a nonaddict would be. If he is sent to prison he, of course, will be abstinent (unless the prison is inefficient or corrupt enough to enable him to obtain drugs), and on his release he will hopefully remain abstinent. If he is initially placed on probation rather than being committed to prison, or if he is paroled following his release from prison, his probation or parole officer will try to see that he remains abstinent. Although this approach has been by far the most widespread method of treating addicts in this country at all periods of time since 1914, as mentioned earlier, it is almost totally unsuccessful.

A variant of the straight punitive approach is the punitive-medical approach, where the addict who has committed a crime is permitted to go to a hospital-type facility rather than to prison. The federal government has had a prison-type hospital at Lexington, Kentucky, since 1935, which has attempted to rehabilitate drug addicts.* The record at Lexington is dismal. If success is defined as abstinence by the addict after his release, follow-up studies consistently indicate failure rates of considerably more than 90 percent. The experience of the New York State Narcotics program has been similar. In 1966 New York State established a program whereby an addict against whom criminal charges were filed could elect to enter a controlled hospital facility for treatment of his addiction with a view toward becoming totally abstinent. The program has been an admitted massive failure for many reasons, including the inability of the state to provide sufficient controlled hospital facilities, sufficient skilled staff, the hostility of local residents in the areas in which facilities were to be located, and the enormous potential cost of the program were it to be fully implemented. The program has published very little data from which to gauge its success, but such fragmentary reports as are available indicate results as appalling as those at Lexington. Mayor Lindsay's office reported in 1971 that of 526 persons who had left the New York State program between April and September 1970, only 18 per-

* The United Public Health Hospital at Lexington, Kentucky accepts three categories of addicts: self-committed addicts who do not have criminal charges pending against them, who may leave the hospital at any time; addicts who have no criminal charges pending against them who previously were self-committed; and prisoners who have been committed by a federal court. The latter two categories may not leave the hospital at their own pleasure.

cent had completed the after-care phase of the program without relapsing or absconding. This does not mean, of course, that 18 percent were cured; it means only that 18 percent had followed the prescribed course of treatment. The other 82 percent had not done even that, and the 18 percent had still to prove whether they would remain abstinent.[16]

A third approach to the handling of drug addicts is a recent response to the mushrooming drug addiction figures in the United States. This has been the attempt to set up drug-free therapeutic communities which will withdraw the addict and teach him how to live an abstinent life in society. Daytop Village, Synanon, and Phoenix House all are residential facilities for addicts who wish to be cured of their addiction. Although the program in each institution varies somewhat, all are based on the assumption that the root of addiction is an emotional sickness, and that the sickness and addiction can be cured by some therapeutic group process. All encourage outspoken criticism of each individual by members of the group for the purpose of breaking down the defenses that the individual has erected to shield himself from the reality of his addiction and his rationalizations concerning it. For some individuals this approach is very successful in that they are enabled to live a drug free life. It is doubtful, however, whether such persons can be considered "cured," since the evidence available suggests that they are able to remain drug free only so long as they remain attached to the community. Few, if any, seem to have been able to return to the outer world and remain drug free. Their condition is somewhat analagous to that of alcoholics who are involved with Alcoholics Anonymous, i.e., they are in a state of remission that is maintained only so long as they enjoy the support of the community.[17]

The number of addicts for whom even this partial remission occurs is not large. Administrators of drug-free communities are rather defensive of their programs and are loathe to publish statistics on their success rate, but from the incomplete data that are available, it appears that a large percentage of those admitted to the program drop out within a few weeks or months. A fair percentage of those who remain more than one year are helped. The number who remain more than one year, however, is very small. Worst of all, from the point of view of treating addicts on a large scale, is that even the sponsors and firm supporters of the drug-free community approach concede that their programs can work only with subjects who are willing, and even anxious, to participate. This type of program cannot be imposed by court order or any other type of coercion on an unwilling subject, and it is generally conceded that probably fewer than 10 percent of all addicts are willing to attempt the austere, somewhat monastic type of life that is characteristic of such communities.

The most recent, and in some ways the most hopeful approach to the handling of drug addicts has been the development of methadone maintenance programs. The pioneering in methadone maintenance was begun in 1965 by Drs. Vincent Dole and Marie Nyswander. Dr. Dole of Rockefeller University came to the study of drug addiction through his interest in the control of obesity. Dr. Nyswander, a psychiatrist, had been stationed in the United States Public Service Health Hospital at Lexington, Kentucky, during World War II, and became interested in addicts as patients. Dr. Dole, in his search for the metabolic explanation of obesity, became interested in the biochemical explanation of heroin addiction. In the course of his search through medical literature he came upon an article by Dr. Nyswander, "The Drug Addict As a Patient," which suggested that for many addicts drug maintenance was the only feasible method of handling their addiction. Dole's biochemical expertise and Nyswander's psychiatric approach eventually merged into the first methadone maintenance program in New York City.

The original program had fewer than 100 patients, all of whom were in-patients. Within five years, by March 1970, the program had expanded to 2,300 addicts, most of whom were out-patients. By March 1971 the program included 82 ambulatory or out-patient facilities and 13 in-patient facilities in New York City and Westchester County. Seven thousand patients were under treatment and the admission rate reached 700 patients per month, of whom 70 percent were out-patients. This program was mounted through the cooperative efforts of the Columbia University School of Public Health and Administrative Medicine, the New York City Health Department, and the Beth Israel Medical Center. By 1968 both Chicago and Philadelphia had instituted methadone maintenance programs, and by 1970, at least twenty-five cities were known to have such programs.[18]

While individual methadone maintenance programs vary in the details of their operation, all of them attempt to stabilize the addict on a quantity of methadone administered orally once a day sufficient to block the craving for heroin, keep the addict comfortable, and enable him to function normally. Some programs are in-patient units, and the addict is treated for whatever illnesses from which he may be suffering. He may also be offered social casework and counseling help. Out-patient units may or may not provide such ancillary services, but most frequently, they are the center to which the addict reports to receive his daily dose of methadone. In well run units, precautions are taken to see that the addict does, in fact, swallow his medication, and does not save it to sell to other addicts on the street. Addicts are tested periodically to see if they are using heroin or other drugs along with methadone.

Methadone is, of course, an addicting drug, being a synthetic narcotic developed by the Germans during World War II. Its virtues as compared to heroin are that it can be administered orally; its effects are sufficiently long-lasting so that it can be taken only once a day and, it is relatively easy to stabilize a patient on a maintenance dose. There is some disagreement as to whether addicts are equally willing to take methadone or heroin. Methadone, unless it is injected intravenously, does not produce the same "high" as heroin. On the other hand, most confirmed addicts apparently use heroin not to obtain a high but simply to feel "normal" again, or to avoid the pain of withdrawal. Methadone performs these latter functions admirably. Methadone has even fewer physiological side effects than heroin, the principal one being a tendency toward constipation.

Methadone maintenance programs have, however, achieved a number of very positive results. In the first place, a very large proportion of those who enter the program remain in the program in contrast to drug-free programs like that of the United States Public Health Service Hospital in Lexington, Kentucky, or Synanon, where probably as many as 90 percent of those who enter drop out of the program. Methadone maintenance programs report retention rates that range between 70 and 90 percent. Most of those who do defect are chronic alcoholics or addicts who continue to be multiple drug users. Secondly, patients on methadone show a marked decrease in antisocial behavior. Dr. Frances Gearing, director of the Methadone Maintenance Evaluation Unit of the Columbia University School of Public Health and Administrative Medicine, reports that in the first 1,000 patients admitted, there was a 92 percent decrease in antisocial behavior during the first four years of the program. This figure was reached by comparing the number of arrests accumulated by the patient population during the four years prior to their admission to the program, with the number of arrests which actually occurred during the four years after their admission to the program. While one could challenge the use of arrest figures as an absolute indication of antisocial behavior, nevertheless, the standard is sufficiently reliable to indicate a very substantial decrease in criminal activity.[19] Dr. Gearing's results are borne out, moreover, by accounts of other methadone programs throughout the country which report similar findings.[20]

Third of all, those patients who remain in the program show a decided increase in employment rates. Of the first 1,000 men (all inpatients) admitted to the program, 26 percent were employed at the time of admission. At the end of six months 51 percent were employed, and at the end of one year, 61 percent were employed. Similarly, of the first 500 ambulatory patients admitted, 60 percent were employed at the time of the admission. At the end of one year, the percentage had increased to 72 percent, after two years to 79 percent, and after three years to 88 percent. Fewer than 5 percent were employed by the program itself.[21]

In addition to lower arrest rates and improved employment rates, the New York City Methadone Maintenance Treatment Program reports a death rate of addicts of approximately 1 percent in the first year and .6 percent per year for ensuing years. While this is high for the age group involved, these patients have multiple health problems, and typically have been living apathetic and physically dangerous lives. The death rate is low as compared to the death rate for those who left the program, which was 4 to 5 percent within one year after discharge.

In evaluating methadone maintenance as a technique for handling heroin addicts, it must be kept in mind that the initial programs were somewhat selective in their choice of addicts for admission to the program. These programs were also very well run in the sense that they offered therapeutic and rehabilitative services along with drug maintenance, and they had highly motivated, well-trained staffs. It is possible that programs that are not selective, that accept any addict who walks in off the street and whose addiction can be verified, may not achieve as impressive results. There is also a very distinct danger of abuse from poorly run programs: that nonaddicts will be given methadone; that addicts will not be supervised sufficiently to insure that they do not divert supplies to a black market; or that record keeping and staffing will be corrupt or sloppy enough so that illegal operations can take place. Nevertheless, the initial results of rather large-scale methadone programs have unquestionably been more hopeful and more impressive than any other previously tried approach to drug addiction in the sense of returning addicts to normal functioning. There have been consistent reports of a drop in the crime rate in New York City at the same time that methadone use has increased sharply. While there is no proof of a causal relationship between these two phenomena, it is sufficiently suggestive to warrant close scrutiny.

The British Experience—How Relevant Is It in America?

The United States and Great Britain have used widely divergent methods to handle the problem of drug addiction. By 1973, after nearly sixty years of regulation, it was apparent that American methods, which had been largely punitive had failed to deter addiction from spreading, and had created a host of undesirable side-effects, the most serious of which was an increase in crime and antisocial behavior among addicts. The British, by way of contrast, consistently have been far more successful in preventing the spread of addiction and have experienced very little criminal activity associated with drug addiction. One cannot, unfortunately, draw the obvious conclusion that Americans ought to switch to the British approach and all will be well. England and the United States are two very different countries—different in economy, in culture, in population. If we are to learn something from the British experience, we must take account of those differences and then decide how much of the British experience is relevant to the American problem.

As of 1973, there were fewer than 3,000 persons addicted to opiates in Great Britain. Most of these addicts were nontherapeutic addicts, i.e., those whose addiction was unrelated to the practice of medicine or to treatment for a disease. Of this nontherapeutic group, most of the addicts were young (under age thirty-five) and male. They cut across all class and ethnic lines, and were in fact, except for age and sex, a representative cross-section of the general population. They were largely native born, and most lived in the London area.

As indicated before, addicts report to an out-patient clinic attached to a hospital once a week. A prescription for a weekly supply of drugs to be dispensed on a daily basis is mailed to their neighborhood pharmacies, where they report daily for their supplies. At the clinic itself arrangements are made for appropriate auxiliary treatment where indicated: medical treatment for hepatitis, malnutrition, or any other physical disease when present; psychiatric therapy where indicated; vocational training or counseling where appropriate; and help with family problems, housing, job seeking, etc., if necessary. The emphasis in the handling of addicts is always on producing maximally functioning individuals, rather than ex-drug addicts. The aim of the British system is to produce a person who can take care of himself, his family, and his obligations to the greatest possible extent, rather than to produce individuals who can achieve abstinence.

Addicts are, of course, asked if they wish to become abstinent, and if they do, they are no doubt given help along these lines. The great majority of addicts, however, are stabilized as quickly as possible on a maintenance dose of either heroin or methadone that will keep them sufficiently comfortable to get on with the normal routines of living. The fact of addiction is not treated as a disgrace, a scandal, a weakness, or an irreversible calamity. The addict is instead treated as an individual with a chronic condition requiring constant though fairly routine treatment. Drug clinics are attached to hospitals that provide for many other types of patients. No great distinction is made between heroin and methadone, and the decision to use one rather than the other is based on expediency (e.g., methadone can be administered only once a day, while heroin requires more frequent administration), more than the moral superiority of methadone over heroin.

There are some problems connected with the British method of handling opiates addicts (though by American standards they are not very serious). One of these is the problem of determining who is truly an addict; another is preventing the diversion of prescribed drugs to the black market; and a third is establishing the proper dose for each individual addict. To some extent all three of these problems are interrelated, and are connected to the larger problem of preventing the spread of drug addiction to youngsters not yet addicted. When a patient appears at a clinic and declares that he is an addict, it is sometimes difficult to determine with absolute certainty that he is really physically addicted to heroin. Tests such as thin layer chromotography (a form of urinalysis) can determine whether he has used heroin in the immediate past, but only the patient's testimony can tell the physician for how long such use has continued. Similarly, it is very difficult for the physician to know objectively how large a dose the addict should receive. The dose is established initially experimentally, and from the patient's reaction the physician subsequently adjusts it. Again, if the patient lies, the physician may give him more than he actually needs, in which case the addict may attempt to sell some of the excess on the black market. On the other hand, if the physician ignores his patient's complaints, he will force the patient to seek illegal sources.

There are no pat formulas for dealing with these problems. Those practitioners involved in the running of drug clinics are, on the whole, satisfied with the results. Patients seem to be reasonably well satisfied with their treatment and surveys show an increase in employment, and a decrease in criminality among those treated at the clinics.[22] At the same time the British Home Office and Scotland Yard are both satisfied that only a minor black market in illegal heroin or methadone exists. These practitioners concede that it is possible to cheat the system. They argue, however, that an individual who is determined to become an addict will become one, one way or the other. They also recognize the problem of establishing the appropriate dose for each addict, and the risks of either undersupplying or oversupplying addicts. They feel, however, that while a small black market is probably inevitable, its size is limited ultimately by the existence of readily available, inexpensive, legal narcotics at the clinics. Indeed, rather than worrying about undersupplying addicts, some physicians have questioned whether it is the physician's duty to sit in moral judgment on his patient and deny him sufficient drugs so that he may use them for pleasure rather than simply normal functioning; and some police officials have wondered whether more freely prescribed narcotics might not tend to shrink, rather than to expand the black market, since every addict will be provided for generously. Thus far both of these arguments have been rejected, and physicians such as Thomas H. Bewley, an eminent British authority on problems of addiction, recognize that this sometimes leads to strains and inconsistencies in the physician-patient relationship.

When treating a patient dependent on drugs the aims of the doctor may not be those of the patient. A person who is using drugs or who wishes to use drugs may want to use them, not to alleviate illness or suffering, but for their pleasurable effect. If this is the sole reason he wishes to use the drugs (for example, taking amphetamines intraveneously at a party) it is unlikely that a doctor would accede to the request to provide drugs for this purpose. Most doctors would not consider it their function to provide pleasure at low cost to the individual through the National Health Service. In general, as doctors, our aim is to deal with such states as pathological depression. Doctors may aim to make unhappy people "normal" but not to make normal people euphoric or give them a "buzz" or a "high."

This prescribing role has both advantages and disadvantages. Doctors working in treatment clinics are dealing with captive patients who must attend weekly to obtain their drugs—an unusual doctor-patient relationship. In other situations a patient who is dissatisfied with his doctor can go to another doctor, but if a patient attending one of the treatment clinics is dissatisfied and goes to another clinic, that clinic will check with the Home Office and contact the first clinic. The second clinic may accept the patient or advise him to remain at the first clinic since the treatment first prescribed would be continued no matter what clinic he attended. In practice the patient who is attending a treatment clinic has little choice.[23]

The American approach for handling addicts is, of course, very different from the British, and this difference stems in part from quite different assumptions as to the nature of addiction and the effect of addiction on the addict; and in part from the cultural and numerical differences between our addict population and that of Great Britain. We have roughly 100 times as many addicts in this country—300,000 as opposed to 3,000—with a population that is only 4 times as large. While our addicts, like the British, are largely young and male, unlike the British, they are not otherwise a representative cross-section of the population. They are instead predominantly poor and nonwhite.

Not only is our addict population different, however, our perception of the problem posed by these addicts is also very different. We assume that addiction is morally evil and that as long as a person is addicted he is completely lost to society and to himself. He is the total fallen man and his only redemption lies in the possibility of his purging himself of the evil that is within him by renouncing drugs forever. The possibility of achieving abstinence, however slight the empirical basis for it, has been the underlying theme of American policy toward addicts. With the exception of the recently developed methadone programs, all our methods of handling addicts are focused on making the addict abstinent. The British, on the other hand, see addiction as a personality problem rather than a moral evil. They do not see addiction as the total destruction of individual capability. They believe the addict can function reasonably well even while he remains an addict and their prognosis for the future of a stabilized addict is very much the same as it would be were he not an addict.

Paradoxically, the American approach, which is far more harsh, condemning, and punitive, in a strange kind of way is more gratifying to the addict's ego. We label him a criminal, we call him evil, weak, depraved, we mobilize our social resources to deal with the problems he is creating, and in the course of doing all these things, we glorify him—we make him a very important man. Most poor boys from the ghettos are born to live and die in anonymity. Poor boys who become addict bad boys achieve a moment of fame—perhaps not the fame the middle class thinks they ought to achieve, but nevertheless a respite from deadening anonymity and facelessness. By making drugs so hard to get, by forcing addicts into association with each other for mutual self-help we create an addict society within the larger society, a subculture in which the deviant becomes normal and the criminal becomes the hardworking upright member of the community.

> [Addicts in New York are] engaged in meaningful activities and relationships seven days a week. The brief moments of euphoria after each administration of a small amount of heroin constitute a small fraction of their daily lives. The rest of the time they are aggressively pursuing a career that is exacting, challenging, adventurous, and rewarding. . . . The heroin user walks with a fast, purposeful stride, as if he is late for an important appointment—indeed, he is. He is hustling

(robbing or stealing), trying to sell stolen goods, avoiding the police, looking for a heroin dealer with a good bag (the street retail unit of heroin), coming back from copping (buying heroin), looking for a safe place to take the drug, or looking for someone who beat (cheated) him—among other things. He is, in short, taking care of business. . . . *For them . . . the quest for heroin is the quest for a meaningful life, not an escape from life. And the meaning does not lie, primarily, in the effects of the drug on their minds and bodies; it lies in the gratification of accomplishing a series of challenging, exciting tasks, every day of the week.*[24]

The British addict is not a big man. He is not an important man. He is an unfortunate man who has a problem, a "condition." He goes to a clinic once a week in a hospital where there are other clinics that treat people with allergies, venereal diseases, and respiratory complaints. He goes to the drug store every day and he picks up a small vial of medication. There is no excitement, no challenge, no comment, no criticism, no labeling. His life, such as it is, goes on in much the same way as it did before he became addicted. His problems are still there, he still needs to cope. The clinic will help him if he will accept help. If he won't he will have to cope some other way. He may or may not be successful, but he will be judged by the same standards and in much the same way as if he were not an addict.

Can the British approach be used in the United States? No one can answer this question with any certainty. Certain conclusions, however, seem to be beyond dispute. In the first place, the traditional American punitive approach is a total failure, and is highly counterproductive. We cannot force abstinence on confirmed addicts, nor can we persuade most addicts to give up their addiction. Secondly, addicts can continue to take drugs and function as reasonably stable, competent, productive members of society. Heroin used in reasonable amounts does not cause physical or psychological damage, and addicts can be stabilized on doses sufficient to make them feel and act "normal." Thirdly, stabilized addicts consistently show patterns of increased gainful employment and decreased criminality. This is true both in Great Britain and in the United States for addicts enrolled in methadone programs. This is not to deny that even stabilized addicts tend to show a disproportionate amount of criminality, which is understandable in light of the fact that well adjusted maximally functioning individuals do not turn to drugs in the first place, unless under extraordinary stress. Most drug addicts are troubled individuals before they become drug addicts, and stabilization does nothing to improve their chances of success in life other than to remove addiction as a potentially insuperable stumbling block.

The details of the British method of handling addicts may not be applicable in the United States. It is hard to say whether, for example, addiction clinics can be attached to municipal or voluntary hospitals throughout the city. The large numbers of addicts involved will produce logistical problems: the need for space, equipment, public transportation, traffic control, etc. Similarly, it is hard to say whether one could adequately supervise the large numbers of pharmacies that would have to be involved in dispensing prescribed drugs. Surely, however, some type of medical handling can be devised *if we will finally accept the notion that medical rather than legal-punitive handling is the proper approach to the problem.* We must accept the fact that medical handling does not imply social approval of drug addiction, nor does it mean that drugs will be freely dispensed or obtainable on demand. At the same time we must give up the twin notions that addiction is a moral disease and that addiction is necessarily curable. The addict is a person with a particular kind of problem. He needs help, not punishment. And he may or may not be able to overcome his dependence on drugs, particularly while he is young.

At the same time we must recognize that there are no simple solutions to a problem as complex as drug addiction. Even if we accept the principle of medical handling, this does not indicate that only one type of program should be available for addicts. Methadone maintenance, heroin maintenance, Synanon, the development of a chemical heroin antagonist, private psychotherapy, religious conversion—all of these approaches are useful for some individuals, and all should be available. Some addicts can and will overcome their addiction; some can be successfully stabilized and lead productive lives; others cannot be stabilized, or will turn to other drugs or alcohol; still others will continue to commit serious antisocial acts even if they are stabilized. Different kinds of problems require different kinds of solutions. And the indispensible first step toward society's coping with the problem of deviance is to remove the artificial restrictions on utilizing any approach that may be useful. If we can give up the cheap morality of sitting in judgment on "sinners" our reward may be the better morality of helping people to live decent lives.

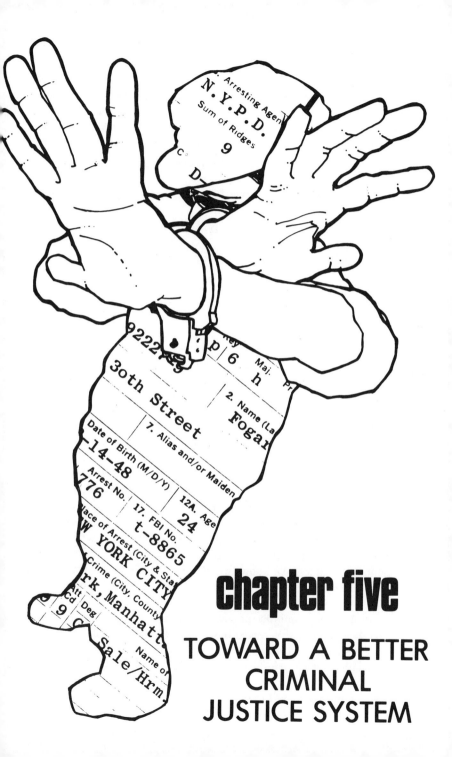

chapter five

TOWARD A BETTER CRIMINAL JUSTICE SYSTEM

It is better to prevent crimes than to punish them.

Cesare Beccaria, *Dei Delitte e Delle Pene.*

Never use a preventive means of a nature to do more evil than the offense to be punished.

Jeremy Bentham, *Theory of Legislation*

Crime is normal because a society exempt from it is utterly impossible.

Émile Durkheim, *The Rules of Sociological Method*

If the law, as Oliver Wendell Holmes has said, is the product of "felt necessities" rather than logic, it is understandable that the system of criminal justice based on that law has grown by accretion rather than plan. There is probably no one in public life in the United States today who would say that he is satisfied with the way we handle the problem of law-breaking. Complaints about the shortcomings of our criminal justice system are universal. They come from liberals and conservatives, from the poor and from the rich, from blacks and from whites, from police, prosecutors, prisoners, and from the general public. The law's delay is the rule, not the exception; plea bargaining, a term once familiar only to criminal court personnel and lawyers practicing criminal law, is now discussed freely at Rotarian luncheons, civic association meetings, and communion breakfasts. Criminal justice reform, like tax reform, has become a staple ingredient of campaign oratory. We know that there are many things wrong with our criminal justice system; what is not clear is what we ought to do about it.

A colossal number of suggestions for criminal justice reform have been tendered in recent times. These proposals fall largely into two categories: *procedural* reform, i.e., improving the efficiency with which police make arrests, prosecutors bring cases to trial, and judges adjudicate cases and sentence those who are convicted; and *substantive* reform, i.e., changing the substance of the law itself in order to improve the overall working of the system, generally, by removing *malum prohibitum* crimes, i.e., morals offenses, from the penal code. The observations made in this book, of course, fall into this latter category, as do the arguments of those reformers who think that prostitution, obscenity, gambling, and consensual sodomy ought to be legally permissible activities. Despite the multiplicity of the suggestions for reform, however, the pace of reform has been very slow. It has perhaps proceeded a bit more quickly in the procedural field than in the substantive field, but much more needs to be accomplished in both areas.

Paradoxically, although the public is concerned almost to the point of hysteria over the failure of the criminal justice system, one of the obstacles to reform is public apathy. The public is highly receptive to dramatic, demagogically appealing suggestions such as a policeman on every corner, mandatory life sentences for drug sellers, "stricter" (not soft-headed) judges, and the like. It is very hard to make the general public understand why these measures will not work: that even a policeman on every corner will not prevent crimes committed indoors, and in addition would make life both unbearable and unbearably expensive; that drug sellers simply are not deterred by threats of life sentences; and that American judges on the whole are already very harsh as compared to judges in Western Europe. It is very hard, in short, to tell the public that there are no simple solutions to the crime problem, because public reaction to that message is withdrawal and apathy.

To complain of public apathy is perhaps but another way of noting that reform in this country has to be accomplished politically. Normally, this means that the legislature (either state or federal) must take some kind of action: or if not the legislature, then to a lesser extent the courts or the administrative branches. To obtain political action, one must have political clout. Again, those most concerned with reform of the system have very little effective political clout. The two groups most directly involved with the need for reform are those who are the victims of crimes, and those who are subsequently arrested and prosecuted for the commission of crimes. The first group, victims, are very much concerned with making the system more effective, but they are a politically and sociologically fragmented group.

The average victim of a crime is likely to be poor, but even if he is middle or upper class, his first-hand observation of the shortcomings of the system (as for example, the need for witnesses to appear at multiple hearings none of which leads to anything but further delay) can only frustrate him. He has no way of obtaining the information or building the organizational structure necessary to achieve effective political action leading to reform. He has, in short, nothing in common with other victims except the fact of their victimization, and he has no expertise other than his sad personal experience which in no way enables him to deal with the political problem.

Those accused (or convicted) of crimes, on the other hand, are a more homogeneous group. They are, for the most part, poor and nonwhite and they share many interests including their common entanglement in the toils of the law. Despite these common interests (and thus a potential for organizational involvement), this group too is politically powerless because its members for the most part are poor, nonwhite, and may frequently be social pariahs such as derelicts, alcoholics, or homosexuals. As a rule such persons are also lacking in political consciousness. Politicians are normally unresponsive to such a group, and indeed those efforts at reform which have been made have been successful only when made by middle-class people on their behalf. Prison riots are an exception to this rule. Attica and the Tombs were examples of political pressure mounted directly by convicted persons. Even here, however, such reforms as resulted were accomplished in part through the assistance of middle-class lawyers and legal defender groups.

It is not only public apathy, however, which discourages criminal justice reform. Any proposal relating to substantive reform—suggesting that any mode of conduct currently considered criminal be removed from the penal code—arouses deeply felt fear in the average person. To many laymen, decriminalizing conduct is the equivalent of endowing it with a government stamp of approval. Thus, to declare that prostitution will no longer be a criminal offense is to announce that henceforth the frequenting of prostitutes is appropriate conduct for all members of the community. Such a notion is, of course, untrue, but it is very difficult to convince the public that the penal code is only one way, and perhaps not even the most effective way of discouraging undesirable conduct. To most people the criminal law is a statement of social policy, and they want included in it every form of conduct of which they disapprove. The criminal law *is* a statement of social policy, but it is not the *only* statement of social policy, and most of our conduct is regulated by the rules formal and informal, stated and unstated, promulgated by our families, by our churches, by our peer groups, and by our work groups. When a mode of conduct is decriminalized, it is simply moved from one category of controls to another. Most wives would object to their husbands consorting with prostitutes even if such conduct were decriminalized, and it is doubtful that the town high school principal would openly consort with the local street walker even if she had the legal status of a small businesswoman.

Not only public attitudes, but also legislative attitudes have slowed down the pace of criminal justice reform. Even where the public has largely overcome its resistance to change, frequently legislators out of an exaggerated fear of unfavorable reaction hesitate to initiate, or even go along with suggested changes of the law. This can best be seen perhaps in regard to changes in birth control, divorce, and abortion laws. Long after the use of contraceptives was widespread and highly acceptable, and long after divorce had been accepted in our most respectable families, state legislatures in some states refused to make obviously needed legislative changes. The mere existence of a highly organized pressure group, in this case the Catholic church, was sufficient to frighten legislators into maintaining the status quo, even though it was doubtful whether the church was sufficiently supported by its own members to punish its opponents at the polls. A similar situation in relation to abortion has been resolved only recently, largely through the application of countervailing pressures by organized proponents of reform. In relation to the criminal justice system, legislatures have a pathological fear of being thought permissive, soft-hearted, or worst of all, wanting to weaken our moral fiber, and there are very few countervailing pressures to help stiffen their backbones. It is hard for a legislator for example, to advocate the legalization of all gambling including numbers betting, without laying himself open to the charge that he does not care if the poor gamble the food out of their children's mouths.

On a somewhat different level, some reform has been opposed by public officials because, while they agree with the need for change, they genuinely do not know of viable alternatives. Many public officials recognize, for example, that our methods of handling hard drugs are disastrously wrong, but they don't know of alternatives that they can comfortably espouse. Even after the decision to decriminalize certain forms of conduct has been made, some type of regulation may be necessary, especially for certain kinds of tangential activity. For example, even if restrictions on pornography and obscenity were removed for adults, should they be removed on dissemination of such materials for children? How freely should producers of such materials be permitted to advertise on theater billboards, in bookstore windows, etc.? If we legalize gambling, should bookmakers be licensed? How do we protect children from homosexual exploitation? If alcoholics are not arrested, what should be done with drunks sleeping in subway stations, gutters, and hallways? If prostitution is a legal activity, is pimping likewise a legal activity?

Many suggestions are made to legislators as to viable alternatives for criminal regulations of morals offenses. Some of these suggestions are made on the basis of sociological and psychological research. Some are based on studies of how other countries handle similar problems. Some suggestions are made by practitioners in the field, others by academics and those who approach the problem conceptually. No one, however, can give the legislator a guarantee of how suggested reforms will work out in practice, and it is the legislator who is the person on the spot—the person who must bear the ultimate responsibility for any adverse social consequence. It is understandable that under these circumstances many legislators, even those who are compassionate, intelligent, and courageous, hesitate to move forward into what are essentially untried areas. In many cases reform comes only when the status quo is so disastrous that there is nothing left to lose.

Finally, reform of the criminal justice system is hampered by a factor that hampers reform of any system—the opposition of vested interests, of those who would be, or think they would be, adversely affected by change. If heroin were legalized, for example, those who operate drug-free programs probably will construe such a change as threatening the size of their potential clientele. The legalization of gambling will probably affect adversely race track owners and operators, as well as bookmakers and those involved in the numbers game. Policemen, prosecutors, judges, court attendants, probation and parole officers, and correction personnel, to some extent all owe their jobs to the large numbers of accused and convicted persons handled by the system. Any decrease in the number handled would threaten somewhat existing jobs and income, and in any case would minimize the well known tendencies of established bureaucracies toward empire building. In addition to those who have legitimate interests in the system, there are, of course, a large number of persons who have an illegitimate interest in the status quo in that they make a living from illegal activities. The principal sources of income from organized crime are thought to be gambling, loansharking, and drug dealing. Our knowledge of the organization and operation of organized crime is fragmentary, but it is reasonable to assume that this segment of the underworld opposes decriminalization of those morals offenses from which they earn money in precisely the same manner as bootleggers in the early thirties opposed repeal. It is also a safe assumption that organized crime is capable of wielding some political influence, and that that influence will be exerted to discourage substantive reform of the criminal justice system.

These obstacles to reform—public apathy, confusion and fear, legislative hesitation, and the footdragging of those with vested interests in the status quo—are not likely to disappear in the immediate future. Nevertheless, the prospects for reform are perhaps brighter than they have been for many years, largely because the social cost of the unreformed system has become so great. We are literally approaching the point where we have very little to lose by reform. Public unhappiness with our unresolved problems is to some extent overcoming public fear and apathy, and even those with legitimate vested interests, such as the police, prosecutors, and judges who normally might be expected to resist change are finding their positions to be increasingly untenable and unsatisfactory as the problems that beset the system increase its irrationality. It is very demoralizing for a policeman to recognize that the suspect he has arrested will be out on the street committing crimes before the policeman is back in the precinct; and it demeans a judge or a prosecutor to be forced to strike a debasing bargain with an obviously guilty accused person. If viable alternative reform policies can be presented, there is some reasonable hope for their implementation. Perhaps the best way of exploring these proposals is to take note of the direction in which our handling of certain kinds of problems has been moving. By evaluating the effect such movement has had, we can then make an educated guess as to the potential impact of further change.

Prostitution

Prostitution is currently a criminal offense in almost all jurisdictions, the principal exception being some parts of Nevada. Prostitution is usually defined as the performance of sexual acts in return for money. The application of the law, however, is reserved almost exclusively to women (although male prostitutes do exist), and to street walkers rather than call girls. In fact, it is the act of solicitation rather than the sexual act per se that leads to most prosecutions. Not only are call girls seldom prosecuted, but their activities go virtually unnoticed and therefore uncriticized unless they become involved in some larger scheme of corruption involving prominent politicians or businessmen.

Most police activity against prostitutes results directly or indirectly from the distastefulness of public solicitation by street walkers. Residents of areas where such women congregate, businessmen, and even casual visitors object to the garish appearance of prostitutes and to their sometimes embarrassing overtures. These objections are transformed into a low-level but persistent pressure on the police to keep the area in question reasonably "clean." Respectable residential and business districts are, of course, kept cleaner than run down downtown areas which, in major cities, usually become the haunts for a number of undesirables: prostitutes, alcoholics, drug pushers, homosexuals, and pornography purveyors. Even in these areas, however, when the situation becomes too unpleasant, the mayor will generally sound an alarm, and for a few days or weeks the police will conduct a general roundup.

To most policemen, prostitution has a rather low priority in terms of allocation of police time, and in fact, police activity is geared to the level demanded by public criticism or political pressure. In general, there is a tendency to ignore prostitution if possible and the number of arrests and prosecutions is far less than in previous times. At the turn of the century prostitution was an important source of income both for organized crime and corrupt policemen. It is considered to be only a minor source today.

Prostitution is, of course, the classic example of victimless crime. Neither participant in the transaction is coerced, and the morality of the conduct in question is probably no more dubious than the morality of many acts, sexual and otherwise, that are noncriminal. There is no objective measurable harm to society in the practice itself, and for these reasons a strong case can be made for the removal of prostitution from the criminal code. Certainly, it should be removed if we are concerned about the reform of the criminal justice system and the most rational use of social resources in this area: police, prosecutors, courts, and corrections.

Simply removing prostitution from the criminal code, however, is not a sufficient recommendation. Certain problems remain that must be handled in some way. If prostitution is legalized, for example, will street walking then be a permissible activity? While prostitution itself may involve two willing participants, street solicitation frequently does not. The person solicited may be embarrassed, annoyed, or distressed, and residents and visitors to areas where prostitutes congregate are quite reasonably repelled by the sight of girls looking for customers. Most reformers, therefore, recommend that solicitation remain as a criminal offense. If, however, solicitation is to be forbidden, how are prostitutes to do business? How can they make their availability known to those who wish to employ their services? Some European cities handle this through the establishment of red-light districts. Most Americans, however, find this solution rather repugnant even in principle, and in practice no one wants his district to be zoned for prostitution.

The alternative is to adopt the English system, which is to allow prostitutes to advertise their services in magazines and newspapers. Prostitutes in London, for example, like other small business-persons, rent suitable space in areas convenient to their prospective clientele. While walking through Soho, for example, one may observe discreet signs that "Madame Yvonne," may be found on the second floor. Madame Yvonne, presumably has placed ads in selected publications to inform the interested public, albeit in guarded euphemistic terms, that she is available for business. Whether to opt for red-light districts, or to permit advertising, is a decision that will have to be made by each affected community, and while neither solution is without drawbacks, either seems preferable to the hypocritical and anachronistic practice of keeping prostitution in the criminal code.

Another problem that arises in connection with the decriminalization of prostitution, is whether prostitutes should be licensed. Proponents of licensing base their position, usually, on one of two grounds. One argument is that if prostitution is to be a legal business, then prostitutes should be taxed, much as are other small businesses. This means not only that the prostitute must pay a personal income tax, with its concomitant record keeping, appointment book, etc., but that she must pay small business taxes, franchise taxes, occupancy taxes, and the like. Some critics find the notion of government "profiting" from the earnings of a prostitute very distasteful; yet, the notion of taxation of gamblers is very popular, and is indeed one of the reasons for growing public pressure for legalized gambling. There may, of course, be many administrative problems in terms of enforcing tax statutes applicable to prostitutes, but if our revenue agents can cope with other service establishments that do a largely cash business, such as beauty shops, automobile repair shops, lawyers, and physicians, presumably there will be ways to overcome such difficulties.

Another argument for the licensing of prostitutes is that they constitute a public health danger, being a source of infection for venereal diseases. The empirical evidence is ambiguous on this point. On the one hand, prostitutes certainly do encounter a large number of sexual partners daily, and an infected prostitute will broadcast her infection widely. On the other hand, even a licensed prostitute required to report for periodic health examinations can be infected minutes after receiving a clean bill of health, and will spread disease until her next examination. Gonorrhea is especially difficult to detect in its early stages in women. The spread of venereal disease, moreover, while it has reached epidemic proportions in recent days, is due almost entirely to nonprostitute contacts. Prostitution seems to account for only a very small percentage of venereal disease cases in this country. On these grounds many critics, including some women's lib spokesmen, feel that singling out prostitutes for licensing and health examinations is irrational and discriminatory. On the other hand, if beauticians and food handlers are subject to health controls, it would seem hard to sustain a charge of invidious discrimination against such regulation of prostitutes.

Finally, if prostitution is a legal activity, does this mean that procuring (pimping) is also legal? If it is legal to be a prostitute, should it be legal to live off the earnings of a prostitute? Logically, the answer would have to be affirmative, since if it were not, it would be impossible for a printer, for example, to print advertising for a prostitute, or impossible even for a landlord to rent premises for her business. A pimp is in effect a business agent for a prostitute. He helps her to do her business, which, under the present system, means that he helps her to carry on an illegal activity by soliciting business which she has insufficient opportunity to solicit herself; and he provides her with legal protection when she is arrested. If prostitution were legal, the second function would disappear entirely, and the first function would be transformed from a shady, dubious activity to an occupation very similar to that of a press agent or public relations functionary. The exploitative, brutal part of the relationship between the prostitute and her pimp would be substantially diminished by the fact that the prostitute, as a legitimate business person, would be free to seek an agent on the best possible terms for herself, rather than being forced to accept the quasi-criminal candidates who normally are willing and anxious to act as pimps.

This is not to say, of course, that procuring for a prostitute will or should have the status of other ancient professions such as law or medicine; nevertheless, it need not be quite so distasteful an occupation as it is today. Actually, psychologists and sociologists tell us that the pimp performs other less obvious functions for the prostitute. Besides being her business manager and protector, he is frequently her companion, her confidant, and her lover. Even though he may beat her and spend her money recklessly for personal adornment or even other women, nevertheless, he is one of the few human beings who accepts her for what she is, knows her problems, and helps her to cope with them. There are not many people that the prostitute can talk to and relax with at the end of her working hours. If prostitution is legalized, presumably the prostitute will have a wider choice of companions than she has at present. The net effect of removing prostitution from the penal code would, in short, be to eliminate the occupation of pimping as we know it.

Obscenity

The basic question in regard to regulation of obscenity is not whether a particular movie, book, picture, or exhibit is obscene; it is whether there ought to be any legal suppression of obscenity at all.

The cases that come before the courts invariably present the issue of whether some allegedly offensive material ought to be suppressed or its purveyors punished, and the courts, in the first instance at least, usually examine the material in question to determine whether it is, in fact, obscene. Such determination, however, has proved to be very difficult to make, and the reason underlying this difficulty is that the basic question of whether *any* form of communication ought to be censored has yet to be resolved. One Supreme Court justice, Hugo Black, consistently took a clear-cut position that all regulations of obscenity were invalid because the First Amendment forbids *all* regulation of speech. Indeed, Justice Black went so far as to refuse to examine the allegedly obscene exhibits that constituted the evidence in the cases brought before him, on the ground that the content of the material was irrelevant since *no* regulation of speech (in the larger sense, books, periodicals, films, live entertainment—all communication, written and oral, verbal and nonverbal) was permissible. His fellow justices were not so fortunate or unfortunate. Their view of the problem led them to read, look, listen, or otherwise to examine all the titillating tidbits brought before them.

Historically, the struggle between the state and individuals who wish to say things the ruling authorities consider impermissible has been a long one. Originally, most regulation of speech occurred in the political or religious arena. In Tudor England, for example, censorship was concerned mostly with speech that attacked either the monarch or the church—treason or heresy. As the British political system matured, political criticism became more legitimate; and as religious authority became further separated from secular authority, criticism of religion and the church was likewise less subject to regulation. In the eighteenth and nineteenth centuries, however, British censors became increasingly concerned over antireligious material with a *sexual* theme. The first successful obscenity prosecution of a publisher was of Edmund Curll in 1727 for a book entitled, *Venus in the Cloister, or The Nun in Her Smock;* and the landmark case of *Regina* vs. *Hicklin* [1] dealt with an antireligious tract entitled *The Confessional Unmasked.* This pamphlet, published by a militant Protestant society, purported to publicize the improper questions put to women in the confessional, and also described actual seductions of women during confessions.

The *Hicklin* case was important because it was the first test of an 1857 act that provided a mechanism for police seizure of obscene material; but its greater significance lies in the fact that for the first time the presiding judge attempted to define obscenity. The so-called Hicklin Rule states that

> . . . (T)he test of obscenity is this, whether the tendency of the matter charged as obscenity is to deprave and corrupt those whose minds are open to such immoral influences, and into whose hands a publication of this sort may fall.[2]

The Hicklin Rule became the standard for American obscenity prosecutions for almost a century. It was applied to all disputed materials with a sexual theme regardless of their religious content. And it was interpreted to mean that parts of books, as opposed to a work as a whole, could be taken out of context and declared obscene if they were likely adversely to affect the most susceptible and easily influenced groups in the potential audience as opposed to that audience as a whole. Thus, purple passages in any work, no matter how respectable, might be the basis for legal suppression of that work if somebody, anybody, were shown to be unhealthfully stimulated by such passages. Indeed, a photograph of the ceiling of the Sistine Chapel in the Vatican was seized as obscene by custom officials in New York City. The great antivice crusader Anthony Comstock was characterized by one of his critics as a man who tried to make the world safe for a fourteen-year-old school girl with pronounced erotic tendencies. This, in effect, is what the Hicklin Rule attempted to do in relation to materials with a sexual theme for British and American society.

In the United States, rebellion against such censorship took the legal form of challenges to official suppression under the First Amendment, the argument being that suppression of communication is forbidden by the very definite statement that "Congress shall make no law . . . abridging the freedom of speech or of the press."* These challenges did not take the form of a head-on attack on all obscenity regulation. They took, instead, the more customary route of chipping away at a particular suppression based on a particularly undesirable

---

* Although the First Amendment refers only to Congress, after *Gitlow vs. New York,* 268 U.S. 652, in 1925, it was widely accepted that the states (and localities) were bound by the standards of the First Amendment.

standard. In 1934, in a case involving the suppression of James Joyce's *Ulysses*, Morris Ernst, on behalf of Random House, the publisher who attempted to import the book, argued that the book as a whole, rather than particular passages, should be considered in a determination of obscenity. Judges Learned and Augustus Hand, sitting in the United States Federal Court for the Second Circuit, agreed that "the proper test of whether a given book is obscene is its dominant effect," and that the

> *relevance of the objectionable parts to the theme, the established reputation of the work in the estimation of approved critics, if the book is modern, and the verdict of the past, if it is ancient are persuasive evidence . . .*[3]

The net effect of the *Ulysses* decision was to base future obscenity verdicts on a work in its entirety rather than on titillating passages.

A further modification of the *Hicklin* Rule came with the *Roth* decision in 1957.[4] Samuel Roth, a New York publisher convicted for mailing obscene advertising and an obscene book in violation of the federal obscenity statutes, challenged the conviction on the ground that these statutes *"on their faces and in a vacuum,* violated the freedom of expression guarantees . . . of the Constitution." The court, unfortunately for Mr. Roth, affirmed his conviction but agreed with a good many of his philosophical arguments by specifically rejecting the *Hicklin* test.

> *The* Hicklin *test, judging obscenity by the effect of isolated passages upon the most susceptible persons, . . . must be rejected as unconstitutionally restrictive of the freedoms of speech and press.*[5]

The court went on to cite with approval the standard of the trial court that had convicted Roth:

> *. . . The test is not whether it would arouse sexual desires or sexual impure thoughts in those comprising a particular segment of the community, the young, the immature or the highly prudish or would leave another segment, the scientific or highly educated or the so-called worldly-wise and sophisticated indifferent and unmoved . . .*

The test in each case is the effect of the book, picture or publication considered as a whole, not upon any particular class, but upon all those whom it is likely to reach . . . you determine its impact upon the average person in the community.[6]

Roth thus dealt the *coup de grace* to *Hicklin* by requiring not only that a work be considered in its entirety but that its impact on the *average, normal person* constitute the relevant standard.

The problem with *Roth*, however, was that the unresolved issue of whether there should be regulation of obscenity at all became increasingly more insistent as the lower courts attempted to apply the liberalized standard in an increasingly libertarian era. It became apparent quite soon that contemporary community standards of what was desirable and what had "redeeming social value" were impossible to apply from the standpoint of police and prosecutors since fewer and fewer works seemed to fit the definition of what was obscene. In cosmopolitan areas like New York and San Francisco, relatively few prosecutions for obscenity resulted in convictions since there was insufficient consensus as to what was offensive to the community and what was totally worthless from a social or literary point of view. Subtly the burden of proof became increasingly difficult for police and prosecutors to sustain. At the same time there was no general agreement to eliminate all obscenity prosecutions, and so the courts were faced with the problem of finding yet another rationale for limiting the distribution of obscene materials.

That rationale appeared with the case of *Ginzburg* vs. *United States*.[7] In 1962 Ralph Ginzburg, an independent publisher who previously had been highly successful in promoting and circulating popular periodicals such as *Look* and *Esquire*, undertook to merchandise three obscure, erotic publications: *Eros*, an expensive, artfully contrived magazine on sex directed toward an upper-middle-class audience ($25.00 annual subscription, $10.00 per single issue); *The Housewife's Handbook on Selective Promiscuity*, which purported to be a sexual autobiography detailing with complete candor the author's sexual experiences from age three to age thirty-six; and *Liaison*, a rather trivial biweekly newsletter. These three publications, while highly erotic in content, were hardly pornography, and might indeed have circulated unmolested by the United States government had not Ginzburg chosen to publicize his publications in a manner that was not only somewhat lewd, but that hinted slyly that it was permissiveness in relation to sexual materials on the part of the United States Supreme Court that permitted their publication and circulation. Like a bad boy who has learned words he knows he shouldn't use, Ginzburg applied for mailing privileges from both Blue Balls and Intercourse, Pennsylvania. When those facilities refused his application because of their inability to handle a large volume of mail, he applied to Middlesex, New Jersey. Worse yet, in the advertisements he subsequently sent out, he boldly proclaimed that

> Eros *is the result of recent court decisions that have realistically interpreted America's obscenity laws and have given this country a new breath of freedom of expression.*[8]

Ginzburg ran into trouble when a number of complaints were made to the post office by recipients of his advertisements who were highly offended both by the description of the advertised publications and by his statement that he planned to go as far as recent Supreme Court decisions allowed. He was indicted in 1963 for violation of postal regulations forbidding the mailing of obscene material. He was convicted in the Federal District Court for the Eastern District of Pennsylvania and sentenced to five years in prison and personally fined $28,000. On appeal to the United States Supreme Court, Ginzburg argued that by the standards of *Roth* none of his publications was obscene because all had at least some redeeming social value if taken as a whole. The prosecution, however, had argued that the offense, i.e., the merchandising of these materials, had to be considered in the context of the circumstances of the production, sale or publicity, even if the publications themselves, standing alone, might have not been obscene. The court agreed, holding in effect that what Ginzburg said about his materials was as relevant as the materials themselves. Justice Brennan, writing for the majority, told Ginzburg "thou sayest it":

> *This evidence . . . was relevant in determining the ultimate of obscenity. . . . The deliberate representation of petitioners' publications as erotically arousing . . . stimulated the reader to accept them as prurient; he looks for titillation, not for saving intellectual content. . . . The circumstances of presentation and dissemination of material are equally rel-*

> evant to determining whether social importance claimed for
> material in the courtroom was, in the circumstances, pre-
> tense or reality. . . . Where the purveyor's sole emphasis is
> on the sexually provocative aspects of his publication, that
> fact may be decisive in the determination of obscenity.[9]

The court had a new rationale. Obscenity had become a question not only of erotic materials themselves, but of the way they were
merchandised. If the material was of borderline permissibility, and if
the purveyor chose, in his advertising copy, to describe it in terms
which, if true, might render it impermissible, the advertiser's description, rather than the material itself would form the basis for the
determination of obscenity.

Poor Ginzburg! Even admirers of the Warren Court must admit
that Ginzburg got less than justice from that body. Until the decision
was rendered there had been no suggestion outside a concurring
opinion by Chief Justice Warren alone in *Roth* that merchandising
might enter into a determination of obscenity. Ginzburg was, in fact,
convicted on the basis of an *ex post facto* standard. Furthermore, it is
hard to escape the impression that Ginzburg was convicted not for
being a purveyor of lewd materials, but for being a smart aleck. The
court seemed far less offended by the "artiness" of *Eros* than by the
slip inserted in each advertisement labeled "GUARANTEE" and
reading "Documentary Books, Inc. [the publisher] unconditionally
guarantees full refund on the price if the book fails to reach you
because of United States Post Office censorship and interference."

Nevertheless, the court had bumbled its way into a new guide-
line for the permissible, legitimate suppression of communication:
that such suppression was justified when offensive material is inflicted on an unwilling audience through unsolicited advertising.
The court, in effect, was justifying the infringement of the publisher's
civil liberties by the protection of the public's civil liberties. It was
putting restrictions on those who would speak in the name of the general public's right not to have to listen. Certainly, if any restriction of
the First Amendment could be made palatable to its civil libertarian
defenders, this one, based on the protection of a competing civil liberty, might succeed. In fact, while the injustice to Ginzburg himself
created a furor, the notion that the general public had a right not to be
exposed to the "leer of the sensualist" proved quite palatable, and for

a time it seemed as if the matter of obscenity regulation might be handled on the basis of tight controls on pandering and advertising, with few if any controls on private consumption. The decision in *Stanley* vs. *Georgia*,[10] where the Supreme Court affirmed the right of an individual to show an obscene film in his own home, conformed to this principle.

The problem, however, once again lay in the application of the principle to the real world. It was easy enough for police and prosecutors to handle panderers, offensive bookstore and movie theater displays, and mailed advertising. This left, however, virtually no restriction on discreetly advertised pornography: films such as *Deep Throat*, stag movies sold in "sex boutiques," hard-core pornographic novels in plain, unadorned covers, etc. Unadvertised obscenity, in short, had ceased to be regulated, and many people objected. The result of these objections was a June 1973 Supreme Court decision relating to a group of obscenity cases.[11] These cases involved various situations: the mailing of unsolicited sexually explicit material in violation of state law; the showing of an allegedly obscene film to a consenting adult audience in a commercial movie theater; the importation of obscene material (8 mm. film) for the private use of the importer in violation of federal law; the knowing transportation of obscene material by common carrier in interstate commerce in violation of federal law; and the sale in an adult bookstore of a plain-covered, unillustrated book containing repetitively descriptive materials of an explicitly sexual nature.

In five lengthy, rather turgid, majority opinions written by Chief Justice Burger for the majority (over the vigorous dissents of Justices Douglas, Brennan, Stewart, and Marshall), the court held that there was something called obscenity which is not protected by the First Amendment. The guidelines for recognizing such obscenity were essentially a stricter version of the guidelines enunciated in *Roth* and *Memoirs* vs. *Massachussetts.** To be considered obscene, a

---

* *A Book named "John Cleland's Memoirs of a Woman of Pleasure"* v. *Massachusetts* 383 U.S. 413 (1966) was the case in which the United States Supreme Court held the novel popularly known as *Fanny Hill* to be not obscene. The standards for the determination were essentially that of the *Roth* case with increased emphasis on the requirement that to be found obscene, the material in question, must be found to be utterly without redeeming social value.

work taken as a whole must appeal to the prurient interest in sex; portray in a patently offensive way sexual conduct specifically defined by law; and, taken as a whole, may not have "serious" literary artistic, political, or scientific value. Such "obscene" works may be prohibited by localities on the basis of local standards, either on general principles, or because of local fear that antisocial conduct might result from the dissemination of such works. Expert testimony need not be introduced in the determination of whether the work is, in fact, obscene, nor is the burden of proof on the community to show that antisocial conduct may result from such works. If communities have widely divergent standards as to the same work, such divergence is not in and of itself a basis for a claim of First Amendment infringement.

The net result of these decisions was to revert to the status quo ante Ginzburg, i.e., the standards prevailing at the time of *Roth* and *Memoirs* with the added complication of varying local standards rather than one national standard. Unfortunately the problem with the *Roth-Memoirs* standard is that it runs squarely into the First Amendment. Despite the court's semantic gymnastics, obscenity *is* speech.* Wishing won't make it so, and no matter how many times the court says that pornography is nonspeech, in the real world it *is* speech, and its relationship to the First Amendment must be handled in as rational a manner as possible. Restrictions on other forms of speech have been legitimatized at the United States Supreme Court level in recent years by variants of the clear and present danger formula: that the speech in question will lead imminently and probably to antisocial action, usually riot or revolution. The effort of the Burger court to suggest that the states have a legitimate interest in preventing the antisocial action that might result from obscenity would, of course, be consistent with this rationale. The problem here, however, is one of proof. There is virtually no widely acceptable evidence that crime, sexual or otherwise, is a result of the "consumption" of obscene materials. The Burger opinion seeks to avoid this dilemma by suggesting that the burden of proof is on the distributor of the questioned material to show that it is *not* socially harmful. To shift the

* If you call a tail a leg, how many legs has a dog? Five? No, calling a tail a leg don't *make* it a leg.

Abraham Lincoln

burden of proof in this manner, however, undercuts substantially the impact of the First Amendment. The absolute prohibition in the wording: "Congress shall make *no* law . . . abridging . . . freedom of speech," suggests strongly that the burden of proof must be on the government when it violates this express prohibition, and this indeed has been the interpretation of the court, *de facto* if not necessarily in theory, for at least the last two decades.

Not only have the recent obscenity decisions run squarely into the theoretical First Amendment problem, but the reluctance of the court to establish a national standard, and its reversion to the specious comfort of local standards will undoubtedly have not only a chilling effect on publication and communication in this area, but will give rise to a host of practical problems as well. In a nation where publishing and film making are nationally based commercial enterprises rather than small local businesses, how can such enterprises be carried on when publishers and exhibitors have no way of knowing in what communities their output is legal and in what communities it is not? The effect on this type of commerce will be similar to the effect on commerce in general, of the chaos prevailing immediately prior to the adoption of the United States Constitution when each state was free to regulate commerce idiosyncratically. The net effect of relying on local standards is to force every community to the lowest common denominator of the least tolerant and accepting community, because only at that level can a national market be assured. This, of course, would no doubt be precisely what those who view the dissemination of obscenity with alarm would prefer. But the conflict with the First Amendment and the implications for American society as a whole cannot be shrugged off lightly. Critics have suggested that although these decisions relate to explicitly sexual materials, the rationale may well be extended to other controversial and offensive communications. A minor, though perhaps, significant example of this tendency occurred in New York City in connection with a controversy over a speaker whose ideas were profoundly repugnant to a large section of the metropolitan community. Dr. William B. Shockley, a professor of physics at Stanford University, and a Nobel Prize winner, with very unorthodox views on genetics, was invited to speak at Staten Island Community College in New York. Dr. Shockley believes that intelligence is largely inherited and that the disadvantaged place of blacks in our society is due more to heredity than environment. Such views understandably are highly controversial and abrasive, the more so since Dr. Shockley's expertise and professional credentials lie in the field of physics rather than genetics. When the invitation was announced, a sizeable group of students at the college protested vigorously, denouncing Shockley for his racist views, calling him a charlatan, his views unscientific, etc. They urged the president of the college to withdraw the invitation. One student went so far as to justify this request, which clearly was an infringement of academic freedom, by saying that since the Supreme Court had turned over the setting of moral standards to local communities in its obscenity decisions, there was no reason why localities should not set standards for local speakers.*

Perhaps it is unfair to take seriously a comment which extended a decision that the Supreme Court very specifically applied to the obscenity area only, to the area of political speech. Yet the pressure to do so is very great. If a community can determine what kind of sexually oriented communications it wishes to receive, why indeed

---

* Tom Wicker, "The Shockley Case," *New York Times*, November 16, 1973, p. 41. The invitation was not withdrawn despite student protests. When Shockley appeared, however, hecklers in the audience made it impossible for him to speak, and he withdrew without having addressed his audience.

Another spin-off of the 1973 Supreme Court obscenity rulings is a comment expressed in a letter to the editor of the *New York Times* regarding the "book-burning" in Drake, North Dakota. The Drake local school board made a determination that Kurt Vonnegut's *Slaughterhouse Five*, which had been assigned reading in the local high school, was pornographic. They removed the books from the school bodily and apparently for want of better disposal methods, burned them. This incident gave rise to considerable criticism in view of the fact that the book, which is a work of serious literary reputation, was generally not regarded as pornographic, and the burning led to some unpleasant memories of fascist performances in Nazi Germany. The letter writer took exception to the criticism of the actions of the school board by saying "I have noted your editorial comment about the so-called book burning at Drake, N.D., and while the rights of man and freedom of the press are precious, *so are the rights of a community, according to the Supreme Court, to determine what is and what is not pornographic.*" (emphasis added, December 7, 1973, p. 40.) The point is, however, that while a school board assuredly has the right to select appropriate materials for its students, the words of the First Amendment say that the *community per se* has *no* rights in the matter of determining what any individual may or may not say.

should it not determine what kind of politically oriented communications it wishes to receive? The 1973 Supreme Court obscenity decisions have started us down a very dangerous path because they have ignored the central meaning of the First Amendment: *that what is to be communicated in a democratic society is not a decision for majorities to make.* The First Amendment protects *minorities,* meaning precisely that unpleasant, abrasive, stupid, and provocative individuals can say what they wish without the approval of the communities of which they are a part. Though the court would like, through semantic sleight of hand, to say that obscenity is not communication and therefore the rules don't apply, in the real world and in the public mind, the transition between obscene communications and other undesirable types of speech is logical and easy. The price of suppressing *Deep Throat* very possibly is the suppression of Dr. Shockley, and after Dr. Shockley, George Wallace, George McGovern, and eventually anyone else who does not please the ruling establishment.

The regulation of obscenity has a certain superficial attractiveness to those who see such regulation as a way of elevating the moral tone of society at very little social cost. The social cost is greater than appears at first blush, and the effects of such regulation are complex and far-reaching. Obscene communications—books, films, pictures, plays, or whatever—are highly distasteful to many, perhaps to most people of the United States. Many others overtly or covertly enjoy such communications. Certainly, those who find such material offensive can and should be protected against having those materials inflicted upon them. The attempts to limit "pandering" are a proper and legitimate way of protecting those who don't want to see or hear erotic presentations. In addition, if the consumption of the obscene or pornographic does indeed lead to antisocial action—crime or sexual deviance—then it should be regulated to the extent necessary to prevent such social deviance. Before this can be done, however, respectable, honest research must be done to ascertain the impact on the public at large, or special publics, such as juveniles, of such materials. If such undesirable impact can be shown, then reasonable regulation will be relatively easy to frame. The gravamen of this approach should be not to define what many people consider poor taste, but to determine that which is demonstrably and measurably socially harmful in the sense of causing aberrant behavior. The

burden of proof of demonstrating that such impact exists, however, must be on the regulating authority. Expression of any kind should not be forbidden except for reasons the state can demonstrate.

Aside from protecting the sensibilities of those who do not wish to partake of obscene materials, and protecting the public from those materials that have demonstrably led to antisocial conduct, as a practical matter there is little that can or should be done to regulate obscenity. Attempts to create a category of nonspeech for obscene materials are dangerous because they are little more than circumventions of the First Amendment, and the social cost of such circumvention is far higher than any foreseeable undesirable impact obscenity may have. Aside from that, moreover, the desperately strained conditions of our criminal justice systems in the United States simply precludes any diversion of resources for such purposes. A 1970 survey of police and prosecutors in seventeen major cities in the United States for the President's Commission on Obscenity and Pornography found that whatever their private opinions might have been with respect to regulating obscenity and pornography, from the standpoint of performing their day-to-day jobs, almost all such officials felt that such efforts must have a very low priority in terms of the use of the resources at their command.[12] Similarly, the responses to a questionnaire sent to the prosecutors of the major metropolitan areas of the United States, indicated that not one of the prosecutors assigned the regulation of obscenity first priority after the prosecution of major crimes. In other words, of the *malum prohibitum* offenses (gambling, obscenity, drug use, consensual sodomy, drunkenness, etc.), no prosecutor felt that regulation of obscenity was most important. Most prosecutors rated obscenity relatively low, or simply did not rank it at all.[13] On the other hand, it is undoubtedly true that prosecutors are quite sensitive to political pressure emanating from antiobscenity groups and all prosecutors will react favorably, at least rhetorically, to requests for vigorous prosecution emanating from such groups. Certainly, the 1973 Supreme Court decisions seem, as of this writing, to have generated an increase of prosecutorial and police activity. The wisdom of such increased activity is doubtful; the permanence of such an increase will depend largely on how sustained the political pressures may be, how receptive the courts are, and how much such prosecutions impinge upon more urgent activities of the police and prosecutors.

Gambling

Gambling is ubiquitous in the United States, the contents of our penal codes notwithstanding. In 1962 the late Robert Kennedy estimated that the American people spent more on gambling than on medical care or education.[14] In 1972, the New York City Police Department estimated that $1.5 billion was spent on illegal gambling; in 1973, $691 million was bet legally through the government sponsored Off-Track Betting Corporation.[15] Not only is private gambling widespread, but public lotteries have been in existence at least intermittently from early colonial times onward. Indeed, lotteries were instrumental in financing such educational institutions as Harvard, Yale, and Columbia. Even today one of the most persuasive arguments for state sponsorship of lotteries is that the proceeds can be used to support educational institutions. In 1964 New Hampshire adopted a state lottery on these grounds; in 1967 New York, and in 1970 New Jersey followed suit. Despite its popularity, however, gambling is either prohibited or strictly regulated in every state of the union, thus attesting to the ambivalence of our feelings: on the one hand, people like to gamble, and generally will find a way to gamble despite legislative restrictions; on the other hand, a fairly vocal part of the public considers gambling harmful and suitable for regulation through the criminal process.

Various reasons have been advanced to explain the almost universal urge to gamble. Robert D. Herman, a sociologist, suggests that gambling provides

> An escape from the routine and boredom of modern industrial life in which the sense of creation and the "instinct of workmanship" has been lost. "Taking a chance" destroys routine and hence is pleasurable.[16]

Another view is that gambling keeps alive a hope for social betterment among people who are least capable of fulfilling their mobility aspirations through conventional avenues. A related observation is that gambling occasionally allows the bettor to beat the system and demonstrate that for a brief moment he can control his fate. A Marxist view is that gambling represents a safety valve so that the poor, instead of attacking their economic oppressors, who are the source of their deprivations and unfilled aspirations, can relieve their frustrations. Some psychologists have suggested that "gambling uncon-

sciously revives . . . the old childish phantasy and megalomania," and activates the latent rebellion against logic, intelligence, and renunciation.[17] Perhaps Judge John M. Murtagh has come as close to the mark as anyone in saying that

> *Gambling is essentially the poor person's means of satisfying a normal human instinct. It puts a spark into his daily existence—an important item when you think of the boredom and the lack of homelife of the underprivileged.*[18]

Gambling, in short, is fun, especially for poor people who haven't got much else, and for many people it is a way of coping with boredom, frustration, feelings of powerlessness, and the reality of their own inadequacy.

On the other hand, it is the very fact that gambling is used as a crutch and an escape, and that poor people are so heavily involved, that causes much of the criticism and antigambling legislation in our penal codes. Realistically, of course, the gambling public taken as a whole cannot win, because the odds are so fixed as to provide a substantial margin of profit for the entrepreneurs of gambling. For the most part these entrepreneurs are operating illegally, and it is known that gambling profits are one of the chief sources of income for organized crime. Even, however, where the gambling operation is run by a public authority for the purpose of financing schools or some other worthy cause, many people feel such an operation to be reprehensible; "Any society that bases its financial structure on the weaknesses of its people doesn't deserve to survive." [19] Basically, such critics feel a revulsion against the self-delusion that is involved in gambling, along with a strong feeling that gambling prevents people from meeting their proper obligations. Unquestionably, most of the money bet in the numbers games that flourish in our black ghettos should rationally be spent for food, clothing, or shelter for the gambler's family. But here, as in so many areas, man does not live by bread alone, and to the numbers player his daily bet represents excitement, visions of the impossible coming true, and a spot of brightness in a drab world. Gambling on this level is obviously an attempt to cope, counterproductive though it may be by making the gambler even poorer than he was before.

In any case, historically it has proven impossible to eradicate gambling, and a realistic social policy must be based on this fact. Our

past policy has consisted largely of forbidding gambling. Gradually, certain types of exceptions were made in response to social pressures, as for example when Bingo was permitted as a means of raising money for church activities. Race track betting has been widely permitted. By and large, however, lotteries, sports betting, bookmaking, numbers games, and casino-type betting have been illegal. Since World War II, there has been a gradual erosion of antigambling laws, so that now a number of states have publicly sponsored lotteries, New York State has a highly successful public betting corporation for off-track horse race betting (OTB), and pressure is mounting steadily to legalize sports betting and the numbers game. (Nevada, of course, has had both legal gambling casinos and houses of prostitution for many years.)

Given the ubiquitous nature of gambling, police and prosecutors could probably spend a good portion of their time doing nothing but arresting illegal gamblers and bookmakers if they so desired. Obviously, since far more serious problems exist, and must receive priority, the police for the most part can do no more than try to control large-scale gambling operations, and in particular those operations that are linked to organized crime. Their success is somewhat comparable to Hercules' in cleaning the Augean stables: as fast as one operation is cleaned up another springs up to take its place. Gambling provides, moreover, probably the most frequent source of police corruption in our big cities, and the handling of police officials who are supposed to be suppressing gambling is a major administrative headache to top municipal officials. At the same time the police cannot ignore gambling because to do so would further increase contempt for the law and its processes among the citizenry that is fully aware of the universality of betting of one kind and another.

As publicly sponsored betting increases, moreover, the pressure on removing gambling from the penal code must inevitably increase. Already the contradictions in public policy are so many and so obvious as to further demoralize our already demoralized police, and to lead to the very disrespect for law on the part of the public that everyone agrees is disastrous. In New York City, for example, there is an OTB office on 125th Street in the heart of Harlem, which legally accepts bets on horse races at local tracks. At the same time, an army of numbers runners illegally accepts bets the winners of which some-

times are determined indirectly by the outcome of these very same horse races. From the point of view of the runner, who makes his living as low man on the totem pole of illegal gambling operations, why should an employee of OTB have a legal job complete with salary, vacations, pensions, and other fringe benefits, when he, who performs a very similar service, is subject to harassment, arrest, and labeling as a criminal? * Not only does this seem irrational to the numbers runner, but it is equally irrational to the policeman on the beat, the prosecutor's office, and even to the courts. Similarly, why is it legal to bet on horse races either at the track or through OTB, or to bet on the outcome of a lottery through the various state sponsored gambling operations, but illegal to bet on the outcome of football games, baseball games, or prize fights? The irrationality and contradictions are such that it is hard to see how we can avoid removing gambling from our penal codes unless we wish to enact a complete prohibition and get rid of Bingo, race tracks, and even Las Vegas. Complete legalization may at this time seem unlikely; complete prohibition of gambling is, however, much more unlikely.

The benefits of removing gambling from the penal code would be substantial. For one thing, considerable relief of the criminal justice system would result in those jurisdictions where there has been even a reasonable attempt to cope with the gambling problem. Even in those cities where the police have not made large numbers of gambling arrests, a major source of police corruption will be eliminated. Every police administrator acknowledges that if he didn't have to worry about his men being reached by gamblers, he would run his department more efficiently. Most periodic shakeups are counterproductive in terms of morale and effectiveness, but are necessary to break up illegal associations that spring up very quickly between gambling interests and the local police. Illegal gambling is also considered to be the chief source of capital for many organized crime enterprises, such as drug traffic and even loansharking. While removing gambling as a source of income will not cause organized crime to disappear, nevertheless, gambling is an operation that can

* Numbers runners, of course, earn more than OTB employees. Among other things the runner customarily receives from the delighted customer 10 percent of the proceeds of any winning number he may have sold.

be undertaken with a relatively small financial investment, and presumably will make business life harder for underworld elements.*

Not only does the legalization of gambling have negative value in that it corrects certain existing problems, but it holds possibilities of positive values in the sense that the widespread desire to gamble may be used to further worthwhile social purposes through the taxation of gambling activities. The excise taxes on alcohol and tobacco have long been lucrative sources of revenue for the federal and state governments, with relatively little protest from those who are paying the tax. The taxation of gambling would probably be equally painless and prove highly profitable. There is, to be sure, a considerable body of public opinion that feels that society ought not benefit from "immoral" activities. Again, the legitimacy of this response depends on one's view of deviance. If society is willing to benefit from those who drink whiskey and smoke cigarettes, practices which are highly detrimental to physical health and which lead in the case of liquor to extensive antisocial conduct, why is it wrong to benefit from gambling? For most people gambling is a form of recreation, and probably the chief objection to this form of recreation is that it is unwise for poor people to spend their money this way. It is also unwise for poor people to smoke and drink. Yet they do smoke and drink and aside from the wisdom or morality of middle-class dictation of standards of conduct for the poor, as a practical matter it can't be done. Middle-class legislation in this area has never been successful. Under these circumstances it is very hard to see why gambling should not be subject to the same kind of taxation other luxuries bear.

The legalization of gambling does, however, present some questions of public policy that have probably received insufficient consideration. Until now, decriminalization has been largely in the context of the government's entering the field itself. Except for the legalization of Bingo and slot machines and the Nevada casino-type

* Some critics allege that this is a false hope. A statement in the *New York Times* by the New York City Police Department claims that OTB has *increased* the levels of illegal betting and the income of organized crime by creating an atmosphere conducive to betting. If all betting were legal, however, presumably all betting money would flow through legitimate channels. In the area in which OTB operates, i.e., bookmaking on horse races, the take of illegal operators has been markedly reduced. It is in the areas that remain illegal that their income has increased.

operations, the change in the penal code has simply made it possible for the state, or an agency thereof, to conduct certain types of gaming enterprises, e.g., lotteries or off-track betting. This need not be so. The state does not have to become the proprietor of a gambling business. Betting of any type can simply be removed from the penal code so that private individuals can go into business, as for example, the turf accountants in England. Even if the state does wish to conduct gambling operations moreover, it need not do so on a monopoly basis. Gambling can be both a public and private enterprise, and proprietors of gambling businesses can be regulated, taxed, or licensed in any appropriate manner.

Another related issue is the question of advertising. In the spirit of American free enterprise, in those areas in which the state has gone into the gambling business, it has made strong efforts to ensure the financial success of the venture and to that end has usually engaged in extensive advertising campaigns. Again, this need not be so. Gambling can be made available, under public or private sponsorship, to those who wish it with *no* advertising permitted, in much the same way some states run liquor stores. The location of gambling outlets can be confined to appropriate areas sufficiently accessible to meet demand, but not intrusive enough to promote gambling that might not otherwise take place. If the emphasis is to be merely on making a service available, then the operation will be less lucrative and less public money will be raised. This is certainly, however, a legitimate policy for a state to adopt. While the state should not attempt to criminalize conduct that is widespread, and for the most part relatively harmless, it need not act as a sponsor or a promoter of an activity that has little intrinsic merit. Neutrality is a perfectly feasible stance.

One further problem related to the decriminalization of gambling is the compulsive gambler. Critics fear that making gambling widely available will create large numbers of persons who will not be able to control their wagering. This fear assumes that compulsive gamblers are ordinary people who never had a previous gambling problem because the opportunities to gamble were lacking. This is not so. The compulsive gambler has very deep seated personality problems which would manifest themselves in any event.[20] Such a gambler bears the same relationship to gambling that the alcoholic does to drinking. Just as social drinkers cannot be handled in the

same way as alcoholics, compulsive gamblers must be treated differently from ordinary gamblers. Those for whom gambling has become an obsession, and who have created situations in which gambling threatens to destroy their lives, need some kind of therapy either in small groups or on a one-to-one basis. These are seriously deviant individuals with problems they cannot handle, and even if gambling had never been invented their inability to function would take another form. Some can be helped, some cannot, but in either case, the regulation of gambling is almost irrelevant to their personal problems. To outlaw gambling because of compulsive gamblers is as irrational as to forbid the manufacture of candy because some people are too fat.

Homosexuality

The greatest conceptual difficulty in handling homosexuality is how to define the nature of the problem. Homosexuality is deviant conduct, but is the deviance merely statistical and insignificant, or is the deviance pathological? In our society most of us are heterosexual; some of us are homosexual. Homosexual behavior is "different" because it is unusual, but is this difference comparable to being left-handed, or is it comparable to being tubercular? Is a homosexual a fully functioning human being, albeit functioning somewhat differently from the rest of us, or is he a sick man? To decide on a rational social policy toward homosexuals, one must first determine whether homosexuality is an unimportant variation in conduct or a disease, and if it is a disease, whether the disease is catching or not. If it is an unimportant variation like left-handedness, then no social policy beyond accommodation need be formulated; if it is a disease like arthritis, then therapy must be provided; if it is a disease like active tuberculosis, preventive measures as well as treatment are indicated.

Homosexuality up to the present time has been handled essentially as though it were a pathological condition that could be spread by contact with those as yet uncontaminated. Not only have social and legal policy been structured so as to "cure" or reform homosexuals by converting them into heterosexuals, but precautions have been taken to prevent close contacts between homosexuals and heterosexuals especially in large single sex groupings or institutions such as the military, the priesthood, dormitories, and prisons. The restrictions on homosexuals have taken the form both of laws forbid-

ding and punishing homosexual activity; administrative regulations forbidding hiring of homosexuals in certain capacities; and a whole host of socially discriminatory practices. The penal codes of most jurisdictions forbid homosexual practice on any level, even between two consenting adults, and certainly where force is involved or where one partner is under the age of consent. In practice, however, consensual sodomy that is discreet and carried on strictly privately is rarely, if ever, prosecuted. Prosecutions result almost invariably from complaints by those who have been offended by some public manifestation of homosexual activity: solicitation in public toilets, transvestitism, obviously effeminate conduct, openly seductive or flirtatious behavior. Female homosexuals, in fact, are almost never prosecuted simply because their conduct is so much less obvious and noticeable. Homosexual behavior involving force or duress, or with underage partners, is prosecuted in much the same way as in heterosexual behavior of this type. It is the equivalent of rape or statutory rape, or child molestation, and while it may arouse even more disgust on the part of police and prosecutors than its heterosexual counterpart, its criminality stems essentially from considerations other than that of homosexuality.

Administratively, most jurisdictions have rules that forbid the recruiting of homosexuals for the armed services, the police, as teachers, firemen, and a host of other positions, particularly those of a sensitive nature. Homosexual marriages are not recognized and homosexuals are not eligible for the benefits of married couples in relation to sections of tax laws, customs regulations, and inheritance laws based on the marital relationship. Homosexual couples may have difficulty in making contracts such as leases and in buying homes, or obtaining mortgages or consumer credit.

On an extralegal level, homosexuals are subjected to a great deal of social disapproval and derision. Very few homosexuals will openly proclaim their identity as homosexuals because they will be scorned and mocked by many people; they may lose their jobs even where no statutory restrictions against homosexuals exist; they may have difficulty in obtaining further employment; they will be treated as pariahs and be cut off from social contacts with many nonhomosexuals; and at best, those who are more sympathetic will look upon them as sick people worthy of pity and understanding but rarely of acceptance. Most psychiatrists, for example, would consider a homosexual patient, no matter what his complaint, to have an additional dimension to his problem in his homosexuality, i.e., a depressed homosexual would need treatment not only for his depression, but for his "sexual aberration" as well.

The lot of homosexuals is obviously not a happy one, but in practical terms their difficulties stem far more from administrative regulations and social discrimination than from the harsher provisions of the penal law. Consensual sodomy has all but disappeared as a cause for arrest or prosecution in our big cities, if, as previously indicated, the conduct in question is strictly private. A discreet homosexual, in short, is a legally safe homosexual. Should his activities, however, come to the attention of the outside heterosexual world, he may still be prosecuted for his solicitation, transvestitism, or whatever. Such prosecutions do not receive high priority from either police or prosecutors. For the most part, the criminal justice system would be happy to ignore homosexual activity if it could do so without public comment. Not only do the police and the courts feel their time could be better spent, but homosexual prisoners are a nuisance in the institutions in which they are confined and require special handling.

Society, however, inflicts severe penalties on homosexuals, and in self-defense in recent years homosexuals have banded together in organizations such as the Gay Activist Alliance to secure and protect their rights. The very fact that enough homosexuals have been willing to identify themselves openly to make the existence of such an organization possible, indicates a less repressive and more tolerant social atmosphere than formerly existed, and given this atmosphere, homosexuals have made a modest amount of headway in alleviating some of the discomforts of their condition.[21] Harassment of homosexuals by police has been declining, except for the most blatant kinds of solicitation in public.

Success in overcoming discrimination imposed through administrative regulations or social practices, however, has been difficult because the underlying public attitude toward homosexuals is still that they are sick people, and that the sickness is catching. Gay Activists, for example, as of February 1974 had not yet succeeded in getting specific legal reassurances of their right to employment on equal terms with heterosexuals in New York City, one of the most tolerant and accepting of communities in the United States.[22] In this connection, there is considerable significance in a statement by the

American Psychiatric Association that homosexuality per se should no longer be considered a "psychiatric disorder," and should be defined instead as a "sexual orientation disturbance." [23] The meaning of this erudite statement is not clear, but apparently the psychiatrists are attempting to convey the message that a homosexual who is satisfied with his sexual orientation and is functioning well is not, *ipso facto,* a "sick" person. Nevertheless, the statement is ambivalent in that it implies less than total acceptance of homosexuality as an alternate state to heterosexuality.

The *New York Times* asked two psychiatrists, Dr. Robert L. Spitzer of Columbia and Dr. Irving Bieber of the New York Medical College to state their positions on the question: Is homosexuality a psychiatric disorder? After some preliminary sparring, the worthy doctors met in the following head-on confrontation:

> *Dr. Bieber:* I say homosexuality is a psychiatric injury to function and belongs in any psychiatric manual. Now that doesn't mean I consider it an illness any more than I consider frigidity an illness. As long as something like frigidity will be in the manual, disorders of sexual functioning and homosexuality belong there. . . .
>
> *Dr. Spitzer:* . . . You have as your value system that everybody should be a heterosexual.
>
> *Dr. Bieber:* You think it's a value system? Do I think all homosexuals today should become heterosexuals? Definitely not. There are many homosexuals . . . for whom heterosexuality is no longer possible.
>
> *Dr. Spitzer:* But should they feel that their heterosexuality is injured or crippled?
>
> *Dr. Bieber:* If they want to be accurate, they can take the view that their heterosexuality has been irreparably injured.
>
> *Dr. Spitzer:* Injury is already a value.
>
> *Dr. Bieber:* Injury is not a value. A broken leg is not a value.
>
> *Dr. Spitzer:* I cannot function homosexually but I would not regard it as an injury. You wouldn't either.
>
> *Dr. Bieber:* That is not a counterpart.
>
> *Dr. Spitzer:* Well I believe it is. . . . I don't regard homosex-

uality as optimal as heterosexual development. I would agree with Freud that something has happened in the development of the sexual instinct that leads one to be incapable of or not interested in heterosexual functioning. I am loath, however, to apply the word disorder because of its many implications.[24]

If the above colloquy still does not provide a clear-cut answer to the question "Is homosexuality a psychiatric disorder?" it would appear to be a fair conclusion that while there is disagreement among psychiatrists about how dysfunctional homosexuality is, most would agree that heterosexuality is still the optimal state.

It is quite clear that given the state of medical opinion and the general tolerance of moderate deviance in manners and mores, it is a cruel anachronism to punish consensual homosexual conduct between adults, and such provisions of our penal codes should be dropped immediately. Administrative practices that discriminate against homosexuals are a somewhat more difficult problem. Tax laws, for example, frequently reflect the kinds of social organization that the general public wishes to encourage, e.g., income taxes that discriminate against single persons, encourage homeowning, reward philanthropy, etc. It is questionable whether the general public wishes to offer equal incentives to heterosexual and homosexual marriage as long as there is no respected group of opinion leaders that is willing to declare unequivocally that homosexuality and heterosexuality are equally desirable states.

Similarly, job discrimination is a complex problem. Certainly, the unwillingness to hire homosexuals for sensitive jobs because of their proneness to blackmail, should be eliminated if legal penalties for homosexual behavior are removed and social discrimination becomes less oppressive. Whether homosexuals should be hired as teachers, policemen, soldiers, etc., however, depends on several considerations. One is the degree to which their sexual conduct intrudes itself on their professional or business lives. Promiscuous or acting out heterosexuals are frequently unwelcome in many types of positions, as witness the concern of boards of trustees over scandalous faculty behavior on college campuses. Assuming, however, that the candidate for a given position is discreet and private in his homosexual activities, should the mere fact of his homosexuality bar him from certain jobs? A sense of fairness would seem to indicate that it should not, unless and until research proves that homosexuality is "catching," i.e., that the mere presence of a homosexual as an accepted human being will lead others, particularly susceptible young adolescents, to opt for homosexuality rather than heterosexuality as a way of life. Thus far, this notion is in the not-proven category, and until we have more scientific evidence to support it it is hard to see why discreet homosexuals should not enjoy the same rights and privileges as heterosexuals. Homosexuals should be restricted in their behavior in much the same way heterosexuals are: aggressive seductive behavior toward the unwilling or defenseless should be discouraged or punished, and private behavior should be left within the zone of privacy that a free society with a limited government, by definition, guarantees to each of its citizens.

Alcoholism

Our laws in relation to alcoholism, in some ways, are more enlightened than laws in relation to any other morals offense, largely because the public has come to accept moderate alcohol consumption as permissible behavior and to look on excessive use of alcohol as a disease. Indeed, it is the very acceptance and widespread use of alcohol in social situations that leads to problems for which we must resort to the penal codes. While drinking per se is not and should not be an offense, and while alcoholism is a serious disease and not a crime, antisocial conduct stemming from the use of alcohol, may very well be criminal. The two chief categories of such criminal conduct are drunken driving and assaultive behavior. While neither type of conduct is perhaps as reprehensible as premeditated murder, forcible rape, or arson, the social cost of drunken driving and alcohol-related assaultive crimes is tremendous because such crimes are so numerous. The President's Commission on Law Enforcement and the Administration of Justice states that "two million arrests in 1965—one of every three arrests in America—were for the offense of public drunkenness," [25] and the *FBI Uniform Crime Reports* for the same year indicate that 52.6 percent of all arrests in the nation were for alcohol-related offenses: drunkenness, liquor law violations, drunken driving, disorderly conduct, and vagrancy. (Disorderly conduct and vagrancy are frequently related to drinking.)

The handling of alcohol offenses by the criminal justice system is, moreover, complicated by certain procedural problems: the difficulty of obtaining evidence of drunkenness without conducting an unconstitutional search of the person; and the problem of fixing responsibility on one whose capacities are diminished by drinking which in itself is legal.

There have been numerous court tests of the right of the police to determine the sobriety of a suspected drunk by taking blood samples, giving performance tests, analyzing the subject's breath, etc. The objection of some critics to these tests has been generally that they force the suspect to incriminate himself and thus violate the Fifth and Fourteenth Amendments. The courts, however, have not been sympathetic to this argument, and the United States Supreme Court has held that the use of this type of nontestimonial evidence is similar to the use of fingerprints and visual identification; and that the Constitutional prohibition against forced self-incrimination applies to oral and written statements rather than physical evidence of this type. It is to be noted, however, that in both the cases involving blood tests that came to the United States Supreme Court the facts were such that in neither case did the suspect physically struggle against the taking of the blood sample (although in one case the accused was unconscious, and in the other case he protested verbally); nor was there any indication that the blood samples had not been properly obtained by authorized medical personnel.[26] It is by no means certain that blood samples taken in a police station from a kicking, screaming, protesting suspect would be equally approved.

Some law enforcement agents have argued that it is not necessary for the niceties of due process to be observed in drunken driving prosecutions where the punishment is only license revocation since the issuing of a driver's license is in the nature of the grant of a privilege rather than an inherent right of citizenship. Without entering into the thicket of the right-privilege argument, the argument fails because regardless of whether the obtaining of the driver's license is a right or a privilege, when any governmental authority acts to curtail the freedom of action of any citizen, such action must be fair and not arbitrary or capricious, which is another way of saying that the standards of due process must be observed. In general, however, the courts have held consistently that reasonable tests for sobriety are fair and that convictions can be obtained on the basis of such evidence.

More difficult perhaps is the problem of fixing legal responsibility for antisocial behavior resulting from intoxication. Public policy generally has been to arrest those who are inebriated in a public place either because they might harm themselves or others, or because their presence is distasteful to the public. Thus chronic alcoholics and derelicts who wander from the skid row area to the better parts of town are arrested because people don't like to step over bodies in the streets. Gradually, however, as the public has come to view alcoholism as a disease rather than a personal weakness, it has become apparent that it is not appropriate for the law to punish a disease. In 1966 two United States Courts of Appeal ruled that a homeless alcoholic cannot be punished for his public intoxication,[27] and in June 1968, the United States Supreme Court in *Powell* vs. *Texas* made a similar ruling.[28] A majority of the court agreed that alcoholism is a disease and that an alcoholic drinks involuntarily as a result of his illness. They held that a homeless alcoholic may have no choice but to be drunk in public, and therefore cannot constitutionally be convicted of public intoxication. Powell, unfortunately, had a home and family and therefore his conviction was upheld. This decision strikes the observer as somewhat illogical. If alcoholism is a disease, why should one be required to be sick in private? If one happens to be sick in a public place, why should he be punished? The answer, obviously, is that as stated above, the public does not like to step over bodies in the street. But the Constitutional imperatives of the public's squeamishness are not clear. Surely, if the public wants derelicts removed from the streets, would it not be more humane and constitutionally more logical to require localities to establish *nonpunitive* agencies to undertake such removal in an assistance capacity for all publicly inebriated persons, homeless or not, rather than to permit punishment of drunks with homes, and allow homeless alcoholics to lie in the streets?

More serious than the problem of public drunkenness is the problem of assaultive behavior resulting from drunkenness. If a person drinks involuntarily because he has a compulsion to drink, can he be held responsible for his conduct while under the influence of this compulsion? A defense of this nature against a criminal charge is very similar to an insanity defense. It is a claim of diminished responsibility, and in fact one of the earliest important insanity decisions in the United States, *State* vs. *Pike*,[29] involved an alcoholic defendant. The courts, however, with the exception of the very early *Pike* decision, have not been sympathetic to this claim and have held generally that only alcoholism which amounted to insanity could provide a defense to a criminal charge.[30] The implication of this rationale is that the accused must have been out of touch with reality (psychotic from the point of view of a psychiatrist), not at the time the offense was committed, *but at the time he took the first drink*. The refusal of the courts to accept such a defense probably reflects the reality that most persons who commit crimes while inebriated are not psychotic, and indeed are no more than social drinkers who are somewhat immoderate in their habits. It is doubtful, however, if even a confirmed alcoholic could successfully maintain a defense of diminished capacity due to disease.

The problem, thus, does not lie in a legal inability to prosecute for crimes committed under the influence of alcohol, but in the burden that such offenses through their inordinate numbers place on the criminal justice system as well as on other social institutions. The answer certainly cannot be the resurrection of prohibition. It must lie instead in an attempt to make the public aware of the price that society pays for inappropriate consumption of alcohol. We need to mount campaigns not against the evils of drink, but against the evils of drinking at the wrong time. There is nothing wrong with public acceptance of alcohol consumption; there is something very wrong in the public insensitivity to the problems caused by drunken driving and assaultive behavior due to drunkenness. The public is aware of these problems and verbally deplores immoderate drinking, but there is insufficient opprobrium and disgust attached to the drunken driver or brawler. At a social gathering, it is considered puritanical to expect those who will be driving home to remain virtually abstinent, and the reaction of guests to an ugly drunk is to keep out of his way. When those who drink inappropriately are treated with the same contempt and disapproval as are petty hoodlums or thieves, the social constraints on drinking will be more effective. In much the same way as the antismoking campaign has tried to change the image of the smoker from a suave man-of-the-world to a self-indulgent shortsighted fool, the image of the social drinker who is not meticulous about the potential consequences of his drinking must be made far more unacceptable than it is today. This approach is evident in countries like Great Britain and Sweden where social drinking, even heavy drinking, is at least as acceptable as it is here, but where there is considerably less tolerance for those who commit offenses as a consequence of their drinking.

In relation to chronic alcoholics, particularly homeless derelicts, more and more effective, therapeutic facilities are needed. The usual process whereby the police make periodic sweeps and pick up unfortunates lying on the streets, relieves the sensibilities of the general public and keeps derelicts from freezing to death in cold weather, but accomplishes very little else. The police are probably the only available agency for actually removing inebriates from the street, but they should be used in their capacity of rendering aid to citizens rather than handling the unfortunates as criminals. It follows then that some kind of shelter with a rehabilitative component must be available into which the police may transfer the drunk from the street. Handling such chronic alcoholics is a social problem of major proportions which requires adequate support from public and private sources.

Drugs

The first priority in formulating a viable policy in relation to drug abuse is to establish clear and realistic goals for such a policy. *A drug-free society is not a clear and realistic goal.* Enabling people who use drugs to cope with their lives with as few deleterious side effects as possible *is* such a clear and realistic goal.

People who use drugs, do so because drugs seem to them the easiest way of coping with life's problems. They use drugs for much the same reasons that people drink alcohol, smoke cigarettes, or overeat—in an effort to cope. Drugs are, in many cases, perhaps most cases, a bad way of handling life's tensions. But they cannot be removed via the penal code. It is no more possible to ordain a drug-free United States than an alcohol-free, or a tobacco-free United States. What we can do is regulate the supply of drugs so as to discourage the use of the most harmful drugs; prevent nonusers, particularly young people, from unthinkingly acquiring a drug habit; and offer therapeutic and rehabilitative service to those who have become addicted, and who either wish to end their addiction, or to function as normally as possible while addicted.

Essentially, a viable drug policy must be two-pronged: medical and legal. From a medical point of view, drug abuse is a much more complex problem than heroin use. Most people in this country take drugs in one form or another. The spectrum of use ranges from the confirmed coffee drinker or patent medicine pill popper, to the mainliner who injects heroin, cocaine, or whatever esoteric substance reputed to give a high is on the market. Some drug use is, of course, legitimate. Prescription drugs properly ordered by physicians, and used in an appropriate manner, are literally life-savers. Such use does not concern us. All other drug use, however, is to some extent, at least, undesirable, and the way we discourage such undesirable drug use must vary with the characteristics of the user and of the drug taken. Drinking too many cups of coffee, or taking too many Alka-Seltzers is probably best handled by an educational program directed at the general public, but more serious drug abuse requires more formal handling.

The drugs that cause the greatest concern to us today are marihuana, amphetamines, barbiturates, cocaine, and opium derivates such as heroin. Marihuana, smoked in reasonable quantities, has to date no scientifically proven harmful physical or psychological effects. The conventional wisdom has it, of course, that marihuana is not only harmful per se, but is also the first step in the downward path that leads to heroin use. Much research has been undertaken to substantiate this popular belief. To date, none has succeeded in proving either physiological damage, or a "stepping stone" pattern to heroin use.* Many marihuana users, of course, have physical ailments, are psychologically disturbed, and eventually become addicted to heroin. What has not been established is the causative relationship, if any, between these two sets of phenomena. Until such time as such a relationship has been established, there is no medical problem in relation to the use of marihuana, and there is no apparent justification for legal prohibition.

Amphetamines and barbiturates, on the other hand, are extremely dangerous though useful drugs which are legal when sold by prescriptions. When used improperly, they cause severe personality disturbance such as depression, wild and erratic behavior, irrational

---

* A recent study suggests that marihuana may weaken the immunological defenses of the body. These findings have not yet been confirmed, but if they are, marihuana will then become a legitimate medical problem, which so far it is not. *New York Post,* January 26, 1974, p. 12.

functioning, and a whole host of psychological derangements, some of which can be fatal. Two problems are apparent in relation to the amphetamines and barbiturates: first, that they are overprescribed by physicians; and second, that they are readily available and widely used illegally. Some much needed self-policing is obviously in order on the part of the medical profession and by the manufacturers of pharmaceutical products. Sufficient medical research indicating the dangers of overuse of amphetamines and barbiturates has been published to provide the basis for investigation and censure by the medical societies of physicians who are careless in prescribing such drugs to their patients. In 1972, the case of a Dr. Max Jacobson, an Upper East Side (New York City) physician who treated many well known affluent people in governmental and entertainment circles, received a great deal of publicity when it was revealed that Dr. Jacobson had been ubiquitously injecting amphetamines along with vitamins as "pick-me-ups" for his patients. Although the doctor attempted to defend his prescriptions as sound medical practice, he was subsequently investigated with a view to censure by his medical society.[31]

At the same time it is well known that pharmaceutical companies are manufacturing far more of these types of drugs than is necessary for legitimate purposes in this country. Much of this excess finds its way, frequently by export to Mexico and subsequent illegal reimportation, into underground channels where "uppers and downers" can be purchased. If the drug manufacturers cannot handle this problem by themselves, then it would be appropriate for the government to establish quotas and police the production of amphetamines and barbiturates so as to cut down on the supply of illegitimate drugs.

Amphetamines and barbiturates cause such profound personality changes that, like alcohol, their overuse frequently leads to antisocial behavior. Their overuse, however, is not especially associated with crime, partly because the users for the most part are middle-class people whose aberrations take other forms (suicide, school failure), and partly because they are so freely available at a moderate price that users need not turn to crime to obtain the money for their purchases. Those who overuse amphetamines and barbiturates, however, need medical care in handling their addiction, which in many ways is more serious than heroin addiction since these drugs cause lasting physiological damage, and the addiction is very difficult to overcome.

Under no circumstances, however, should the use of amphetamines and barbiturates be forbidden by law. Such a policy would be highly counterproductive since it would have little realistic effect on reducing consumption and would raise the price of the drugs and lead to criminal behavior on the part of users.

Heroin use, of course, is the most publicized and the most serious drug abuse problem in this country. The chief difficulty in relation to heroin use is its association with criminal behavior which is due, not to the use of the drug per se, but to the need to obtain money for the drug which is wildly expensive because it is totally illegal and cannot be medically prescribed in this country. In medical terms, heroin use is not as difficult a problem as the overuse of amphetamines, barbiturates, or even alcohol, because heroin used in reasonable quantities and in a reasonable manner does not have adverse physiological or psychological effects. Heroin is, however, addictive, a serious consequence that does not preclude normal functioning, provided the user has access to a stabilized dose administered hygienically. Several medical approaches should be available to addicts. For those who wish to overcome their addiction, programs such as those offered in drug-free communities should be made available. Religious groups, such as the Black Muslims, who offer highly emotional psychological support to ex-addicts (somewhat similar to the role of Alcoholics Anonymous in relation to drinking), can be very helpful to certain personalities. Group therapy or individual psychotherapy by themselves are effective in a small number of cases.

For the majority of drug addicts who do not wish to be, or cannot become abstinent, however, the most important type of program is a heroin or methadone dispensing program, patterned on the British model. The determination of whether heroin or methadone is to be used should be left to the medical authorities in charge. At present, the American public is willing to accept the prescription only of methadone, not of heroin. In reality, though they are different drugs, when the doses are adjusted, both are very similar in their effects on the user. In proper doses, both are highly addictive; both can produce a temporary euphoria; neither is physically harmful; and both will allow addicts to function normally on stabilized amounts. The morality of use is the same for both; it is not more moral to take methadone than heroin, even though culturally it is, in the United

States, today more acceptable to take methadone than heroin. In part, this is because methadone is a legal drug, while heroin is not. Methadone's legality, however, is due to the fact that the public has been led to believe that it is somehow different from heroin, and its use somehow not as wrong. The only appreciable difference between methadone and heroin in use is that methadone is more long lasting in its effects, and can be taken orally and less frequently than heroin.

Methadone programs have become increasingly popular in large cities in the United States in the last five years. It is difficult to say precisely how successful they have been in the absence of thoroughgoing evaluations of such programs. New York City, however, probably has the most extensive methadone treatment programs in the country, and it is possible to estimate the effectiveness of the methadone approach from the data available there. As of 1973, about 25 percent of the funds distributed by the New York State Drug Abuse Control Commission (the funding agency for all publicly supported drug programs in New York State) were allocated to the support of methadone programs which serviced approximately 60 percent of the clients helped by the DACC. About 37,000 addicts were enrolled in New York State (34,000 in New York City and 3,000 elsewhere) in such programs. While no precise figures are available as to what proportion of these clients are working, have ceased their criminal activity, and have remained with the program, the overall impression of workers in the field, according to Commissioner Meyer H. Diskind of the DACC, is that in the ten-year period since the inception of the New York State methadone program, at least half of the addicts treated in properly run clinics can be said to have been restored to normal functioning in terms of working and noncriminal behavior. In the short run, the percentages of success are probably considerably higher, and even allowing for reversion to former behavior, a very substantial proportion of those in the program have been helped materially.

Methadone programs, however, to be effective must be properly run. This means usually that methadone must be dispensed through a clinic where patients are given their supplies daily which they are then seen to consume by trained personnel. It also means that supportive services such as job training, psychotherapy, and family counseling are made available so that the underlying problems that led initially to addiction may be resolved. Experience has shown that some physicians have profiteered by dispensing methadone privately to virtually all comers, collecting on a per patient basis from federal and state Medicaid funds. This kind of program is disastrous, in that it feeds a black market in methadone and it creates neighborhood hostility to drug treatment programs. When unsupervised, addicts frequently sell, rather than use some of the methadone they are given, to people who want methadone but who don't want to be bothered going to the clinic, registering, or otherwise complying with regulations. A poorly run program also evokes neighborhood protests because addicts tend to congregate and do business in the street which arouses fears for the safety of the children of the community and of an increase in crime. Many of the neighborhood complaints are unjustified, but in well run programs they are kept to a minimum by avoiding unnecessary congregations in the street. In short, most of the criticisms of methadone programs are not of the methadone approach itself but of poor implementation of that approach.*

Methadone programs are, at present, in the United States the most important and useful technique for dealing with heroin addicts. They are not, however, a substitution for the decriminalization of the use of heroin. Heroin should be handled as methadone is, by physicians on a prescription basis, and possibly through hospital clinics only rather than through private practitioners. The reasons for decriminalizing heroin are complex and do not relate mainly to giving the addict his choice of drugs. Indeed, in Great Britain most addicts are given prescriptions for methadone rather than heroin, even if they are heroin addicts, largely because methadone can be taken orally and less frequently than heroin. Drugs that need to be injected into a vein present health problems unless the injection is carried out under medical supervision.

One important reason for decriminalizing heroin is to facilitate medical research into the problems of drug addiction. Methadone and heroin are similar in their effects on the user, but they are not pharmacologically the same. It is important for scientists to have access to supplies of heroin for experimental purposes if they are to

* Much of the above discussion is based on data obtained from Meyer H. Diskind, Assistant Commissioner of the New York State Drug Abuse Control Commission.

investigate the physiological aspects of heroin use. Such questions as what causes addiction; why some persons are capable of using heroin without becoming readily addicted, and others are not; why there is a craving for the drug even years after use has terminated; why addiction seems to lessen with increasing age, have not been answered. To do the kind of research that may shed more light on these questions, it is absolutely necessary to have heroin available. It is not sufficient, moreover, to have a central authority release small quantities of heroin for a limited time for experimental purposes as was proposed recently for a Vera Institute of Justice program that anticipated maintaining addicts on decreasing doses of heroin for one year.* The record keeping and the institutional effort involved in obtaining permission to use the drug is enormous, and the uncertainty of being able to continue an experiment once it has started is very restrictive of research. Under those circumstances, most scientists shy away from involvement in the field, and even worse, very little research money is liable to become available. If heroin were handled like morphine, manufacturers would be licensed to produce it and authorized users to purchase it. It would by no means be readily available to the general public but would be accessible with reasonable record-keeping controls for authorized research.

A second reason for decriminalizing heroin is more subtle but possibly even more important. As long as it is illegal to possess heroin, the user must remain part of the criminal subculture. This makes the user a law breaker and his friends and associates become a ring of outcasts and criminals. While to many people, particularly if they are middle aged, middle class, and white, this seems a dreadful status, to adolescents, particularly black adolescents who are angry or frightened or confused by a world that is not treating them very well, there is a certain glamour to such status. To be a bad boy is a way of making people notice, and the "badder" you are the more attention others will pay to you. To make heroin a medicine to be dispensed by a physician in a clinic is to rob its use of this glamour. To make the bad boy a handicapped person is to change his self-image and role expectancy from criminal to patient. The cement that binds him to his associates in the drug subculture is loosened because the strongest

* For many reasons, including claims of genocide by the black community, this program never got off the ground.

element in that cement is the illegality of the venture. If an addict needs a fix, he needs his connection. He cannot go out into the city at large to purchase what he needs just anywhere. He needs his friends or his group, and because these friends are all like him, fugitives from the law, their relationship becomes almost total as well as highly personal. The relationship is total because the use of heroin is a total occupation in the sense that the "hustle" to obtain the drug and the social interaction surrounding the injecting of the drug, and the release and relaxation that follow the injection, occupy all of the addict's time and emotional and physical energies. The drug and the people who helped him get it and use it are literally his whole world.

Heroin in the clinic setting is entirely different. For one thing, obtaining it takes only a fraction of the time and energy and poses no challenge at all. For another, while the addict may establish personal relationships among the staff and with other patients at the clinic, the social interaction is much more limited, is likely to be of a professional rather than a personal nature, and constitutes a small part of his total existence rather than being central to it. Strenuous efforts will be made to have him fill the remainder of his daily routine with activities such as work that relate to the outside world rather than to his drug habit. The methadone clinic, of course, to some extent offers an addict these alternatives already. As long as heroin remains illegal, however, it will be attractive to those whose personal needs require the rebellion of breaking the law and the intense closeness of the illegal drug subculture. If our efforts are to be directed to teaching addicts acceptable ways of coping with their habits and the problems that led them to become addicted in the first place, then we must remove, as far as possible, the unacceptable alternatives that illegal heroin generates.

In addition to methadone and heroin prescription programs, moreover, research should continue into other approaches for handling the problem of addiction, such as the development of chemical antagonists to heroin, like cyclazocine. A heroin antagonist acts through blocking the effect of heroin on the body. Thus, an addict who injects heroin while on one of these drugs will not perceive any effect. The hope of research in this field is that if a long-lasting antagonist can be developed, a single injection would effectively prevent an addict from taking heroin for a period of weeks or even months. (This approach is somewhat similar to the use of antabuse for the treatment of alcoholics: the alcoholic who takes a drink of alcohol while on antabuse will experience unpleasant side effects which will effectively prevent him from continuing to drink.) Chemical antagonists, while a worthwhile field for research, do have certain built-in limitations. They may help the addict be heroin abstinent but unfortunately they leave untouched the basic disturbances that led to addiction in the first place. The addict may not be able to take heroin, but he may nevertheless be plagued by the same anxiety and depression from which he originally sought surcease, and this anxiety may lead him to try other methods of obtaining relief, such as barbiturates or alcohol, which may be even less desirable. Again, while blocking agents for the treatment of a willing patient may have some value, their use as a compulsory treatment poses very grave civil liberties problems.

> *What the large-scale use of a long-acting narcotic antagonist would in fact produce, is a horde of men, women, and adolescents, assailed by anxiety and depression, with a continued craving for heroin—and no way to assuage their distress. . . .*
>
> *An ethical consideration is also involved in the use of long-acting narcotic antagonists: why is it* wrong *to provide an addict with an addicting drug such as methadone—that is, one that carries a built-in pharmacological compulsion for continued use—but* right *to use legal compulsion even imprisonment, to force continued use of a non-addicting drug?* [32]

Cocaine is a drug that is used to some extent interchangeably with heroin by heroin addicts, although it is pharmacologically quite different and is classified as a stimulant rather than a depressant. Unlike heroin it is not physically addictive, though unfortunately, again unlike heroin, it can produce severe psychotic reactions in the user. During these psychotic episodes assaultive behavior and other antisocial conduct sometimes occurs. Cocaine is somewhat similar to the amphetamines and in fact is not widely used, partly because it is very expensive and difficult to obtain, and partly because the amphetamines provide a cheap and more readily available substitute.[33] Like other dangerous drugs, it should be available on a prescription basis and manufacture and sale should be government regulated.

To say that heroin use should be decriminalized, and that addiction should be handled medically rather than legally, does not mean that the criminal justice system has no part to play in the control of drug abuse. In the first place, medical handling presupposes a number of administrative regulations of manufacturers, physicians, and others who handle regulated substances, as well as import restrictions on these pharmaceuticals, and the criminal justice system must be used to enforce these regulations. The decriminalization of heroin does not mean that heroin will be available at the corner candy store. The intent, in fact, is quite the opposite: to make heroin available *only through legitimate medical channels.* Though illegal, heroin is widely available today. The aim of decriminalization will be to eliminate this availability. The British experience suggests, moreover, that heroin be dispensed through clinics rather than through individual practitioners.

Illegal smuggling must also be stopped, not only of heroin, but also of amphetamines and barbiturates. Thus far, attempts to stop this smuggling have for the most part been failures, probably because of the lure of the enormous profits to be made selling illegal drugs. Once legitimate medical access to all drugs is provided, however, the black market price will drop sharply so that the number and persistence of potential smugglers should be likewise greatly reduced. Decriminalization should make the job of law enforcement authorities easier and more feasible, but will by no means eliminate the need for policing by agents of the criminal justice system. It should also make enforcement more effective by reducing sharply the opportunities for corruption of police and custom inspectors.

A second important role for the criminal justice system is in the handling of criminal behavior that results from the use of drugs. It is fatuous to suppose that decriminalization of heroin and the medical handling of other mood affecting drugs will make solid law abiding citizens of those who take them. Most addicts are multiproblem people. They had problems before they took drugs, and they will continue to have problems even after they obtain medical help for their addiction problems. Many had prior criminal records and will not necessarily be reformed by stabilizing their use of heroin or methadone. The hope of decriminalization is to eliminate the crime that is a result of the economics of heroin use, i.e., the need to support a very expensive and demanding habit, but there is no question that the incidence of crime among drug users, particularly lower-class drug users, would be higher than among the normal population even if heroin were sold like sugar in the supermarket. Just as repeal put the bootleggers out of business and reduced crime, organized and otherwise, connected with the illegal use and sale of alcohol, but did not reduce the antisocial conduct of those who drink excessively, decriminalization of heroin will not reduce the antisocial conduct of all heroin users. The criminal justice system is still necessary to control and deter such individuals. Hopefully, decriminalization will cut down the size of the job to manageable proportions.

Conclusions

In the last analysis, the success of the approaches suggested here for the decriminalization of many morals offenses—heroin use, prostitution, gambling, obscenity, etc.—depends on the responses of what Mr. Nixon fondly used to call "the silent majority." Imperfect though it may be, American government is responsive to the electorate, at least to the extent that government action profoundly distasteful to most people is not likely to succeed in the long run. Reform of the criminal justice system depends on the successful resolution of a political problem: the need to convince the general public that *removing* some undesirable modes of conduct from the penal code may be a more effective way of maintaining high moral standards within the community than is control by threat of severe punishment. There is a limit to the effective reach of the criminal law, and when we transcend that limit we get less effective regulation rather than more. There are sanctions other than our penal codes. We still have homes, mothers, fathers, clergymen, teachers, workmates, political leaders, friends, and peers—all of whom profoundly shape and regulate our daily existence. Above all, the very foundations of democratic theory presuppose that man is at least minimally rational and if not inherently good, at least not inherently evil. These assumptions may be false, and if they are then the whole attempt to create a viable democratic society is an illusion doomed to failure. Perhaps there is no future for self-government in an age as technologically advanced and as beset with the kinds of problems engendered by that technology as our own.

On the other hand, nearly two hundred years ago in Philadelphia there were, no doubt, even among the founding fathers, many who were skeptical as to the possibility of the common man having the wisdom to make correct choices among social policies. Over one hundred years ago, Abraham Lincoln reflected on the same doubts in his Gettysburg Address when he asked whether it was possible for "any nation so conceived, and so dedicated" to long endure. Fifty years ago, Oliver Wendell Holmes said,

> . . . when men have realized that time has upset many fighting faiths, they may come to believe even more than they believe the very foundations of their own conduct that the ultimate good desired is better reached by free trade in ideas—that the best test of truth is the power of the thought to get itself accepted in the competition of the market, and that truth is the only ground upon which their wishes can be safely carried out. That, at any rate, is the theory of our Constitution. It is an experiment, as all life is an experiment.[34]

The outcome of the experiment is still in doubt, but two hundred years have passed, and the United States as a self-governing society is still in business, while many elitist, autocratic systems have long since crumbled.

There is still much work to be done. The general public, outraged over crime, corruption, and what is perceived as excess permissiveness, reacts by adopting increasingly punitive attitudes. In 1973, a survey conducted for the *New York Times* by Daniel Yankelovich, Inc., of 1,341 residents of New York City revealed that in the most liberal city of the United States, 57 percent of the public opposed legalizing marihuana, 67 percent favored life sentences for drug pushers without possibility of parole, and 53 percent favored cracking down on pornography.[35] These responses can mean only one thing: that despite our signal failure to control this kind of behavior punitively the general public knows of no other response but more of the same—more of the same unsuccessful punitive approaches that have failed in the past. The public needs to be shown that there is a way out of the frustration, fear, and failure that are the results of the criminalization of modes of conduct that should be handled nonpunitively. Our blind use of the penal code is self-defeating. There are other ways, decent, kindlier, more compassionate and above all, more effective ways. It is time to try them.

chapter six
COURTS, THE LAW, AND POLITICS

The Law, wherein, as in a magic mirror, we see reflected not only our lives, but the lives of all men that have been! When I think on this majestic theme, my eyes dazzle.

Oliver Wendell Holmes, Jr., Address to the Suffolk Bar Association.

A court must resolve all conflicts presented to it, with or without adequate knowledge.

David L. Bazelon, "The Awesome Decision," *Saturday Evening Post*, January 23, 1960.

No mather whether th' constitution follows th' flag nor not, th' supreme court follows th' iliction returns.

Finley Peter Dunne, *Mr. Dooley's Opinions*

The central theme of this book has been the need to reform the substance of the criminal law. The law and its impact have thus far been discussed largely in sociological terms: the nature of deviance, the impact on individuals of different methods of handling deviance, the best ways of mediating cultural clashes, etc. But there are other dimensions to the criminal law. The law can be looked at historically to discover how it came to assume its present form; it can be looked at philosophically as a statement of what the relationship between the individual and the state ought to be; it can be looked at politically to demonstrate the allocation of power—who gets what, when, and how—and it can be looked at structurally to define the institutions that have been established to implement the law.

Perhaps one way of understanding the implications of the plea for legal reform is to consider the problem from several vantage points. How different, for example, would the suggested changes be from the kinds of changes that have occurred in the law in the past? Would such changes redefine the theoretical relationship between the individual and the state, or shift the balance of power among groups in society? Institutionally, how would such change be handled? Would such a reform be radical or conservative, i.e., would the law be pushed in a new direction, or brought back to its original course? If we could answer these questions, we could perhaps, better assess the likely impact of such reform. To that end, therefore, a brief discussion of the history, philosophy, and institutions of the American legal system seems in order.

The foundation of our criminal justice system is, of course, the criminal law, and the most important social institution connected with the handling of the criminal law is the criminal court system; yet, the criminal law is only one branch of our overall network of laws, and the criminal courts are only those courts which may, at times, handle criminal cases. We cannot speak of reforming the criminal justice system without understanding that the criminal justice system is only a part of a much larger legal system. We cannot suggest a pattern for the future without tracing the path by which we came to be what we are today.

American Law: The Beginnings

Every school boy knows that the English Common Law is the foundation of American law, but very few people really know what Common Law is. When questioned, students in the classroom will frequently mumble something about the Common Law being "unwritten" law. This conjures up fascinating visions of elderly jurists on their death beds whispering the Common Law to their disciples. The vision is, alas, false because the Common Law has been committed to writing. What students mean when they call the Common Law "unwritten" is that it was never composed by a group of legislators or by a sovereign. It is judge-made law, and is contained in the decisions of the judges who presided over the courts of medieval England.

The development of the Common Law started under the Norman and Angevin kings during the eleventh and twelfth centuries. It replaced earlier tribal and feudal law in which justice had been in the hands of popular assemblies known as folk moots. As feudalism developed, folk moots evolved eventually into shire moots, local courts whose membership included the elite of feudal society: large landowners, bishops, lords, and shire-reeves. The first step in the nationalizing of the courts was taken when William the Conqueror attempted to consolidate his power by sending his own representatives to the local shire moots. William also separated lay from ecclesiastical courts, so that two distinct legal systems emerged: state law and canon law (church law). State law came to be called Common Law and was judge-made (as opposed to king-made or parliament-made), and was common to all England in the same way that canon law was common to all Christendom. The law was also "common" because it had been derived by the royal justices from the customary practices of the realm.

The Common Law is thought to have developed over approximately four centuries from about 1100 to 1500 A.D. During this period judges, in deciding cases brought before them, relied heavily on decisions made by other judges in handling similar earlier cases. This heavy reliance on precedent is known as the doctrine of *stare decisis*. The Common Law developed a pragmatic orientation: decisions were based on the facts of the case rather than on a generalized statement of principle. Decisions also rested solidly on centuries of local practice, apparently sanctified into acceptability by time. The Common Law, however, suffered from two basic flaws: it tended toward rigidity, since new sets of facts were difficult to handle under the old precepts; and it could not handle satisfactorily cases where damage inflicted by a wrongdoer could not be compensated by money. These two defects in the Common Law led to the growth of equity, a parallel system of judge-made law which originated in the appeals of litigants to the Royal Chancellor (the keeper of the king's conscience) for justice. It was in the courts of Equity that such devices as the injunction to prevent the commission of a wrong, rather than to compensate for it later on, originated. Thus, by the end of the fifteenth century a fairly comprehensive system of law had developed in England based in large part on the decisions of generations of judges in the crown's courts of Law and Equity.

When the English settlers came to America in the seventeenth century they brought with them, of course, the English legal system of which the bedrock was the Common Law. The English system already had embodied within it some notions of protection of the individual against the power of the state, as for example, the restrictions on the king imposed by Magna Carta, or the feeling for the inviolability of private property which William Pitt expressed so eloquently:

The poorest man may in his cottage bid defiance to all the force of the crown. It may be frail; its roof may shake; the wind may blow through it; the storms may enter, the rain may enter—but the King of England cannot enter; all his forces dare not cross the threshold of the ruined tenement!

The colonists further refined these ideas by adding to customary legal practice certain procedural protections (such as bail, the right of confrontation, and the right not to incriminate oneself) that were derived from sources other than the Common Law. Professor Gerhard Mueller, a legal scholar, points out that many of the early settlers were more familiar with manorial law and the Bible than with the sophisticated legalities of the English courts.[1] Their English experience and their deep religiosity formed the basis for these distinctively American accretions to the Common Law base. Further accretions came from the royal charters establishing each colony, which provided a kind of fundamental or constitutional law; the acts of the colonial legislatures; and the edicts of the royal governors.

Most law in both America and in England continued to be made by the courts rather than by the executive (president, governor, or king) or the legislature (Congress, state legislatures, or Parliament). It was not until well into the nineteenth century that statute law, i.e., law made by legislative bodies, began to acquire dominance over judicial rulings.

Law: Form and Substance

The law, in a certain sense, is what is found in the law books. Anyone who has given the matter any thought knows, however, that this is only a partial truth. To begin with, the statutes that are printed in the books are modified by the interpretations of the courts. The law is what the judges say it is. Indeed Oliver Wendell Holmes went so far as to say that "the prophesies of what the courts will do in fact and nothing more is what I mean by law."

Courts change their interpretations of what laws mean. Adoption laws in most states, for example, require that the courts, in ruling on applications for adoption, shall act "in the best interests" of the child. What these "best interests" are, however, has varied markedly from one court to another, and from one time period to another. Twenty-five years ago, interreligious adoptions were virtually impossible in New York and Massachusetts, although this is not true today. Interracial adoptions are only now becoming acceptable in some parts of the United States. The point obviously is that although the wording of the statute on the books has not changed, in the real world the substance of the law *has*, and this change has occurred through the process of judicial interpretation.

To cite another example, in 1949 the leaders of the United States Communist party were prosecuted for violation of the Smith Act in that they had conspired to advocate the violent overthrow of the government. The evidence introduced against the defendants was that they taught and preached from four classical works of communist literature: *The Communist Manifesto* by Karl Marx and Friedrich Engels; *The State and Revolution* by V. I. Lenin; *Foundations of Leninism* by Joseph Stalin; and *The History of the Communist Party of the Soviet Union.* Judge Medina of the Federal Court for the Southern District of New York decided that as a matter of law, the evidence introduced was sufficient to sustain the prosecution's charges, or in other words, that such preaching was what the lawmakers had in mind when they forbade advocacy of the violent overthrow of the government.[2] Eight years later in 1957, in *Yates* vs. *United States*,[3] the United States Supreme Court in reviewing the convictions of fourteen "second string" Communist party officials for Smith Act violations based on the same type of evidence as in *Dennis*, reversed those convictions and declared that this type of advocacy or preaching was *not* what Congress had in mind when it passed the Smith Act. . . .

> (W)e are unable to regard the District Court's charge upon this aspect of the case as adequate. . . . The essential distinction is that those to whom the advocacy is addressed must be urged to do something, now or in the future, rather than merely to believe in something.

> We recognize that distinctions between advocacy and teaching of abstract doctrines, with evil intent, and that which is directed to stirring people to action, are often subtle and difficult to grasp, for in a broad sense, as Mr. Justice Holmes said in his dissenting opinion in Gitlow: "Every idea is an incitement."[4]

As a result of the *Yates* interpretation, the Smith Act, while still on the books, has been virtually repealed as far as effective enforcement is concerned.

Not only do the courts change law through interpretation, but administrative officials, i.e., police and prosecutors, change the impact of the law through differential enforcement. The police cannot and should not enforce equally every law on the books. If they did, we would need a police force of mammoth proportions and scarcely a citizen would go through the day without official reprimand or arrest. Indeed, there would be so many policemen waiting in court to testify against accused persons there would be no one left on the streets for patrol duty. The question then is not whether the police *should* use discretion in enforcing the law, but *how* they exercise that discretion, i.e., what their criteria are. Most observers would agree that poor people, and especially poor blacks, are handled more strictly and punitively than middle-class WASPS. Political heretics, especially of the left, homosexuals, mental defectives, hippies, and skid row bums also feel the weight of the law disproportionately. Such people are more likely to become suspects or defendants in criminal cases. When arrested they are less likely to be released on bail or to be discharged on their own recognizance. If tried, they are less likely to have the assistance of good quality counsel; if convicted, they are less likely to appeal; if sentenced, they are more likely to receive prison sentences rather than fines or probation; and when sentenced to prison, their sentences tend to be longer than those given well-to-do defendants.

Such differential handling does not necessarily indicate malevolence or antipoor or antiblack bias on the part of the police, although such bias undoubtedly plays a considerable role in determining police patterns of enforcement. The police themselves explain their actions by pointing to the crime statistics that indicate the high incidence of crime among the groups most punitively handled. While crime statistics are notoriously unreliable and to some extent become self-fulfilling prophecies, if attention is focused on the victims of crime, it is hard to escape the conclusion that poor people generally commit more, and more violent crimes than do the middle class or well-to-do. The most victimized groups in our society, in terms of crimes against both persons and property, are those who live in our black ghettos. Well-to-do white men do not come into the ghetto for purposes of mugging, burglary, or assault, although there is no doubt a considerable amount of "white-collar crime" in the form of fraudulent business dealings between merchants and customers or landlords and tenants.[5]

Prosecutors similarly do not prosecute every accused person. Many cases are dropped before trial for lack of evidence or for other reasons. If there are racial and class discriminatory patterns underlying the exercise of prosecutorial discretion, they are not nearly so clear-cut. Probably a more important factor affecting prosecutors is the state of public opinion and the likely repercussions of the decision whether or not to prosecute on the prosecutor's career.

The law, thus, is hardly a fixed quantity. It varies from place to place, from era to era. It changes with judicial interpretation, and its impact is intensified or muted through differential enforcement. It would be fallacious, however, to assume that the law is entirely related to time, place, and circumstance. There is an underlying consistency to our law that transcends these variables. To understand this consistency, however, one must examine the philosophical basis of the law itself. The law basically exists to prohibit conduct that is seriously disruptive of society. It does so by prohibiting certain kinds of acts. In addition, however, the law embodies within itself the notion of "fairness" or justice. It concerns itself not only with the acts that are committed by individuals, private or public, but the manner in which those acts are committed. On the one hand, we are concerned not only that the state takes away a man's liberty, but with the procedures by which the state does this. By the same token we ask not only what one person did to another, but his motive in doing it. It is from the notion of prohibited acts that our penal codes arise; it is from the concept of justice or fairness that ideas such as due process and *mens rea* stem. It is easy to understand why killing is a prohibited act. We are concerned with more than the act of killing, however. We want to know why the killer killed; what was his intent; whether it was truly evil; and we want to know by what authority the police arrested the killer; how he was treated in custody; by what method his guilt was adjudicated; and how reasonable his punishment was.

These notions of acts that are right or wrong, acceptable or not acceptable on the one hand, and of the importance of intent and procedural fairness on the other, sometimes conflict with each other and cause ambiguities in our criminal justice system. The fuzziness of the line of demarcation between civil and criminal litigation is an example of one of those ambiguities. To the layman the distinction between civil and criminal cases is clear-cut and easy to define. While in most cases this may be true, there are areas in the law where the distinction is by no means clear-cut and where it is hard to say whether a given case should be treated civilly or criminally.

In general, civil cases normally concern disputes between private individuals or corporations. Typically they involve torts (civil wrongs, such as personal injuries from automobile accidents or falling signs), libel, slander, breaches of contract, infringement of trademarks, matrimonial actions, etc. Such cases when they arrive in the courts, are labelled with the names of the parties to the action, e.g., *Brown* v. *Gray*. (Governments can, of course, be party to civil suits. Tax foreclosures, certain kinds of antitrust actions, as well as many other violations of federal and state statutes come to court as civil cases.) The outcome of a civil case involves the assessment of liability and imposition of damages. In short, the purpose of most civil suits is to obtain legal redress for personal injuries, such redress normally taking the form of money damages, or in the cases of injunctions or matrimonial actions, changing the responsibilities of the litigants toward each other. Civil cases are frequently heard without juries, and many more are adjusted by out-of-court settlement between the parties, such settlements frequently being reached with the aid of the court. The standard of proof required in a civil case is that of a "fair preponderance of the evidence." This means that on balance a reasonable, prudent person would tend to believe, rather than disbelieve, the successful litigant. There is no presumption as to the guilt or innocence of either party.

Criminal cases, on the other hand, involve public rather than private wrongs. Strictly speaking, the victim, i.e., the person raped, murdered, or assaulted, is not the wronged party. Action is brought not in his name, but in the name of the community, i.e., the government. In early feudal times, crime was indeed considered to have been a tort, a private wrong to be avenged by the victim or his kinfolk. In the time of Henry II, however, in one of the great forward steps of Anglo-Saxon jurisprudence, the concept of crime as a *public* wrong developed. The peace that was shattered was no longer the local lord's peace, but the king's peace.

The king was now the source of law. He had jurisdiction in every case. The State, and not the family or the lord, now was the proper prosecutor in every case.[6]

Underlying the concept of crime as a public wrong is the notion that the community has been injured more grievously and more substantially than the victim, even if the victim has lost his life, for what is at stake in a crime is not only the fate of two individuals, the criminal and his victim, but the fate of society itself. Blackstone makes this distinction:

The distinction of public wrongs from private, of crimes and misdemeanors from civil injuries, are an infringement or privation of the civil rights which belong to individuals, considered merely as individuals; public wrongs, or crimes and misdemeanors, are a breach and violation of the public rights and duties, due to the whole community, considered as a community, in its social aggregate capacity.

As if I detain a field from another man, to which the law has given him a right, this is a civil injury, and not a crime; for here only the right of an individual is concerned, and it is immaterial to the public which of us is in possession of the land: but treason, murder and robbery are properly ranked among crimes; since, besides the injury done to individuals, they strike at the very being of society, which cannot possibly subsist where actions of this sort are suffered to escape with impunity.

In all cases the crime includes an injury: every public offense is also a private wrong, and somewhat more; it affects the individual, and it likewise affects the community.[7]

It is understandable, thus, why criminal cases come to court labelled with the name of the state as the plaintiff (aggrieved party), e.g., *People of the State of New York* v. *Sibron*, or *United States of America* v. *Massiah*. It is also understandable why penalties in criminal cases tend to be more severe than those in civil cases, and involve long punishment and even death, rather than merely deprivation of property in the form of fines, reparations, or restitution. The standard for proof of guilt is also more stringent in a criminal case: guilt must be proved beyond a reasonable doubt, not merely by a fair preponderance of the evidence. Because of the potential severity of the punishment and the dread consequences for the accused, moreover, the accused is assumed to be innocent until proven guilty in the legally prescribed manner, meaning simply that the burden of proof in a criminal case is on the state to prove guilt rather than on the accused to prove innocence.

Whether an offense is public or private, civil or criminal, is usually obvious, but ambiguities occur in cases where the act itself is a public wrong but where the actor lacks sufficient capacity to be fairly considered to have had evil intent (*mens rea*) and therefore to have committed a crime. Offenses committed by children, the insane, and, in certain instances, by those addicted to drugs or alcohol, fall into this category. Juveniles, for example, frequently commit acts which, if committed by an adult, would be clearly criminal. Child offenders, however, are not handled in the same way as adult offenders. Instead of being adjudicated in accordance with the formal, rigidly defined rules of criminal procedure designed for the protection of an accused whose liberty may be taken away, the child offender is handled informally by a group of officials whose stated intentions are to act in the place of, and in the role of, the parents who so obviously have lost control of the child. The purpose of juvenile proceedings is to help, not punish, the child. For this reason, it is assumed that the child needs no protection, procedural or otherwise, from these "helpers." The proceedings by which the fate of the child is determined are not criminal procedures. In their relative informality, in their alleged lack of punitive orientation, in their emphasis on negotiation and settlement, rather than on an attribution of guilt, they are more nearly civil in nature. As a result of these "protection" proceedings, however, a child may be confined against his will to an institution for months or years, a period which may even exceed that to which he might have been sentenced had he been an adult criminal. If we say that juvenile offenses are not criminal, i.e., are not of such nature as to pose a threat to the fabric of society, and therefore, may be handled procedurally relatively informally, then how do we have the right to confine a person even a person under legal age, unwillingly in an institution, punishment normally inflicted only for *criminal* offenses? We may say we are "helping" the child, but children, no less than adults, perceive involuntary confinement as punishment, especially since in fact, most juvenile institutions are at best custodial and are seldom rehabilitative.

The injustice of handling children in this way has been apparent for many years, and the courts recently have attempted to modify the procedures by which juveniles may be committed. Recent Supreme Court decisions such as *Gault, Kent,* and *Winship*[8] have affirmed the rights of accused juveniles to such long accepted procedural protections as the right to notice of charges against them; the right to counsel; the right to confrontation and cross-examination; the privilege against self-incrimination; and the "beyond a reasonable doubt" standard for proof of guilt. Are juvenile offenders then, to be treated like adult criminals? The answer obviously must be negative unless we are prepared to return to the days when twelve-year-olds were hanged, and to abandon the reformist ideals of the juvenile justice movement of the past century. The United States Supreme Court itself recognized the danger when it declined to declare a jury trial a procedural necessity in juvenile cases.[9] The resolution of this dilemma is not clear. What is clear is that juvenile proceedings cannot be neatly pigeon-holed in a civil-criminal dichotomy.

In a similar manner questions are being raised about the propriety of involuntary insanity commitments, both criminal and civil. Even though confinement in a mental institution is always for purposes of treatment rather than punishment, people involuntarily confined to such institutions are there against their will. By what standards do we assign them to such custody? What are the standards of proof of incompetency required? Who is qualified to testify? Who shall make the determination? How do we know when or if the patient has recovered? How can he effectuate his release? The problem, in short, is how much protection does the allegedly insane person need from those who are trying to "help" him.[10]

To cite a third example, if society chooses to look at the drug addict as a "sick" rather than evil person, and to provide civil commitment aimed at rehabilitation rather than a prison term, problems arise in relation to the proper procedures for handling such offenders. In New York State, for example, an attempt was made in cases involving addicts charged with misdemeanors, to place such persons in hospital-like facilities rather than prisons. Typically, the addict would agree to commit himself to the hospital in return for which the prosecutor would drop the pending misdemeanor charges against him. Problems arose when the "hospitals" turned out to be far more punitive than rehabilitative and the "patients" found themselves detained against their will for periods of time far longer than their sentences on the original misdemeanor charges would have been. Again, it may be humane for the state to declare an addict a sick person and to formulate a policy for helping him, but fairness requires adequate procedural safeguards to ensure that he is really being helped rather than punished. In short, whenever any person is detained involuntarily for whatever reason, relatively loose administrative procedures are highly questionable.

As previously indicated, these problems in the handling of juveniles and others of diminished legal responsibility are difficult to resolve because basically they stem from contradictions inherent in the philosophical basis of the law. The theory of natural law that underlies our penal codes defines not only those acts which are good and bad, right and wrong, but also encompasses notions of fairness and justice from which the concept of *mens rea* has developed, i.e., that a crime is more than an act, it is an act accompanied by an evil intent. It is at this point that the contradiction occurs in regard to the handling of those with diminished responsibility. On the one hand, our moral code says we must punish those who commit evil acts. On the other hand, the code also says we cannot punish, or we ought not punish those who had no evil intent in committing the act. The intent could not be formed because the individual was a child, an insane person, or another incapable of assuming full responsibility. How then is such a person to be treated? If our only method of curbing such antisocial conduct is, in fact, punitive, what do we do?

In practice, we attempt to resolve such dilemmas as best we can. The United States Supreme Court, for example, has given children certain procedural protections, and increasing publicity has been given in recent years to the inadequacy of our programs for juvenile delinquents. The underlying significance of these problems, however, is that when we use the criminal sanction as a method of social control, we must be very cautious indeed because the social price for improper or unwarranted use of the criminal sanction can be very high. In the case of juveniles we may condemn children to a loss of liberty without even the minimal care and solicitude we offer to adult accused persons. In the case of those thought to be insane we may confine individuals who while they may be eccentric or abrasive are mentally well enough to function quite adequately in the world at large.

The use of the criminal sanction against children or the mentally ill is but one side of the coin in relation to the improper use of criminal penalties. Our treatment of morals offenders is the other side of the coin. Where in the case of children the *act* is criminal, but the actor lacks capacity and therefore *mens rea*, in the case of gamblers, homosexuals, prostitutes, and the like, capacity and intent are present, but the *act* is not a public wrong in the sense that it is dangerous to society. The fact that large numbers of people over an extended period of time violate morals laws means two things: one, that such conduct is not truly disruptive, or society would have crumbled long since; and secondly, that regardless of what they say, many people do not truly think such conduct is wrong. If the act, then, is not criminal, it follows that we are using the criminal sanction improperly, and as in the case of those lacking capacity, the social price is high: fostering crime and corruption, creating contempt for the law, and overburdening and rendering less effective our criminal justice system. Worst of all, perhaps, like the wrongful premature confinement of children or the insane, it is cruel; it results in harassing and labelling people who are already weary with struggling to meet the demands society makes and for whom such harassment is simply an additional burden.

The American Court System

In the United States today there are fifty-one court systems: fifty state and one federal. Typically, these court systems operate on a three-tier level: a court of original jurisdiction (trial court); an intermediate appellate court; and a high appellate court. Unfortunately, although the structure of the courts is similar throughout the state and federal systems the terminology used is not. State trial courts are frequently referred to as county or superior courts, but they may have other names as well. (Indeed, in New York State, this court is called the Supreme Court.) These trial courts hear major criminal and civil cases, i.e., felonies or suits involving large sums of money. Misdemeanors and minor civil suits are usually heard in local courts, sometimes called magistrates (criminal) or municipal (civil) courts whose decisions may be appealed to the superior courts. The intermediate appellate court (perhaps most frequently labelled the court of appeals) handles both criminal and civil appeals from the trial courts. The highest appellate courts in the states are usually called supreme courts, and they handle appeals from the intermediate appellate courts.

In the federal system the lowest courts of general jurisdiction are the District Courts of which there are over ninety. Each state has at least one; some of the more populous have as many as four. The intermediate appellate court, of which there are eleven, is called the Court of Appeals, and handles appeals from the District Courts and from the decisions of certain administrative agencies. The highest federal court is, of course, the United States Supreme Court. All federal courts handle both civil and criminal cases.

Of all the courts in the United States, by far the most interesting and politically significant is the United States Supreme Court. It alone, of all American courts, is established in the Constitution itself, Article III of which vests judicial power of the United States in "one Supreme Court" and extends such power to "all cases, in law and equity, arising under this Constitution, the laws of the United States, and treaties made, or which shall be made, under their authority."

In 1789, at the time of its establishment, the powers of the new court were unclear, to say the least. The first chief justice of the United States, John Jay, thought so little of the job that he resigned to become ambassador to Spain. The great John Marshall himself, for a short time, held the positions of both secretary of state and chief justice simultaneously. The Jeffersonian dominated Congress elected in 1800 showed such contempt for the court that it passed a law suspending the court's functions for one entire year. In 1803, however, the court was virtually reborn in what is probably the single most significant decision it has ever rendered: *Marbury* v. *Madison*. The facts of the Marbury case, which originated in a dirty bit of chicanery involving judicial appointments, are no longer relevant; what is important is that in that decision John Marshall claimed for the court the right of judicial review, i.e., the right to sit in judgment on the acts of the executive and legislative branches of the federal establishment, thereby establishing the United States Supreme Court as a fully equal partner in the business of government.

> *If an act of the legislature, repugnant to the Constitution is void, does it, notwithstanding its validity, bind the courts and oblige them to give it effect? This . . . would seem . . . an absurdity too gross to be insisted on. . . . It is emphatically the province and duty of the judicial department to say what the law is.*[11]

Having thus confidently asserted its power, the Supreme Court very prudently refrained from exercising that power vis-à-vis Congress for the next half-century, until the disaster of *Dred Scott* on the eve of the Civil War.*

Scholars have long argued the question of whether the founding fathers intended for the Supreme Court to have the power to sit in judgment on coequal legislative and executive branches. Neither the Constitution nor the Federalist papers, nor any contemporaneous official documents indicate unequivocally that the Supreme Court was intended to have this power. On the other hand, that part of the *Marbury* decision which proclaimed judicial review excited very little opposition even among Marshall's Jeffersonian opponents. Contemporary evidence seems to indicate that the notion of judicial review was well understood and was expected of the Supreme Court. By 1803, state high courts had on previous occasions sat in judgment on the actions of their state legislatures, and during colonial times, disputes over whether acts of a colonial legislature violated the colony's charter had been referred to the Privy Council in England for resolution. On balance, the preponderance of the historical evidence tends

---

* The U.S. Supreme Court does, of course, exercise judicial review over the acts of the state governments as well, and indeed this power over the states is not only exercised more frequently but is probably far more important in shaping the totality of the American political system than its power to review actions of Congress or the president. The right to sit in judgment on the states, however, is not nearly as controversial as the right of judicial review at the federal level, primarily because the Constitution is less ambiguous on the subject. Section 2 of Article VI provides that the Constitution and laws of the United States shall be "the supreme law of the land, and that the judges of every state shall be bound thereby, anything in the Constitution or laws of any state to the contrary notwithstanding." The implication is fairly clear that the U.S. Supreme Court would be the logical agency to supervise the state judges in their duty to uphold the federal Constitution.

to favor Marshall's interpretation of the powers of the court, and in any case the argument today has become almost irrelevant in view of the firm establishment of judicial review as an accepted practice.

There is, however, an ongoing debate as to how activist the court ought to be. Those who favor judicial self-restraint, perhaps influenced by lingering doubts as to the legitimacy of judicial review, argue that the court is essentially an antidemocratic institution inasmuch as it is elitist (drawn from the upper socioeconomic groups), unrepresentative (not elected), and not responsible to the public (comprised of justices appointed for life). As an unrepresentative body, the court ought to confine its activities to the bare minimum required by its role as umpire of the federal system. The court should avoid, wherever possible, involvement in disputes that can be handled by the popularly elected branches of government. The judicial activists, on the other hand, claim an uninhibited, fully active court is necessary to maintain a balance within the system between the right of the majority to govern and the right of minorities to preserve their inalienable rights from infringement by the governing majority. Democracy, activists reason, is not simply majority rule. Individual rights are an important part of the formula, and in a government where both the legislature and the executive are essentially instruments of the majority, it is essential that one branch respond to the needs of those who cannot succeed in influencing either the president or Congress. Were the court to be unduly modest the democratic balance would be upset.

Like the argument over the historical validity of the court's assumption of the power of judicial review, the argument over whether the justices should be restrained or activist cannot be resolved. It is clear, however, that whichever course of action the Supreme Court chooses in a particular controversy, it of necessity influences the outcome of that controversy. Whether it chooses to intervene or modestly declines to participate, the outcome of the dispute will be affected. For the court there is no neutral ground. Once it is agreed that the court could, if it would, intervene, failure to do so is as much a decision as direct intervention. Most partisans in the judicial activism-judicial restraint controversy, choose sides according to their preference for certain substantive results in a current dispute. While it is perfectly proper to advocate that the court not intervene in a given situation because one hopes to preserve the ruling of the lower court, there is no moral superiority in the noninterventionist position. It is, in a negative way, as activist as a more aggressive stance on the part of opponents of the status quo. The ongoing argument over whether the Supreme Court ought to be more or less active generally resolves itself into a question of whose ox is being gored. The New Dealers who railed against the activism of an intransigent Supreme Court during Franklin Roosevelt's first term, were ideological kin to the civil libertarians who praised the activism and "wisdom" of the Warren court.

In any case judicial review is today a fait accompli and an accepted part of American government. The Supreme Court can hear cases brought to it from the highest state courts as well as from the intermediate appellate federal courts. It hears a very limited (largely insignificant) number of cases on original jurisdiction, and a similarly small number of cases from the lower state courts. While the rules of jurisdiction and procedure which have evolved since the *Marbury* decision are fairly complex, two significant features stand out.

In the first place, the court can speak *only in the process of deciding a case. It does not render advisory opinions.* This means that if the court has something to say, it must wait until a suitable vehicle in case form happens to present itself. It also means that if any individual or group in the United States wishes to elicit from the court an authoritative statement or definition of constitutional rights, it may approach the court only by litigating a suitable case. In short, no matter how brilliant, how wise, how urgent the opinions of the justices may be, they will remain forever unheard and unsaid unless a case presents itself wherein these thoughts may be appropriately included. No law, no matter how outrageous, or how patently contrary to the Constitution, is unconstitutional until the justices declare it to be unconstitutional; and they cannot so declare it until it is challenged by a case or controversy that the procedural rules of the court permit it to hear.

Secondly, the case load of the court is almost entirely discretionary; that is, the court has the power, in over 90 percent of cases requesting review, to decide which ones it wishes to hear. Furthermore, the number of cases that the court hears is miniscule compared to the number of cases it *could* theoretically hear, and is a small fraction of even those cases requesting a hearing. For most litigants, thus, the Supreme Court as a court of last resort does not, in reality, exist.

The court itself recognizes that its function is far more subtle and complex than that of the ordinary appellate court. As Justice Frankfurter once said, "After all, this is the Nation's ultimate judicial tribunal, not a super-legal-aid bureau." [12] The court, in deciding which cases to hear, is not primarily motivated by the justice or injustice of the lower court's verdict, or by the fate of the defendant should the review not be granted. Its chief motivation is presumably that the question to be decided is of national significance. The court's formal rules of procedure provide some guidance: for example, cases must arise under the laws or Constitution of the United States and present a federal question for decision; litigants must have suffered a personal injury or damage in order to have standing to sue, and must have exhausted all previous remedies. In the last analysis, however, the rules of procedure are only guidelines to be more or less flexibly applied; the court hears what it thinks is important for the court to hear, and the definition of "importance," like the definition of "national significance," is determined by the justices themselves.

While the members of the court make the final determination as to which cases will be heard in a given term, it is worth noting that almost all the important cases decided by the court (especially in recent years) have been shaped to some extent by judicial pressure groups. To appreciate the roles of judicial pressure groups, it is important to understand that legislatures are not the only sources of law. Courts also make law. As Benjamin Cardozo once said, "Courts legislate in the interstices of the laws made by legislatures." Another way of putting it might be to say that legislatures make law wholesale; courts make it retail. The statutes that the legislature enacts apply to everyone; the ruling that the court makes applies only to the litigant. The *principles* evoked by the court in its ruling, however, *may apply far more widely than to the instant case and the litigants directly concerned.* Although the ruling is binding only on the parties to the case, normally it will be applied by the appropriate governmental authorities to all other cases and individuals similarly situated. Thus, if the courts rule that a trip to Florida is a legitimate medical expense for John Jones, convalescent, every other convalescent who deducts the costs of his trip to Florida will be permitted to do so by the tax authorities.

Even more important, however, is the court's role in setting limits for legislative action through their surveillance of the *sub-*

stance of the law in the course of handling individual cases. Suppose, for example, Congress, in an attempt to thwart income tax cheats, permitted travel expenses for health trips for convalescents except for trips to Florida in winter. If Jones were a bona fide convalescent who needed a warm climate, a court might very well declare that such a legislative exception was unfair and unreasonable, or to use legal parlance, that to forbid Jones the exemption was to take his tax money without *due process of law.*

The concept that the courts, in the United States, have the right and duty to declare that a law is too unfair to stand is of importance, because in effect it provides an alternate way for individuals to shape the law to their liking. It is at this point that judicial pressure groups enter the picture.* Consider, for example, the successful effort to strike down *judicially* the Connecticut statute that made the use of contraceptives a crime. For almost fifty years the Planned Parenthood forces attempted to have the Connecticut state legislature repeal this absurd and unenforceable law only to be defeated by the potential political power of the Catholic Church at the polls. Regardless of their personal sentiments, legislators were unwilling to repeal the statute for fear of not being reelected. Finally, after years of litigation, Planned Parenthood of Connecticut achieved its goal when the United States Supreme Court declared the Connecticut birth control law unconstitutional.

In *Griswold* v. *Connecticut* [13] (the Connecticut birth control case), the appellant Griswold was the director of the Planned Parenthood League of Connecticut, and the allegedly illegal acts charged were committed at her direction while acting in her official capacity; PPLC retained the attorneys who defended her and paid for the entire course of litigation; Planned Parenthood of America, of which PPLC was an affiliate, also entered a brief *amicus curiae* (friend of the court) at the Supreme Court level. The *Griswold* case, in short, reached the United State Supreme Court for adjudication only because of the activities of a group which (at least at that point in its history) existed in large part specifically for the purpose of challenging restrictive legislation in the courts.

---

* A judicial pressure group is a voluntary association of individuals joined by some common interest whose advancement they seek through the courts.

Griswold and Planned Parenthood is perhaps an extreme example, but dozens of others come to mind. The American Jewish Congress has been involved in almost all cases where church-state relations have been challenged; the NAACP has been active in segregation cases; and the ACLU has argued in scores of civil liberties cases. Pressure group involvement can take many forms, but probably the most frequent is the presentation of an *amicus curiae* brief at the United States Supreme Court level, or the providing of counsel or money to defray expenses at any level of the case. Sometimes a group may provide the litigants (as in *Griswold*) or even witnesses. Although the ACLU and the NAACP are currently the most active and well-known judicial pressure groups, not all such judicial pressure groups represent liberal points of view. Many conservative groups on occasion provide either counsel, financing, or *amicus curiae* briefs for cases in which they are interested. Administrative officials, moreover, frequently band together and act in a manner very similar to the ACLU; for example, in the *Miranda* [14] case, involving police procedure, the attorneys general of many states filed briefs *amicus curiae* in opposition to the position taken by the ACLU briefs *amicus curiae*.

Thus, the contribution of judicial pressure groups (whether permanent or *ad hoc*), is to shape the case load of the court by making it possible for certain cases to reach the highest appellate levels, and to influence the thinking of the justices themselves by the arguments made before the court. The attempt to influence the courts, and the United States Supreme Court in particular, in this way is peculiarly available to small and unpopular minorities who find it relatively easy to form effective pressure groups. Even a single private attorney may play such a role, and an examination of the principle criminal procedure cases heard by the Warren Court yields some fascinating insights.

Defendants like Miranda,[15] Rideau,[16] Vignera,[17] et al. collectively present a picture of what most people consider the dregs of society. Miranda, charged with rape, was an unemployed, semiliterate, mentally dull truck driver, with a common-law wife, and a long criminal record going back to his childhood; Rideau was black, uneducated, and accused of a particularly cold-blooded series of killings; Vignera committed a robbery that netted him only ninety-three dollars and handled himself so stupidly afterward that he virtually ensured his arrest and conviction. In all of these cases, the defendants were almost certainly guilty of the crimes with which they were charged but the proceedings by which their convictions were obtained were in some respect faulty. Miranda's confession appeared to have been coerced; Rideau was subjected to unwarranted, prejudicial pretrial publicity; Vignera was unaware of his right to counsel. Each of their convictions was appealed and ultimately was reviewed by the United States Supreme Court.

The attorneys who represented these defendants and others like them were a picture of the elite of our society: well-to-do (sometimes prominent) parents; ivy league colleges and law schools; prestigious and usually lucrative law practices, etc. Victor M. Earle III, for example, who was Vignera's attorney, is the son of a Princeton-educated stock-broker father; an alumnus of Williams College and Columbia Law School; was at the time of his involvement with Vignera associated with Cravath, Swayne and Moore, a leading Wall Street law firm; and in a previous Supreme Court appearance had faced opposing counsel in the person of none other than Richard M. Nixon.

As a group, the defendants and attorneys described above come from opposite ends of the social spectrum. It is true that not all defendants are poor, black, and undereducated. Some are white and rich, like Sam Sheppard. Neither are all attorneys who appear before the Supreme Court in criminal procedure cases from Ivy League colleges and prestigious law firms that provide them with excellent incomes. Some attorneys attended local law schools and live on modest salaries from legal defender groups.

On the whole, however, the picture is true. Those who have appeared as defendants or petitioners in United States Supreme Court criminal procedure cases are at the bottom of the socioeconomic heap. The lawyers who represented them are, on the other hand, a highly elite group. In some respects, perhaps, this is not surprising. We expect that nasty brutish crimes will be committed by nasty brutish people, just as we expect that the cream of the legal profession will practice before the bar of the United States Supreme Court. The interesting question is, however, how does this come about? How does a defendant like Vignera get an attorney like Earle? Even more interesting, is why—why do attorneys like Earle take cases like these? Why do they become involved with men who, on the whole, are not only born losers, but are extremely unlikely to be rehabilitated or reformed in their behavior patterns?

How these attorneys come to be involved in these cases is relatively easy to determine. Some attorneys are affiliated with, or volunteer their services to, legal defender groups such as the American Civil Liberties Union or the NAACP Legal Defense Fund. Some are employed by the Legal Aid Society. Some are appointed by the court, either at the trial level or on appeal—sometimes even by the United States Supreme Court itself, frequently after they have made their availability known to the court. Occasionally, attorneys are recommended to the client by a friend, another attorney, an employer, or even a community figure such as a priest. Some lawyers handle the case from beginning to end; others come in at some point in the appellate process.

To say that these attorneys are either court appointees or associated with legal defense groups, however, is not to explain very much. It only begs the real question of why this type of lawyer is associated with such organizations. While some attorneys take such cases in the same spirit as physicians who serve without pay in clinics for the poor, and some no doubt want the prestige, fun, and excitement that goes with an opportunity to appear before the United States Supreme Court, many attorneys take these cases out of concern for the principle of law involved as distinguished from the interests of the client.[18] Many attorneys perceive themselves in the role of defenders of a system of law and government that they view as threatened by inadequate, incompetent, or immoral government officials.

As an example, in the case of *Aguilar* v. *Texas*,[19] the defendant was arrested on an affidavit from police officers which simply stated that they had "reliable information" from a credible person that narcotics were kept in Aguilar's home. No further information was given to the magistrate issuing the search warrant as to the nature of either the informant or the source of his information. Clyde W. Woody, attorney for Aguilar, commented:

> *It was necessary to fully apprise the Court of Criminal Appeals as well as the trial courts of the State of Texas of the real meaning of the Fourth and Fifth Amendments of the Constitution of the United States. In my opinion the Courts of this*

state, as well as the citizens of the State of Texas, were the victims of a fraud being perpetrated under the guise of law enforcement. The function of the arrest and search warrant in Texas prior to Aguilar had been utilized as a writ of assistance which in my opinion would bring discredit and lawlessness to the Courts and cause the citizens to lose respect for the Constitution as well as the Judiciary. It was obvious that the executive branch in Texas had already succeeded in bringing discredit upon themselves.

In a similar vein, Gretchen White Oberman (then a Legal Aid attorney), discussed *Sibron* v. *New York*,[20] a case involving the New York State "stop and frisk" law which lowered the standards for police searches and seizures of suspected persons.

The Legal Aid Society is assigned to hundreds and thousands of cases at the trial level and this was one of the many. The trial attorney saw the legal potential and asked Mr. Finkel of the Appeals Bureau to handle it personally on appeal. . . . Mr. Finkel had it in the Appellate Term and the New York Court of Appeals. I had handled People v. Rivera, *the first stop and frisk case in the New York Court of Appeals a couple of years before and Mr. Finkel, knowing my commitment to the privacy principle of the Fourth Amendment asked me to collaborate with him on the jurisdictional statement to the Supreme Court, and on the brief and argument when the case was taken by the Court for review.*

Our work together was a true labor of love. We believed every word we wrote in the brief and every statement we made orally before the Court. I would have done the same thing without salary from the Society because I believed that the issue involved was important to the law and ultimately to the entire social fabric of the country.[21]

Many attorneys, however, are reluctant to admit to taking a case for the satisfaction of an ideological consideration rather than to meet the needs of the client. The ethics of the legal profession dictate that a lawyer's first concern must be for his client, and any other consideration permitted to intrude itself into the case might lead to a conflict of interest. Thus, Victor M. Earle III, explained carefully why he undertook to defend Michael Vignera:

> Understand that the principle [activating me] is free service for the indigents, not the particular legal or constitutional issue involved. As it happened, I believed strongly that the police needed to be controlled in their interrogations, and my brief contained the four-part warning which the Court adopted in its Miranda opinion.

Doubtless Mr. Earle was concerned for Vignera. It is not easy, however, to write a brief good enough for the United States Supreme Court to use as the substance of its decision. Such a brief requires more than a casual effort; such an effort requires more than a casual commitment.

In looking at the output of the United States Supreme Court, one is struck by the degree to which it is influenced by minorities organized as judicial pressure groups. These groups operate through their effect on the court's agenda, an effect achieved by efforts to see that cases raising issues relevant to these groups are reviewed by the courts. These issues relate almost always to personal, as opposed to property rights; and concern the large question of the relationship of the individual to the state.

In the quest for reform of the criminal justice system it is to be expected that those who feel that morals laws infringe unduly on the freedom of individuals will turn to the courts for relief when legislatures prove too difficult or too slow. An unsuccessful challenge to the marihuana statutes [22] has already been made and litigation over the permissibility of obscenity has been a hardy perennial in recent years. The *Powell* [23] case involving alcoholics, and the abortion [24] and birth control cases [25] are other examples of challenges to morals laws. Homosexual societies can be expected to mount legal challenges to discriminatory practices soon, and some day even gamblers and prostitutes may organize.

The likelihood of success in these endeavors, however, depends on the receptivity of public opinion. The Supreme Court may not follow the election returns quite as faithfully as the legislative and executive branches do, but follow them they must, because the law basically is not the watchdog of society; it is its reflection. If

Planned Parenthood, or the NAACP or Citizens for Decent Literature or even Victor M. Earle III spoke only for themselves, the court would not hear the cases in which they were involved, nor be influenced favorably if it did. It is only when the court perceives these claims as a *reflection* of substantial attitudinal changes in society, that it is willing to give legal relief.

Thus we have come full circle. Whether through the legislature or through the courts, change will come only when society is willing to accept such change. The willingness to forego the use of the criminal sanction as a method of social control depends to some extent on our belief in our own innate decency and self-restraint. Three hundred years ago Thomas Hobbes wrote:

> *During the time men live without a common power to keep them in awe, they are in that condition which is called war; and such a war, as is of every man, against every man . . . and the life of man [is] solitary, poor, nasty, brutish, and short.*[26]

For Hobbes, the alternatives were the criminal sanction or chaos. John Locke had a kindlier view—of men sufficiently rational and aware of social and individual needs to be capable of self-government. Mill carried Locke's views to their ultimate conclusions:

> *The sole end for which mankind are warranted, individually or collectively, in interfering with the liberty of action of any of their number is self-protection.*[27]

Quoting old philosophies has a somewhat musty flavor and is almost ludicrous in the context of the sordidness of one of our big urban criminal courts. Yet the basic conflict is there and must be resolved. How much control do people need? How much control can the law provide? Can we control except through fear of punishment? So far, Hobbes has had the better of the argument. Let's give Mill a chance.

notes

Chapter one
[1] 367 U.S. 643 (1961).

Chapter two
[1] *New York Times*, January 22, 1974, p. 41.
[2] 6 Wheat. 264 (1821).

Chapter three
[1] Albert K. Cohen, "The Study of Social Disorganization and Deviant Behavior," in Robert K. Merton, Leonard Broom, and Leonard S. Cottrell, Jr., eds., *Sociology Today: Problems and Prospects* (New York: Basic Books, 1959), p. 462.
[2] Robert K. Merton, *Social Theory and Social Structure* (New York: Free Press, 1957), pp. 131–60.
[3] Harold Greenwald, *The Elegant Prostitute* (New York: Walker and Company, 1970), pp. 169–70.
[4] Edward M. Brecher et al., *Licit and Illicit Drugs* (Boston: Little, Brown, 1972), p. 232.
[5] Ibid., p. 25.
[6] Ibid., p. 234.
[7] Ibid., p. 235.

Chapter four
[1] "Heroin Hunger May Not a Mugger Make," *New York Times Magazine*, March 18, 1973, p. 39.
[2] Marvin E. Wolfgang, "Crime in a Birth Cohort," *Proceedings of the American Philosophical Society* 117, no. 5 (October 1973).
[3] See David Burnham, "Murder Rates for Blacks in City 8 Times That for White Victims," *New York Times*, August 5, 1973, p. 1.
[4] Edward M. Brecher et al., *Licit and Illicit Drugs* (Boston: Little, Brown, 1972), p. 51.
[5] Jerome H. Jaffee, M.D., as quoted in Brecher, *Licit and Illicit Drugs*, p. 65.
[6] See John W. Finner, "Army Reports Few in War in 1970–72 Are Addicts Today," *New York Times*, April 24, 1973, p. 1. Some officials who have worked closely with addicts feel that the quality of street heroin is so poor that

many users who think themselves physically addicted are not, and that their continued use of heroin is a result of psychological rather than physical dependence. Whether psychological addiction is easier to break than physical is not clear, but in theory at least, it may be, since physical addiction is also normally psychological as well.

[7] Charles Winick, "Maturing Out of Addiction," *Bulletin on Narcotics* 14, no. 1 (January–March 1962): 5.

[8] Donald T. Dickson, "Bureaucracy and Morality: An Organizational Perspective on a Moral Crusade," *Social Problems* 16, no. 2 (Fall 1968): 149.

[9] 249 U.S. 96 (1919).

[10] 258 U.S. 280 (1922).

[11] James M. Markham, review of David M. Musto, M.D., *The American Disease: Origins of Narcotic Control* (New Haven, Conn.: Yale University Press, 1973); *New York Times Book Review*, April 29, 1973, p. 12.

[12] See, for example, Brecher, *Licit and Illicit Drugs*, Chapters 2 and 5.

[13] For an excellent discussion of the impact of the Harrison Act see Erich Goode, *Drugs in American Society* (New York: Alfred A. Knopf, 1972), Chapter 7.

[14] Harry Campbell, "The Pathology and Treatment of Morphia Addiction," *British Journal of Inebriety* 20 (1922–23): 147. As quoted in Brecher, *Licit and Illicit Drugs,* p. 121.

[15] Thomas H. Bewley, Ian Pierce James, and Thomas Mahon, "Evaluation of the Effectiveness of Prescribing Clinics for Narcotics Addicts in the United Kingdom, 1968–1970," in C. J. D. Zarafonetis, ed., *Report of the International Symposium on Drug Abuse* (Ann Arbor, Mich.: University of Michigan Press, 1970).

[16] Brecher, *Licit and Illicit Drugs,* p. 77.

[17] See David Sternberg, "Synanon House," *Journal of Criminal Law, Criminology and Police Science* 54, no. 4: 447–55.

[18] For a detailed report of the pioneering New York City methadone maintenance program, see Francis Rowe Gearing, M.D., M.P.H. "Methadone Maintenance Treatment Program, Progress Report through March 31, 1971—a Five Year Overview. (Unpublished report submitted to the New York State Addiction Control Commission, May 14, 1971).

[19] Ibid., p. 6.

[20] Paul Cushman, Jr., "Methadone Maintenance Treatment of Narcotic Addiction," *New York State Journal of Medicine* 72, no. 13 (1972): 1752–55; Hartford Institute of Criminal and Social Justice, *The First Year and a Quarter of the Hartford Dispensary's Methadone Maintenance Treatment Program: a Statistical Profile of the Patients and Impact Assessment,* 1972.

[21] Gearing, "Methadone Maintenance," p. 7.

²² Bewley, et al., "Evaluation of the Effectiveness of Prescribing Clinics," pp. 91–92.

²³ Ibid., pp. 76–77.

²⁴ Edward A. Preble and John J. Casey, Jr., "Taking Care of Business," *International Journal of the Addictions* (March 1969), pp. 2–3, cited in Brecher, et al., *Licit and Illicit Drugs*, pp. 40–41.

Chapter five

¹ L.R. 3 Q.B. 360 (1868).

² Ibid., p. 369.

³ *United States* vs. *One book called "Ulysses" by James Joyce*, 72 F2d 705, 2d Cir. (1934).

⁴ *Roth* vs. *United States*, 354 U.S. 476 (1957).

⁵ Ibid., p. 489.

⁶ Ibid., p. 490.

⁷ 383 U.S. 463 (1966).

⁸ Merle Miller, "Ralph Ginzburg, Middlesex, New Jersey, and the First Amendment," *New York Times Magazine*, April 30, 1972, p. 67.

⁹ *Ginzburg* vs. *United States*, 383 U.S. 463 (1966), at 470.

¹⁰ 394 U.S. 557 (1969).

¹¹ *Miller* vs. *California*, 413 U.S. 15 (1973). *Paris Adult Theatre I* vs. *Slaton*, 413 U.S. 49 (1973). *United States* vs. *12 200-t. Reels of super 8mm Film*, 413 U.S. 123 (1973). *United States* vs. *Orito*, 413 U.S. 139 (1973). *Kaplan* vs. *California*, 413 U.S. 115 (1973). (All decided June 21, 1973.)

¹² Alexander B. Smith and Bernard Locke, "Problems in Arrests and Prosecutions for Obscenity and Pornography," *Technical Report of the Commission on Obscenity and Pornography*, vol. V (Washington, D.C.: U.S. Government Printing Office, 1970).

¹³ Survey of prosecutors conducted by authors in twenty metropolitan areas of the United States in 1973.

¹⁴ Robert F. Kennedy, "The Baleful Influence of Gambling," *Atlantic Monthly* 209, no. 4 (April 1962): 76.

¹⁵ Gerald Eskenazi, "Rise in Illegal Gambling Linked to OTB Climate," *New York Times*, January 10, 1974, pp. 1, 52.

¹⁶ Herbert A. Bloch, "The Sociology of Gambling," *American Journal of Sociology* 57 (1951): 217–18.

¹⁷ Edmund Bergler, *The Psychology of Gambling* (New York: International Universities Press, 1958), p. 18.

¹⁸ John J. Murtagh, "Gambling and Police Corruption," *Atlantic Monthly* 206, no. 5 (November 1960): 53.

[19] Lycurgus M. Starkey, Jr., "Christians and the Gambling Mania," *Christian Century* 80 (February 27, 1963): 267.

[20] See Steve Cady, "The Gambler Who Must," *New York Times Magazine,* January 27, 1974, p. 12.

[21] For a sensitive discussion of a homosexual's identifying himself publicly see Merle Miller, "What It Means to Be a Homosexual," *New York Times Magazine,* January 17, 1971, pp. 9–11.

[22] See "City again Rejects a Rights Bill for Homosexuals," *New York Times,* December 23, 1973, Section IV, p. 5.

[23] Charles Hite, "APA Rules Homosexuality Not Necessarily a Psychiatric Disorder," *Psychiatric News,* January 2, 1974, p. 1.

[24] *New York Times,* December 23, 1973, Section IV, p. 5.

[25] President's Commission on Law Enforcement and Administration of Justice, *Task Force Report: Drunkenness* (Washington, D.C.: U.S. Government Printing Office, 1967), p. 1.

[26] *Breithaupt* vs. *Abram,* 352 U.S. 432 (1957), and *Schmerber* vs. *California,* 384 U.S. 757 (1966).

[27] *Driver* vs. *Hinnant,* 356 F2nd 761 (4th Cir. 1966); *Easter* vs. *District of Columbia,* 361 F2nd 50 (D.C. Cir. 1966).

[28] 392 U.S. 514 (1968).

[29] 49 New Hampshire 399 (1869).

[30] For a good discussion of the legal problems relating to the use of alcoholism and drugs, see Peter Barton Hutt, "The Right to Use Alcohol and Drugs," in Norman Dorsen, ed., *The Rights of Americans* (New York: Vintage Books, 1972), pp. 365–79.

[31] *New York Times,* December 4, 1972, p. 34.

[32] Edward M. Brecher et al., *Licit and Illicit Drugs* (Boston: Little, Brown, 1972), p. 160.

[33] Ibid., pp. 304–5.

[34] *Abrams* vs. *United States,* 250 U.S. 616 (1919), at 630 (emphasis added).

[35] *New York Times,* January 15, 1974, pp. 1, 26.

Chapter six

[1] Gerhard O. W. Mueller, *Crime, Law, and Scholars* (Seattle: University of Washington Press, 1969), Chapter I.

[2] *United States* v. *Dennis,* 341 U.S. 494 (1951).

[3] *Yates* v. *United States,* 354 U.S. 298 (1957).

[4] Ibid., pp. 324–25, 326–27.

[5] For a more complete discussion see Alexander B. Smith and Harriet Pollack, *Crime and Justice in a Mass Society* (Corte Madera, Calif.: Rinehart Press, 1972), Chapter 3.

⁶ Frederick Pollock and F. W. Maitland, *The History of English Law Before the Time of Edward I* (Cambridge: Cambridge Press, 1932), Vol. II, p. 448.

⁷ J. W. Ehrlich, ed., *Ehrlich's Blackstone, Part Two: Private Wrongs, Public Wrongs* (New York: Capricorn Books, 1959), p. 284.

⁸ *In re Gault* 387 U.S. 1 (1967).

Kent v. *United States*, 383 U.S. 541 (1966).

In re Winship, 397 U.S. 358 (1970).

⁹ *McKeiver* v. *Pennsylvania*, 403 U.S. 528 (1971).

¹⁰ For a good comprehensive discussion of the handling of insanity see Karl Menninger, *The Crime of Punishment* (New York: Viking, 1968); and Thomas S. Szasz, *Law, Liberty and Psychiatry* (New York: Macmillan, 1963).

¹¹ *Marbury* v. *Madison*, 1 Cranch 137 (1803), at 177–78.

¹² *Uveges* v. *Pennsylvania*, 335 U.S. 437 (1948), at 449–50.

¹³ 381 U.S. 479 (1965).

¹⁴ 384 U.S. 436 (1966).

¹⁵ *Miranda* v. *Arizona*, 384 U.S. 436 (1966).

¹⁶ *Rideau* v. *Louisiana*, 373 U.S. 723 (1963).

¹⁷ *Vignera* v. *New York*, 384 U.S. 436 (1966).

¹⁸ Alexander B. Smith and Harriet Pollack, "Rich Lawyer/Poor Client," *Student Lawyer* (September 1973), pp. 22–25; 62–63.

¹⁹ 378 U.S. 108 (1964).

²⁰ 392 U.S. 40 (1968).

²¹ Smith and Pollack, "Rich Lawyer/Poor Client," p. 62.

²² *New York Law Forum* 14, no. 1 (Spring 1968).

²³ *Powell* v. *Texas*, 392 U.S. 514 (1968).

²⁴ *Roe* v. *Wade*, 410 U.S. 113 (1973).

²⁵ *Griswold* v. *Connecticut*, 381 U.S. 479 (1965).

²⁶ Thomas Hobbes, *Leviathan* (Cleveland: World Publishing, 1963) Part I, Chapter 13, p. 143.

²⁷ John Stuart Mill, *On Liberty* (New York: Appleton-Century-Crofts, 1947), p. 9.

index

National Health Service (U.K.), 108

National security, FBI and, 14n

Nazi Germany. *See* Hitler, Adolf

Nevada: gambling in, 35, 138, 139, 140–41; prostitution in, 120, 138

New Deal, 180

New Jersey state lottery, 136

New Hampshire state lottery, 136

Newman, Edwin, 2

New York City: Court of General Sessions, 54; Criminal Court, 12n; Criminal Justice system, 4n; drug addiction in, 12, 28, 87–88, 153, 162; drug maintenance programs in, 102, 103–105, 155; free speech controversy in, 132–33; gambling in, 138–39; Health Department, 102; homosexuality in, 144–46; housing integration in, 82; New York State Supreme Court in, 4, 45n, 60n; Police Department, 3, 136, 140n; and Sunday closing laws, 10–11; Tombs riots, 4, 116

New York Medical College, 145

New York Post, 152n

New York State: adoption laws, 168; bookmaking establishments sponsored by, 9; Drug Abuse Control Commission, 155, 156n; vs. drug pushers, 81; lottery, 136; morals laws, 34–35n; Narcotics program, 100–101; Off-Track Betting Corporation (OTB), 9, 35, 136, 138–39, 140n, 141; "stop and frisk" law, 186; Sunday closing law, 10–11

New York State Supreme Court, 176; Kings County Probation Dept., 45n, 60n; New York City, 4

New York Times, 76, 133n, 140n, 145–46, 162

New York Times Index, 93

New York Times Magazine, 21n

Nixon, Richard M., 161, 184; and antiwar protests, 6n, 37

Numbers, 7, 13, 117, 137, 138–39. *See also* Gambling

Nyswander, Dr. Marie, 62, 102

Oberman, Gretchen White, 186

Obscenity, 115, 123–35, 161; case history of, 51, 65, 66; laws (*see* Penal codes: and obscenity); U.S. Supreme Court on, 34n, 124–34, 187

Off-Track Betting Corporation (OTB), 9, 35, 136, 138–39, 140n, 141

Organized crime, 119; and drugs, 15, 28, 96, 153; and gambling, 35, 137, 138, 139–40; and methadone, 156; and morals laws, 15, 16; and Prohibition (*see* Bootlegging); and prostitution, 15, 120

Outcasts, 44

Outsiders (Becker), 18

Overeating (obesity), 27, 40, 42, 62–65 *passim*, 71, 151; case history of, 55–56, 57–58; and drug addiction, 102

President's Commission on Obscenity and Pornography, 135
Premarital sex, 29, 30, 32
Pretrial motions, x
Prisoners, 4; rehabilitation of, 7–8
Prison guards, 7, 80
Prison riots, 4, 7, 116
Prisons: defined, 7n; drug addicts in, 79–80, 100; homosexuals in, 7, 144; problems of, 7–8; purposes of, 58–59, 69–72 *passim*. *See also* Jails
Prison sentences, 5, 7–8, 169; as deterrent, 5, 15; and drug addiction, 79; reform of, 115
Probation system, 4, 8, 58, 72; and case histories, 46–56 *passim*; and drug addicts, 100; and morals offenders, 15, 70, 118–19; whites vs. blacks, 79
Procedural reforms, 114–15
Profiteering, 19, 20
Prohibition (Eighteenth Amendment), 11–12, 26, 29, 150; bootlegging and, 12, 96, 119, 161; and drug use, 95
Property crime. *See* White-collar crime
Prosecutors, 169; and gambling, 138–39; and homosexuality, 143, 144; and morals offenders, 118–19; and obscenity, 127, 130, 135; and plea bargaining, 5–7 *passim*; reform of, 114
Prostitution, 10, 19, 29–30, 32, 66–68, 115, 116, 120–23, 161, 176, 187; case history of, 53–54; causes of, 67–68; and crime, 76; and drug addiction, 27, 67, 85,

88; and entrapment, 13; laws (*see* Penal codes: and prostitution); licensing of, 33, 122–23; in Nevada, 120, 138; pimps and, 14, 118, 122–23; and solicitation, 121
Protestant churches, and gambling, 34–35. *See also* Puritanism; Religion
Psychotics, 41, 44, 57. *See also* Personality abnormalities
Public schools, released time programs in, 34–35n
Puerto Ricans, and drug addiction, 79–80, 87n, 96. *See also* Poverty
Pure Food and Drug Act (1906), 93
Puritanism, 25, 34, 35, 69
Purse snatchings, 3

Race discrimination, 19, 20, 36, 37; and housing, 81–82; Shockley's theory and, 132–33. *See also* Blacks; Poverty
Race track betting, 25, 138, 139; off-track, 9 (*see also* Off-Track Betting Corporation [OTB])
Rape, 9, 10, 18, 43, 143, 147. *See also* Serious crimes
Reason and Law, quoted, 40
Rebels, 44n. *See also* Black revolutionaries
Recidivism, 8
Red light districts, 121. *See also* Prostitution
Reformatories, 7n. *See* Prisons
Regina vs. *Hicklin* (U.K.). *See* *Hicklin* rule